Democracy and Domination

Democracy and Domination

Technologies of Integration and the Rise of Collective Power

ANDREW M. KOCH AND
AMANDA GAIL ZEDDY

LEXINGTON BOOKS

A division of
ROWMAN & LITTLEFIELD PUBLISHERS, INC.
Lanham • Boulder • New York • Toronto • Plymouth, UK

LEXINGTON BOOKS

A division of Rowman & Littlefield Publishers, Inc.
A wholly owned subsidiary of The Rowman & Littlefield Publishing Group, Inc.
4501 Forbes Boulevard, Suite 200
Lanham, MD 20706

Estover Road
Plymouth PL6 7PY
United Kingdom

British Library Cataloguing in Publication Information Available

Library of Congress Cataloging-in-Publication Data

Koch, Andrew M., 1953-
  Democracy and domination : technologies of integration and the rise of collective power
    / Andrew M. Koch and Amanda Gail Zeddy.
      p. cm.
  Includes bibliographical references and index.
  ISBN 978-0-7391-2215-0 (hardcover : alk. paper) — ISBN 978-0-7391-3637-9
  (electronic : alk. paper)
  1. Democracy—History. I. Zeddy, Amanda Gail, 1982- II. Title.
  JC423.K584 2009
  321.8—dc22   2008054746

Printed in the United States of America

♾™ The paper used in this publication meets the minimum requirements of American
National Standard for Information Sciences—Permanence of Paper for Printed Library
Materials, ANSI/NISO Z39.48–1992.

Contents

Introduction

What can be observed from the history of civilization is that organization is power. Organization allows for individual acts to be arranged and co-ordinated into the collective behavior of a community or group. This ability to coordinate activity creates a structure of concerted effort in which the outcome, in terms of effect, is greater than the sum of its parts. The organization is a living machine that, as a result of discipline and the orderly assigned activities and roles, allows for the expansion of the group's power.

Organization has been the technical feature of power in the Western world. It has been essential to its scientific progress, its military prowess, and a significant force in the development of its ideological doctrines of domination. It is the disciplinary nature of the organization that creates the material conditions for the rise and expansion of power.

As Michel Foucault stated, every organization is the repository of some form of power. This power comes in the form of rules and structures that replicate the conditions that maintain the organization. Each must construct an internal structure that both carries out a task for which the organization is designed and generate a legitimating narrative that restructures the order of experience in a fashion that embodies the organization's logic.

Our interest in this work is focused specifically on the collective power that exercises sovereignty and, therefore, exerts absolute power over a given territory and its inhabitants. Such a phenomenon is not tied to a particular form of political association. In ancient times, this unit of territorial administration was the polis. In the Middle Ages the feudal estate exercised the exclusive rights of power. In the modern period, the nation-state has the exclusive right of sovereign power over the inhabitants of the earth.

However, despite these differences in form, there are common foundations upon which the exercise and expansion of power rests in each one of these systems. While power is often associated with the use of coercion and force, below the surface the operation of power is more subtle and sublime. Every political unit must have some form of power that can be brought to bear to discipline the population. This may be carried out through direct acts of suppression and violence. However, the most successful collective power structures direct the force of collective action by creating a narrative to which the actors subscribe. Each possesses a narrative that legitimates the central political institution's exercise of power. This means that each, in order to be successful, must have some mechanism for the creation and dissemination of that legitimating narrative. The broader the reach of the discourse, the more people can be brought under the domain of a centralizing agency of power, with its formal codes and written laws.

Therefore, domination may be "hard" or "soft" in nature. Hard forms of domination can be described as those that use the direct application of force. For example, military organizations are mechanisms for the application of hard forms of domination. They create a disciplinary order, backed by force, within their own ranks and for the populations internal to the territories they control. They are also organizations designed for the extension of hard disciplinary power to those external to the territorial unit.

Our interest is primarily in the softer forms of domination. Soft forms of domination are more subtle. At their core they seek to generate an internal mechanism of self-discipline. This causes the actor to behave in a manner that is consistent with the goals and objectives of the organization. Soft power seeks to seduce, or entice, rather than force compliant activity. At its most benign, the soft form of domination relies on socialization. These are the cues passed through the formal and informal mechanisms that inform a populous as to what is acceptable and unacceptable behavior. Such signals are embedded within the signs of the culture, passed on, modified, and fixed within the rules for the construction of knowledge. This form of power is manifested in the creation of a common sense of identity and mission carried out through the various agents of political socialization found within the system.

The fact that systems of domination may create compliance without violence does not mean that they are not systems of domination. Quite the contrary, the best systems of domination act transparently, with the belief of the population that the institutions are acting in a fashion that is both ethically correct and pragmatically effective. The key to this process of identity formation is the process of dissemination.

This dissemination of the rules governing the political order serves to construct the identity of the inhabitants in a given territory. It also serves a gate-keeping function for those that are to be admitted to the system of power within the society. To pass through the structure one must learn the proper construction of the hierarchy, the myths of its history, and the ethic employed within its system of activities. Through this mechanism it has been possible to create people who willingly sacrifice themselves to the organizational unit. The inquiry into such activity constitutes the pathology of the *political*.

Today the dominant form of political association is the nation-state. The state is a structure that applies both hard and soft forms of domination. Domestically, the signs of the culture are manifested in the legal statutes that establish the norms of social behavior. As cultural transmission, the soft side of domination is apparent in the guiding principles of law, and in the socialization patterns of expectations transmitted as *civic culture*. The hard side of disciplinary power within the state is manifested in the force used against those who transgress those accepted boundaries and challenge the status quo.

The contemporary understanding of state power resides in the shadow of the modern period, with a political discourse that is still dominated by the concepts introduced by Machiavelli, Hobbes, and Locke. These authors were writing at a time when the nation-state's institutional structures were still in their formative stages. The fact that political discourse is still under the sway of such ideas is testimony to the parallel developments of modernist ideology and the nation-state as a form of collective association.

State power as a measure of *right* can be found in Machiavelli and Hobbes. The defense of the political order is associated with the rationale of power itself. However, with Locke a fundamental transformation of the concept of power occurs. Locke creates the notion of *authority*. Authority is a mediated concept. Power is transformed into authority only where the mediating process of *consent* is employed.

In his time, Locke was supporting a mechanism under which the emerging entrepreneurial class could share in the decision making. However, the logic he employed would also provide a foundation for universal suffrage. As a result of Locke's formulation, the legitimacy of collective power could now go unchallenged. The genius of Locke was to define a system in which the masses are made complicit in the collectivization and exercise of power within a modern formulation of the nation-state.

Today the acts of collective power carried out in the Western democracy are carried out in the name of the masses. The twentieth century was the century of the masses. However, it should not be forgotten that the twentieth century was the bloodiest century in human history.

Mass production, mass literacy, mass education, and mass democracy were correlated with mass destruction. The twentieth century was the century of extermination camps, ethnic cleansing, gulags, torture, cultural annihilation, and the technological means to carry out these acts with a level of efficiency never before seen in history. What is equally striking about the century of the masses is that they participated in all these actions. The masses were mobilized into national armies, as cultural warriors, religious zealots, economic mercenaries, and soldiers in the struggle for ethnic purity.

What does this tell us? It tells us that the mass forms of association, the political manifestation of which is the modern democratic state, are not sufficient to bring the freedom, peace, and progress promised by Enlightenment modernism. Thus, the historical evidence requires the generation of an alternative understanding of the forces that effect political transformation. Our comprehension of democracy and its relationship to domination must be reconsidered.

Domination is the exercise of power over a person or people. It does not matter whether that domination is the product of deliberation by the one, the few, or the many. However, defining democracy is more complicated. Is it an ethical position, a procedure, a structure, an ideological construction, or a *telos* of social evolution? Naturally, it has all of those elements, but the real questions of democracy involve the causal linkages among these elements.

For the purposes of this study, *democracy* will be treated as a system of domination that contains a political mechanism that engages some formal method of polling the mass population within a fixed unit of association. Given this broad definition, we will assert that democracy contains no inherent structural check on power. Therefore, we will not assume that democracy is antithetical to the centralization and expansion of power.

Further, it will be assumed that the ideal that informs this political mechanism has an individualistic bias. This is the case because the immediate calculation of what constitutes the best interest of the individual is the core value that informs the practice of individual expression. Therefore, democracy is a political ethic based on the individual's ability to exercise choices in the political domain. Conditions that limit the exercise of those choices or constrict the domain of options available are constraints upon the realization of the democratic ideal.

Thus, at its core democracy contains a paradox. Its foundation is based on the essential individuality of choice, but the result is the collective concentration of power in which the individual cedes power to an artificial, collective entity. As a result, all institutional constructs are in a state of tension with the democratic ideal. If Foucault is correct, and we are accepting that he is, then the formation of institutional structures create disciplinary narratives that infringe upon the free exercise of choice, as the content of the narrative is always focused on organizational maintenance. The effect of such a dynamic is the imposition of an externally generated model of subjectivity on the individual.

We are not suggesting that all power and domination can be removed from social and political life. That would be neither possible nor desirable. Even Foucault agued that such a position was not realistic. Rather, our view is that the tension between these forces requires exploration in order that we not generate unrealistic expectations about democracy. It is our view that under the modern epistemological and ontological paradigms, democracy has been essential for the expansion of the systems of domination. Without a critical appraisal of democracy itself, it is impossible to assess the processes that dictate ever larger domains of authority.

With some level of domination necessary to social life there is a need to address the conditions of that need. No society can exist without some rules that order the behavior of the collective. There is a need for temporary and contextually drawn agreements to reduce the chaos within the aggregate of people living in proximity to one another. For example, it may be agreed that all people should drive on the right-hand side of the road. This will require some mechanism in which the power to enforce such a decision is manifest.

However, such agreements do not constitute the wholesale construction of identity as they are not suggested as essentially constituted features of subjectivity itself. The content of such an agreement does not seek to extend itself in a deductive fashion beyond what is immediately necessary and conditionally determined. It is not asserted as a constituent part of our humanness that we drive on the right-hand side of the road, nor is any additional regulatory arrangement suggested by such an agreement.

The same cannot be said for the sovereign political institutions that have evolved in the West. These political units, nation-states, construct and maintain themselves through a complete structuring identity. They reconstitute subjectivity in their image and establish a disciplinary order to further that objective. The result is the ideology of nationalism.

Benedict Andersen makes this point in his work, *Imagined Communities*. Andersen agues that the nation-state as a socially constructed phenomenon, an "imagined political community." This organizational unit generates an ideology that links all of the members together for a common enterprise. Such a view has dominated the modern period.[1] Nationalism is a "state of mind" that revolves around a "group consciousness."[2] But nationalism is a constructed phenomenon that stems from the association of people within a given territorial unit. "Nationalism is not the awakening of nations to self-consciousness: it *invents* nations where they do not exist," declared Ernest Gellner.[3] As a result of this shared sense on identity and fidelity among the members of a nation-state, human beings who identify themselves with a particular state have been willing to kill and die in the name of the continued existence and protection of the state.[4] For this reason, Tom Nairn has even gone as far as to describe nationalism as "the pathology of modern developmental history."[5]

Through bureaucratic administrative structures, modern nation-states have been able to exert increasing control over the massively swelling populations of the twentieth and twenty-first centuries. This is the case, even within democratic states. Nationalism is not incompatible with democracy. To be legitimate, the ideology of nationalism and patriotism must be held by the masses. State institutions generate the symbolic identity and disseminate it to the masses who, in turn, legitimate the process through democratic procedures.

The state as a bureaucratic administrative apparatus has furthered its domination of human beings and has become more effective in its scope due to technological advances. Mass communications technology and the mass media have been able to reinforce nationalist sentiment through the use of various forms of propaganda. Printing technologies, state-sponsored education systems, and mass media have all provided a forum for the transfer of collective identities associated with the nation-state. Mass computer databases and means of intelligence and surveillance have allowed the state increasing influence and control over human populations. Bureaucracies are formed as a means to manage, govern, and oversee human beings as a collective whole, and within the nation-state system have increasingly encouraged the massification of human societies.

For this reason, the establishment of democratic procedures has not been effective in achieving the individualistic ethos contained in the modern democratic ideal, nor has it generated an effective check on the growth and exercise of domination. The historical evidence bears out such a claim. At the end of the nineteenth century, as mass democracy was taking hold, the European and American governments underwent an expansion of internal state power and engaged in some of their most aggressive colonial practices. It is our view that democracy must be examined for the role it plays in the exercise of power. Mass institutions produce a narrative that defends the order of power that they represent. Modern democratic states produce such a narrative.

It is our contention that democracy emerges as a legitimating mechanism for the expression of centralized political power when the right material conditions are present. In this analysis we will be looking at material conditions that extend the exercise of dominion and those that detract from it. Both the ethical claims for a particular configuration of power and the structures that are generated will be treated as derivative of the material conditions of existence. Material conditions affect the construction of human identity, from which the content of *ethics* emerges. In order to be considered legitimate, the structure that is generated within any political system must conform to the identity/ethics nexus. Therefore, the study of democracy must include the conditions of materiality.

Is this approach deterministic or a "new historicism," in the way defined by Jürgen Habermas?[6] In a sense yes, but not in the fashion typically associated with determinism. Our approach rejects the idea that the full range of human choices is available in any circumstance and, therefore, no choice is transcendentally free. They always take place within an environment that circumscribes the limited domain of options. There is simply no mechanism by which we escape our links to the confines of the empirical context in which we live. This is true both of the physical environment and of the socially constructed environment into which we are born. For this reason, it is important to ground research within the empirical events of history.

However, it must be remembered that our understanding of these events, the interpretation that constitute the results of inquiry are also conditioned by the context of the investigator. Any person engaged in study must always recognize the conditions that influence their judgments. Such limitations are explored by Max Weber in his work, *The Methodology of the Social Sciences.*[7]

But there is another component of this method that must also be considered in the discussion of social knowledge and its validity. The historical record *is* the empirical domain of evidence for the development of any inductively drawn hypotheses describing the trends and tendencies of society. But the conclusions of inductively drawn hypotheses must always remain open. They never move beyond the realm of interpretation. In that sense, all such conclusions are limited by the range of human capacities and the extent of human industry.

Such a perspective breeds caution in the discussion of democracy. From this perspective, democracy cannot be divorced from the material conditions of its construction. It is an idea that only has the force of reason under specific views of subjectivity, which only arise if the material conditions for democracy are aligned.

Democracy has both ethical and structural dimensions. The ethics of democracy is based on the assertions that the public is equal in its capacities to participate in the social steering decisions of the political order. Further, for such a claim to carry the weight of this assumption it must further be assumed that the public is capable of acting rationally in a given circumstance. Therefore, equality and rationality are two central pillars of subjectivity upon which democracy is constructed.

These assumptions are ideological in character. Such a view begs a further question. Where do ideologies come from? It is our view that ideologies are constructed as explanations of the material conditions of existence in any given historical epoch. Material conditions affect the construction of identity, as it must be constructed in a manner that is consistent with the prevailing conditions. Therefore, in order to study the rise of the democratic forms of domination the material conditions that give rise to the ideological premises of such standards should be examined.

From this perspective, transcendental components of Enlightenment modernism should be rejected in favor of a historical approach. The narrative of modernity discounts the significance of the historical record by suggesting that history is an enfolding of transcendent reason. In the modern period the continuity of this process is reflected in the rise of democracy and the increasing empowerment of the masses. Since the early days of the Enlightenment it has been asserted that history will be represented by the unfolding of human potential and that cognitive faculties will be manifested in increasingly rational institutions that will be the vehicle for our liberation, even as the power of those institutions continues to expand their hold over ever larger areas of existence. The masses will finally find their freedom, even if it can only be realized just over the horizon. Such a position can be found in such diverse attitudes as those of Kant and Hegel, although the expression of its democratic conclusions reaches its fruition in Rousseau.[8]

However, suppose we put the facts of history in an alternative narrative. Suppose we assume that instead of the unfolding of a transcendent process, the ideological constructions are themselves the product of a material process of history. Such a perspective alters the way in which inquiry proceeds. It also alters the questions that are asked.

What is the relationship between the rise of material conditions of power and the emergence of ideologies? Every transformation of the conditions of power requires some accompanying narrative that speaks to the *rationality* of the project. These narratives redefine subjectivity in a manner that is compatible to the new realities of power relations. As a result, the accompanying ideologies of power serve a legitimating function for the existing set of social and political arrangements evolving in the social order.

Within a material framework, there can be no teleology of history. Our situation is the result of the material transformation of history, a process that continues to evolve. It is necessary to understand the conditions that give rise to power and its particular configurations in order to make sense of our present. This must be accompanied with an understanding of the material forces that generate a transformation of the constructed narratives of political existence.

From this perspective, the nation-state is not the culmination of social evolution. It is treated as such because modern social inquiry evolved along with the nation-state and used it as its reference point. If the nation-state is not the *telos* of our political evolution, then how do we read the history of political institutions? There is no choice but to examine the material conditions that gave rise to any configuration of power. The advantage of such an approach is that one can then ask a further question. To what degree do those conditions still exist?

In this work we will be examining several interrelated topics. We are interested in exploring the material conditions that give rise to the concentration of political power. We will address the material conditions that enhance or detract from the political unit's ability to coordinate the actions of mass numbers of people. We will also be interested in the conditions that provide for the expansion of public power. What are the conditions necessary for the growth of social steering by the demos? Finally, we will be interested in the role played by democracy in the expansion of institutional power more generally. If democracy is the political model of the contemporary age, what does that mean for the expansion of power in general?

The most important causal features will vary with different historical epochs. We have focused on literacy, the technologies of dissemination, forms of production, and the organization of political power. These create a material base that helps define the nature of power and its ideological narratives.

Literacy is important for several reasons. It enhances the functional capacity of the power structures. Without literacy, the ability to extend power beyond a centralized core set of institutions is limited. This requires a trained class of administrators that are lacking in non-literate societies.

Literacy is important in another respect. If power is the result of collective behavior, literacy is part of the process of the collective dissemination of narratives the bind communities together. Literacy has been an important vehicle in that process. This is especially true when considering the soft exercise of power as a process of socialization. The modes of dissemination have changed throughout the centuries and have altered the conditions for creating collective action.

Of course, this is directly related to another material condition for the expansion of power, organized administration. There must be some institution that asserts administrative order and discipline. There are certain core functions that must be performed regarding the succession of wealth and land, the maintenance of an array of social institutions, and the distribution of collective power internal to the system. There must be both the accompanying narratives to legitimate this administrative discipline and a structure of coercion for its violators.

Societies must have a *successful* system of production, distribution, and consumption in place that can meet the material needs of the population. Success in the production of biological necessities allows for the redirecting of resources into material implements for the expansion of collective power. Further, the operation of the economic system itself may provide some material impetus for the expansion of power. As the last two hundred years have demonstrated, it is more likely that an exchange economy would seek to expand its organizational influences than an economy constructed for self-sufficiency.

Ideologies, including nationalism, will be treated as constructions that are derivatives of the material processes in which the lived experiences are translated in cultural narrative. The material conditions provide the structure for the expansion of centralized institutions. Without the infrastructure, power is limited in its scope. Ideologies serve as the legitimating discourse for that expansion. They provide the narrative of power and make the manifestations of power *rational*, expressed as a continuity of human progress. It is our goal to make this process more transparent, and in doing so, to make the transformation of the social world more open to question and critique.

One final methodological point needs to be made. Despite our interest in the material conditions that give rise to different forms of domination it is not our contention that any one can be singled out as *the* transformative force in history. In that regard, our position is closer to that of Weber than Marx, despite our focus on the materiality of history. As Weber stated in *The Methodology of the Social Sciences*, there is no single cause of historical transformation, therefore, no single instrument that determines ideological constructions. What is most causally influential in the creation of concepts and ideologies may vary from age to age.[9] For example, during the Middle Ages the dissemination of church narratives was significant in shaping the constitution of human identity among the masses. Since the seventeenth century, the rise of consumption and commerce has been more influential in shaping ideological constructions. A materialist approach need not be deterministic in a strict sense.

It is beyond the scope of any work of this type to account for all the subtle forces that account for social change. No doubt we will be criticized for using too broad a brush and leaving out significant features of the periods we will be discussing. The complexity of the causal nexus does not allow for complete articulation. However, it is our view that this work should serve as an opening rather than the final word. What we want to establish is a frame of mind for further work, a model by which further questions can be addressed.

Is there a historical direction of power? There is empirical evidence of the waxing and waning of centralized institutions. Empires have come and gone. Are we now on an inextricable path toward the centralization of power? The historical evidence suggests that power expands when the technical capacity of the system can address the size and scope of expanded responsibilities toward system management. There are material conditions that must be satisfied for the expansion of power to occur. Inquiry should proceed with that point in mind.

All of these issues will be addressed over the course of this work. Chapter One focuses on the elaboration of our theoretical model and methodological assumptions. Chapter Two will begin the substantive analysis of the project, examining the emergence and development of centralized power in ancient Greece and Rome. Chapter Three will address the material conditions leading to a breakdown of the Roman Empire and the rise of the feudal and religious modes of collective power. Chapter Four addresses the Renaissance and early modernism, characterized by the rise of trade and the increasing needs for infrastructure and administrative competence. Chapter Five examines the relationship between the expansion of centralized power within the nation-state and the emergence of mass forms of industrial production. Chapter Six explores the transformative nature of technologically advanced forms of dissemination and the creation of global capital and administration in the twenty-first century.

Notes

1. Anderson, Benedict, *Imagined Communities: Reflections on the Origin and Spread of Nationalism* (London: Verso, 1991), 6.

2. Kohn, Hans, *The Idea of Nationalism: A Study in Its Origins and Background* (New York: The Macmillan Company, 1944), 1–11.

3. Anderson, 6.

4. Anderson, 7.

5. Anderson, 5.

6. Habermas, Jürgen, "Modernity: An Incomplete Project," in *The Anti-Aesthetic*, ed. Hal Foster (Port Townsend, WA: Bay Press, 1983).

7. Weber, Max, *The Methodology of the Social Sciences* (New York: The Free Press, 1949).

8. Today, even in scholarly discourse, there is often a failure to see that the writings of some of its seminal authors are reflections of a material reality that the world has left behind. Today, what is referred to as political theory is particularly guilty in this regard. This creates the illusion that such works describe a process in which the rational agent engages in transcendent thought, disconnected from the conditions of his/her existence.

9. Weber, Max, *The Methodology of the Social Sciences*, 158.

Chapter 1

The Study of Domination

Introduction

In his work, *The Politics*, Aristotle makes a distinction among various configurations of rule. People can be ruled by one, few, or many. Each of these systems of rule has both a positive and a perverted form, largely owing to whether or not the rule is in the best interest of the rulers or of the community. Democracy is described as one of the perverted forms, characterized as rule by the vast numbers of the poor, pursuing their aims of economic redistribution through the power of their numbers.[1]

Today we tend to think in more positive terms about democracy. (It could be argued that the contemporary ideal resembles more what Aristotle had in mind in his description of a "polity.") Nevertheless, Aristotle identifies something about the support for democratic practice that is largely assumed but rarely interrogated in the contemporary discourse. Democracy, as a form of domination, is predicated on some notions of the constructed subject that makes the practice of democracy a rational enterprise. For Aristotle, the component of subjectivity that is of overriding importance is that of equality. To the democrat, the matter of free birth "means equality all around," thus assigning a right to an equal share of all social products and property.[2] Aristotle rejects such a notion, even while acknowledging the link between the construction of subjectivity and the constitution of justice within the state.

In making his distinction about rule by the one, the few, or the many, Aristotle is reflecting a concern for the *who* of power. "Who should rule" is a question that incorporates an ethical dimension. What individual or group has the right to power? This ethical question has always been part of political discourse.

However, the question of *who* cannot be separated neatly from the question of *how*. The *how* of power concerns the conditions that lead to its generation. Power does not occur in a vacuum. It results from the organization of human beings into collective forms of activities. Therefore, it should be viewed as the result of the material conditions that expand the systemic capacity for organization. Human aggregates manifest power as they coordinate collective behavior. In that sense, all systems of coordinated activity are systems of domination.

In this work, the *how* of power will be addressed along a number of dimensions. It will be treated as the result of education and literacy, administrative competence, a system for the dissemination of a common identity, the conditions of technology and production, and the internal system of discipline. These material conditions will be read as causally significant indicators of the ability of organizations to manifest power, defined as the coordination of human activity.

We will follow the general epistemological position of poststructuralist analysis. Central to these assumptions is the view that the exercise of power cannot be divorced from the system in which the knowledge about organizations and power is constructed. Therefore, the construction of knowledge regarding power will be the reflection of the possibilities for the exercise of power in any historical epoch. The outcome of this process of historical reflection is the ideological construction that creates the logic and the rights of power in any age.

Fundamental to the creation of ideologies is the construction of subjectivity. Poststructuralism rejects any notion of transcendent subjectivity. Organizations construct images of the subject that reflect the rationale of the structure from which they spring, creating an image of the subject that legitimates the exercise of power by that organization. Therefore, subjectivity is conditioned by the disciplinary instruments of the organization and the more subtle texts of socialization. From this perspective, the *who* and the *how* of power cannot be separated.

This work will explore the material conditions that promote the growth and spread of sovereign political power. We will carry this out along the material dimensions suggested above. We will also examine the structure of identity made possible by the conditions of power that are manifested in the disciplinary order. It will be our assertion that Aristotle's question of who should rule will be answered differently, depending on the material conditions of power.

As Nietzsche described it in, *On the Genealogy of Morals*, "the doer is the fiction added to the deed."[3] This means that the ideological constructions that legitimate the distribution of power in a society will be the reflection of the conditions of power. From this perspective, ideological struggles over the distribution of power in society are always struggles among competing formulations of human identity.

The Materiality of Organizations and the Rise of Power

There is a tendency in the modern period to think of democracy and domination at the opposite ends of a sliding scale of political practice. At the one end is domination, identified with the threat or use of force as part of maintenance of order and stability. At the other end of the spectrum is democracy, a political practice in which order and stability are maintained by some mechanism by which the sentiments of the population are transformed into the collective action of the political institutions. This view, manifested in writers such as Jean Jacques Rousseau, has tended to equate democracy with freedom, as political participation in the collective processes of decision making fulfill the legitimating conditions for the connection between individual action and collective power.

Such a view of democracy's legitimacy would not be possible without the assumptions regarding subjectivity that emerged in the modern era. The political components of modernity are constructed upon two essential pillars: equality and rationality. Unless human beings are essentially equal, the idea of giving each a voice in collective steering decisions of the social order would be absurd. Only a community of equals can grant equal status in decision making, a central principle of democratic practice. Further, only rational beings can be expected, through some form of rumination and calculation, to arrive at the "best," or most appropriate outcome for a given issue. Therefore, the modern underpinnings of democratic practice are tied to these two fundamental positions with regard to human nature.

However, embedded within these two assumptions is a third. Such a position with regard to the essence of human nature would not be possible without the further proposition that human nature is essentially fixed. This position views the content of subjectivity to be transcendent, beyond the scope of historical influences. The result of such a belief can be witnessed through the documents of Western political philosophy, with the deluded view that every age has discovered what the previous age lacked, the true understanding of the nature of subjectivity from which the new order can be constructed.

For Plato, an aristocracy of wisdom can be constructed if those with talents in the dialectic can be discovered. Conversely, Hobbes asserted that the selfish brutes of society can use the small modicum of reason they possess to save themselves from a violent death. For Kropotkin, the reasonable and benevolent creature is distorted by the institutional power accumulated by the ruling classes. Even for the Marx of the *1844 Manuscripts*, the essential characteristics of the human being are stripped away by the capitalist form of production. In all these examples from Western political philosophy, political prescription is predicated on the fixed content of human identity.

However, there is another means by which the discourse on democracy and domination can be approached. This involves a materialist reading of the relationship between human subjectivity and the historical conditions in which the subject is constructed. Within this view, the text on the subject is constructed in a fashion that makes the prevailing practice, in this case the system of domination, appear rational. From this point of view, the constructed subject is part of the ideological text of any age that rationalizes the distribution of power. This construction is reflected both within the institutional structures, and within the ideological texts that legitimate the existing distribution of power.

Such a perspective is partially developed by Marx in the *German Ideology*, and can generally be described under the title of materialism. However, Marx's formulation is only partially materialistic, as the discussion of alienation is premised on a humanistic reading of subjectivity. Nevertheless, Marx provides a starting point for the generation of an anthropological reading of the historical record. In the twentieth century, the materialist reading of history is developed by the school of poststructuralism.

Poststructuralism and the Logic of Material Inquiry

Epistemology

The development of a perspective on democracy that avoids treating it as fulfilling human essence or as part of a teleology of history requires moving away from the assumptions of modern social theory. This study will use the model of poststructuralism as its central epistemological approach. Poststructuralist epistemology offers a number of advantages. It tends to operate at a more abstract level of generality in its interpretive domain, what Foucault calls *savoir*, and, therefore, is able to engage a broad spectrum of information. Further, poststructuralism views the development of ideology, subjectivity, and political forms as the product of historical forces that manifest the content of those constructions. Such a perspective gives an anthropological reading of the present, a means to try and limit the influence of modernist ideological and teleological biases in the construction of knowledge.

The starting point for such a perspective is the idea that all claims to knowledge are human creations. Human beings see the world through eyes that are strictly human. Therefore, they anthropomorphize the content of that world in seeking to come to an understanding of its forces.[4] Such a position abandons the Platonic/Christian idea that there is a transcendental realm in which the truths about the world are manifest. To paraphrase Nietzsche, there are only creatures in the world who, through a certain relative rightness about the functioning of its systems, enhance their survivability.[5]

All specific claims to knowledge in a subject area, what Foucault calls *connaissance*, are reflections of that underlying condition. We do not capture the essence of the world, the transcendental character of its secrets. Hence, "facts" about the social realm must always be contextualized. They must be seen as linked to the historical conditions from which they are generated. Therefore, our social knowledge must always be viewed as interpretive.[6]

Owing to the fact that human beings are historical creatures, their interpretations must have a historical character. Knowledge is a reflection of the conditions of existence in the age in which it was created. It reflects not only the concerns of a particular society in the content of the knowledge generated, but also contains the more general conditions of *savoir*, the epistemological paradigm in which truth claims receive their validation.[7]

Hence, the production of truth claims is always relative to the epistemological conditions in which those claims receive their validation. For example, in a society in which religious texts are viewed as containing the "word of God," a truth claim that is constructed using scientific syntax is not likely to be viewed as valid. In a society that adheres to a scientific paradigm, the reverse would occur. The poststructuralists view the state of society as a struggle (Foucault refers to it as a war)[8] among these competing epistemological paradigms. The outcomes of these closed systems of inquiry cannot be measured by the quality or quantity of truth claims generated. All are interpretations, even those of science. Each generates its claims to knowledge within a closed system of objects and metaphorical references. In the end, each can only be judged by the conditions of life that it makes possible.

From this perspective, the history of a given culture is one in which the transmission of metaphors and signs, embedded within the language, have been both the way in which truth claims receive their validation and the means by which culture is transmitted from one generation to the next. Nietzsche describes the validation process in *On Truth and Lies in a Non-Moral Sense*. Nietzsche argues that to be considered truthful, our speech must contain the expected metaphors.[9] That is, our statements must transmit the metaphors that have come to us from within the cultural context in which we reside.

Jacques Derrida deals with this notion extensively in the work, *Dissemination*. Derrida's point is that since the time of Plato it has been assumed in the West that our language is constructed as a system of signs that both stand in, and describe, the essence of the object under consideration. Thus, language is assumed to have a metaphysical and transcendent character, ascending to the capturing of essence in the generation of texts about the world.

What is significant about Derrida's contribution is his detailed description of the process by which this takes place. Like other poststructuralists, Derrida begins with the assumption that human beings create knowledge claims about the world. In *Dissemination*, he is particularly interested in their transmission. Language is treated as a system of signs that receive their validity from the fact that they connect to a system of signs that collectively convey the content of a particular culture. These signs do not capture "being" or "essence." They are valid owing to the fact that in their usage they reference a larger system of signs from which they receive their authority.[10]

Hence, language is a system of signs in which the validity of the sign is measured according to its origins within the larger system of signs from which it was "triggered." Thus, texts cannot describe "essence," but only describe other texts in an endless chain of transformation. To this Derrida assigns the term, "grafting."[11]

The notion of grafting onto previous texts assumes the inability to capture "essence," the transcendental truth of being. What is left of knowledge? There can be no knowledge with a capital "K." There is only an endless play of signs and metaphors. If this is the case, there is no "column of being"[12] around which to fix stable identities to objects or people. The assigning of characteristics must remain fluid, open, and substitutable. The field of such substitutions is infinite.[13]

Such a position has profound implications for politics. Derrida articulates a problem that is echoed in the work of Foucault and other contemporary poststructuralists. If it is not possible to assign fixed and stable identities, it is not possible to represent human beings or define "human nature." In such a case, the political prescriptions that arise in the policy-making process can only be historical and transitory.[14] Such a position requires further elaboration.

Representation and Subjectivity

Of particular importance of this epistemological position for the concept of politics is the relationship between language and human subjectivity. If language is historical and metaphorical, then the descriptions of things must have a character that binds the representation of those things to a specific context. In representing human nature, or subjectivity, there cannot be any assertions of content that are not tied to the institutional context that assigns them power. This means that in an epistemological sense, all such construction must remain open.[15]

In considering subjectivity, such a position has several significant implications. The subject is a historical construction. It is a result of the structures of power, the development of the institutional order, and the technological conditions of social existence.

This view reverses the relationship between institutional existence and subjectivity. In the tradition of the "transcendent subject," from Plato to the modern period, subjectivity has been treated as having an independent, ahistorical character. In the view of Derrida, Foucault, and other poststructuralists, subjectivity is the constructed feature of an age carried out through the fabrication of systems of rewards, punishments, inducements, and indoctrination. The order of an age operates only through the dissemination of the constructed subject. It is the rationale that binds together all the features of the system of domination. Within such a domain, the definition of ethical behavior, political action, and the construction of the "normal" subject is reflected and shaped.

Therefore, what is defined as the "human being" is not reflected in the institutional order, but is created by it. Hence, there is no place to stand that is not ideological in character, no transcendent realm in which the construction of the subject takes place outside of its context. Embedded within this epistemological logic, each age tends to create the illusion that it alone has discovered the truth of being in the world.

The politics of such an illusory enterprise is dangerous. This is due to two overriding features. To close off the notion of identity is to deny other possibilities, competing discourses on the subject, and alternative histories. Power creates singularities, not multiplicities. Hence, such a process always contains a totalitarian potential.

Secondly, given that the process is circular, with power generating the means of its own rationality through the construction of subjectivity, the feedback within the system of dissemination engages power in the defense of itself. When the technical capacity of the system will allow the growth and extension of power, there will be no check on the expansion of its domain of action. In fact, such an expansion is contained within the logic of power itself. Such a situation can be seen in the expansion of state power in the contemporary world. For example, the rise of high technology has provided the technical means for the bureaucratic state of the twentieth century to morph into the surveillance state in the twenty-first. The subject will be reconstructed as part of the process, reflecting the changes in the institutional order and its means of centralization and control. It is our contention that democracy will not encumber this process, as its internal make-up will be reconstructed in order to adapt to the transformation of the technical means of control.

This is the case because the institutions of power within any society function through a mechanism by which they generate claims to truth.[16] The content of subjectivity is constituted within the articulation of truth claims emanating from those institutions.[17] Such claims are then reinforced throughout the political order.

This position regarding the relationship between knowledge construction and the political order represent a stance that is clearly *materialist* in its assumptions. Poststructuralism seeks to create a method that moves away from the transcendental assumptions within the modern formulation in the social sciences. This is particularly evident in the development of the genealogical method.

Nietzsche, Foucault, and the Genealogical Method

Given the epistemological position outlined within poststructuralism, the problems of inquiry and analysis seem particularly profound. Any method must begin with the premise that the ideas and concepts embedded within the analysis are going to be contextually transformed. "Democracy" to Aristotle means something very different than the notion of democracy today. Further, given that the content of subjectivity is altered by the conditions of power, it is necessary to locate the field of study away from the particular ideological representations of "essence" or "human nature" that are used as the benchmarks of progress in any particular age. To put this claim another way, if the ideological content of an age is the product of the context in which it is produced, it is necessary to examine the specific practices of an age in order to understand the origins of the ideas that rationalized those practices. Such a method is developed by Nietzsche and Foucault under the name "genealogy."

Foucault describes the genealogical method as:

> . . . a form of history which can account for the constitution of knowledges, discourses, domains of objects etc., without having to make reference to a subject which is either transcendental in relation to the field of events or runs in its empty sameness throughout the course of history.[18]

Foucault clarifies this by saying that the notion of subjectivity needs to be understood as contextually constructed. Within such a framework, the construction of a stable, ahistorical notion of subjectivity is impossible.

As a result, there can be no universal history of the subject and civilization. History cannot be presented as the unfolding of a singular path of development. From the genealogical perspective, history is viewed as a series of successive attempts to impose a hegemonic discourse on the subject. The ability to control the constitution of the subject, and through such a construction reinforce a particular mode of existence over others, solidifies a particular distribution of power relations.

Nietzsche and Genealogy

These methodological assumptions are developed by Nietzsche in *On the Genealogy of Morals*. The guiding question that Nietzsche asks is:

> Under what conditions did man construct the value judgments *good* and *evil*? And what is their intrinsic worth? Have they thus far benefited or retarded mankind? . . . A great variety of answers suggested themselves. I began to distinguish among periods, nations, individuals; I narrowed the problem down; the answers grew into new questions, investigations, supposi-

tions, probabilities, until I had staked off at last my own domain, a whole hidden, growing and blooming world, secret
gardens as it were, of whose existence no one must have an
inkling. . .[19]

Nietzsche's questions demand that the investigator reconsider the whole
study of history and philosophy "as if with new eyes."[20] Genealogy, with
its study of material origins, seeks to discover and reevaluate the most
important and elementary aspects of history and society to ascertain the
true roots of our circumstances, institutions, and values in a manner that
avoids the metaphysics of "essence."

Nietzsche rejected the notion that the origin of political and social
institutions can be found in the realization of a "truth" regarding the nature of human essence. Therefore, there can be no core, no ontological
center around which and from which all social and political life flows.
The very notion of having a center is a construct of human beings. Therefore the belief in a cultural center has no meaning in and of itself. It only
acquires the meaning attached to it.

The result of Nietzsche's stance regarding social reality is that the
distribution of power, the developments in the culture, and the transformation of institutions cannot be explained with reference to a transcendent, universal subject. For Nietzsche, "the origin" should not be perceived to be an event where a quintessential truth is discovered or
realized. This is true even in the discussion of morality.

In *On the Genealogy of Morals*, Nietzsche described the origins of
values in ancient Greece. In Nietzsche's analysis, the content of ancient
Greek values is found within the class relations found in Athens. The
"good" is associated with the values and norms of the most powerful social class.[21] Since the nobles controlled the processes of dissemination,
Nietzsche concluded that the mode of power in this case was "language."
The nobles take possession of language as an expression of power.[22]
Therefore, it is through the ability to control dissemination that an interest can create and spread a discourse on subjectivity that has hegemonic
power. Hegemony comes from the force of dissemination, not the "truth"
of any particular claim. Such a discourse contains the notions of good
and bad behavior and the "proper" distribution of power in the society.

The materiality of this process is developed by Nietzsche as he explores the rise of the Judeo-Christian system of values. Nietzsche rejects
the idea that Judeo-Christian values constitute some necessary progress,
or the development of a truth regarding the human being. Then what explains the rise of Christian morality? Nietzsche focuses on two empirical

developments in the rise of Christian values. The first is the fact that the majority in the ancient Rome was poor and sought an explanation for the conditions of its suffering. Christianity provided both an explanation of suffering and a promise of redemption. Simply put, when the masses realized the power of their numbers, and acquired the rudimentary skills of literacy and organization, they were able to create an alternative discourse on the subject that became the new hegemonic discourse on the subject and its "morality."

The second aspect in the material nature of this development was the rise of an institutional component for the development and dissemination of this doctrine: the institution of the church and the rise of a class of priests as the disseminators of the new values. The priests propagated the new doctrine. Power was maintained, as a disciplinary cruelty became part of the embedded truth regarding the "natural" condition of human subjectivity. The power of the masses was harnessed and controlled by an institution that concentrated power and replicated their collective hopes, fears, and aspirations. As the Roman Empire disintegrated, the priestly class increased its power. This was due to falling literacy rates, and the narrowing of the methods of dissemination. As a result, the scientific knowledge of the ancient world was forgotten and technological advances of Greece and Rome crumbled.

Foucault and Genealogy

Foucault continued the Nietzschean method of genealogy in his own work. Foucault described this method as one in which the inquirer interprets events, giving an overview of the interconnections among fields of study.[23] The investigator does not search for depth, but follows the minor details and slight variations, the "surface" of events.[24] Genealogy is not interested in discovering "origins" of fundamental truths, but in tracing "descent." The genealogical method does not expose a definite beginning. Instead, there is an investigation into the processional thread of "insaturations of power." As a result, events and circumstances must be constantly reevaluated and reinterpreted, with genealogy as the recorded history of these interpretations.[25]

Owing to the fact that knowledge and discourse are treated as human creations, these contextual factors cannot be treated in isolation from the institutions of power. Societies control and discipline their populace by constructing and maintaining knowledge claims and reinforcing these "truths" in the practice of the human sciences. The human sciences endeavor to reinforce the definition of "normality" that maintains the existing institutions of power and discipline. The political system amasses power to reward and punish in the name of the "norm." Laws governing speech, patterns of social behavior, and biological functions, exist as parts of the institutional structures in all states. Tracing those surface practices reveal the underlying foundational claims upon which the institutional order is constructed.

Foucault sought to end the "regime of truth" by developing a means to analyze and probe the mechanisms and institutions in society. All societies have a "political economy" of manufacturing and separating truth from falsehood, techniques for attaining truth, and a status for those who are granted the power to determine the truth. By making those processes visible and transparent, Foucault hoped to weaken the exercise of arbitrary and oppressive power to a minimum and empower alternative knowledges in the social discourse.

Discourse is rule governed. Those in societies who establish the truth are guided by an implicit set of rules that control what kinds of beliefs, concepts, and terminology are satisfactory. These rules also include what credentials and social standing are necessary for a person's discourse to be regarded as knowledge. Hence, there is a central role for a group regarded as intellectuals in the structure and performance of power.

Institutional power manifests itself as the ability to generate and disseminate truth claims regarding subjects, and the exercise of power. It is the concentration and centralization of power within institutions that creates the hegemony that eliminates counter discourses to those of the power structure. As a result, Foucault's position is that genealogical analysis is not the imposition of a more rigorous "science" of empirical analysis, but the movement to delegitimate the power structures that maintain a monopoly on what can enter the domain of discourse in a particular field.[26]

Institutional structures seek to "inscribe knowledges in the hierarchical order of power associated with science…"[27] Given that poststructuralist epistemology views the constructions of scientific knowledge as contextual products influenced by the distribution of power, it is not surprising that Foucault would identify genealogical analysis as "antisciences."[28] However, it should be noted that Foucault's concern was for the operation of scientific inquiry within a set of institutional power relations. In medieval Europe, the institution of the church conducted the Inquisition, burning both books and those labeled as heretics in order to promote a singular, unitary conception of what qualified as truth. To the

poststructuralists, modern institutions, armed with the "scientific method" are engaged in a process of delegitimating and dismantling discourses that constitute alternatives to those of institutionalized power.
After all, who could deny that the latter half of the twentieth century was
dominated by two competing models of the subject, both embedded
within institutional structures that rewarded compliance and punished
dissent, while threatening each other, and the world, with annihilation.
    So Foucault claimed that:

> . . . a genealogy should be seen as a kind of attempt to eman-
> cipate historical knowledges from that subjection [to the pow-
> er of science], to render them, that is, capable of opposition
> and of struggle against the coercion of a theoretical, unitary,
> formal, and scientific discourse. It is based on a reactivation of
> local knowledges ...in opposition to the scientific hierarchisa-
> tion of knowledges and the effects intrinsic to their power. .
> ."[29]

Does such a position mean that Foucault was simply "against science?" The situation is not that simple. Science is a syntactical structure,
a method of generating knowledge that contains no implicit assumptions,
other than the value of its own method. Foucault's position is that the
content produced by the scientific method will serve any master. When
scientific discourse is used in the service of institutional power, it will
reinforce those structures, and the unitary conditions of power, purpose,
and modes of living that constitute the structural components of oppression.
    In Foucault's own genealogical explorations empirical reference
points were essential to his attempts to empower alternative discourses.
In both *Madness and Civilization* and *Discipline and Punish*, Foucault
examined the rise of institutional forms of incarceration and their links to
the emerging view of subjectivity within the structures of power. In his
essay, "Truth and Juridical Forms," Foucault examined the rise of the
"prosecutor" as mechanism that promoted the centralization and expansion of state power.[30] In all of these works, the transformation of social
practices was presented as generating new ideological constructions of
the self, norms of behavior, and the expectations of political life.
    Foucault's objective in genealogical analysis was to reveal the na-
ture and conditions of subjugation. If the social order is the result of social forces, arbitrary rules, petty power struggles, and chance, rather than
the fulfillment of a teleology of existence and the realization of some
underlying principle of human nature, then the methodology that reveals

that condition is a means of liberation. By studying the interrelationship among power, knowledge, and the control of the human body, genealogical study can "unmask the operation of power in order to enable those who suffer from it to resist."[31]

Democracy and Power

As a materialist methodology, poststructuralism seeks to de-transcendentalize the foundational concepts of social practice by moving away from essentialist definitions and replacing them with an understanding of the historical nature of the processes in which they are formed. It is the goal of such research to remove the privileged position of texts that claim a transcendent character. By deconstructing these texts, and historicizing their content, they become unable to command the status of "truth" from which they can direct the collective power of the social order. How many people have been killed in the name of the "truth" of religion, national identity, ethnic purity, the naturalness of cultural hegemony, or the inevitability of historical outcomes? These doctrines have all justified slaughter in the name of the text.

In the nineteenth and twentieth centuries, while the power of some of these texts has declined, a new text has emerged to legitimate the collectivization of power and its exercise. This new transcendental text is democracy. From Napoleon in the nineteenth century to the wars emerging in the twenty-first, there is an undercurrent in which the call of democracy is used to legitimate the actions of the major powers. However, if democracy is a historical construction rather than a truth to be implemented, then its legitimating power is undercut. To put this another way, if democratic practice is bound to the historical conditions that gave rise to it, then it cannot be assigned or enforced as a universal measure of political achievement.

Democracy and domination are not polar opposites on a political scale, but in a relation of genus to species. Democracy is one species of domination. It is the model of domination that emerged along with the material conditions that have come to characterize modernity.

What Democracy Is and Is Not

Before proceeding to a more detailed description of the method to be used in this work, it is necessary to address the matter of definition. What is democracy? What are its defining characteristics? How is democracy connected to the idea of domination? Such questions are more difficult than they appear because of the mythic qualities that have been assigned to democracy as part of the modern understanding of society and politics. Social science, political theory, and contemporary notions of order are products of the development of knowledge that emerged along with the nation-state and its technologies of legitimation.

Such a condition creates a variety of implications. Within this framework there is a tendency to view the pursuit of democratic institutions as a feature embedded within human ontology. The unfolding of democratic practices is, within this model, viewed as the realization of human essence as manifested in political structures and constitutional forms. Democracy fulfills our longing as political creatures.

Another aspect of this ontological position is that democracy is seen as part of an inevitable *telos* of the political order. It is true that since the seventeenth century there has been an increase in the scope and depth of democratic practice. However, it is our contention that such a development can be located within the advance of mass politics, production, and administration. Further, the continuity that is assumed between industrial and postindustrial forms of democratic practice may be more illusory than real. (This issue will be addressed in Chapters Five and Six.)

Along with the notion that the democratic tendency is a component of human nature and that the political history of the species is a fulfilling of that essential destiny is the view that democracy is synonymous with human freedom. The argument's logic following from the assumption that human beings are freedom-seeking creatures and, following Locke, that in a social setting of multiple interests the best that they can achieve is a compromise between having absolute freedom and absolute security. The social freedom secured by this compromise receives its legitimacy from the fact that all consent to a process in which they get some form of input. However, it is our contention that what this actually secures is a majoritarian form of domination. That should not be confused with autonomy and expansion of freedom.

This work will make none of these assumptions. It is our view that democracy must be viewed from a contextualized understanding of history. Following the insights of Nietzsche and Foucault, democracy will be treated as the reflection of social forces in a given society. From this perspective, "human nature" is constructed as an accompanying discourse to the distribution of power, production, and structures of control and domination that are generated and disseminated in a particular epoch. This view rejects the notion of an essence that is fulfilled through adherence to historically contrived structural forms.

Simply stated, democracy is a system of domination in which the masses have some influence over the content and direction in the collective use of power. The "legitimacy" of the exercise of power, described as the transformation of "power" into "authority," stems from the process by which the demos exercises its influence. Thus, the practice of democracy must be accompanied by some technology of social organization for transforming the opinion of the masses into political action for the society.

Such a view of democracy focuses on the procedures of majoritarian rule. Specifically excluded from this discussion are the concepts often referred to as "democratic principles." These principles include such ideas as: tolerance for the opinions of others, minority rights, and respect for the diversity of opinion. It is our contention that such notions are the products of Enlightenment Humanism, and are not necessary components of democracy as a form of rule. Therefore, they should not be treated as essential components of democracy for the purposes of study, regardless of their attractiveness as codes of conduct and social ethics by which to guide political thinking..

Further, the use of the democratic form of domination requires an accompanying discourse on subjectivity, as democracy cannot be divorced from the ideological components that make its practice appear rational. For the purposes of this study, the belief in essential human equality, and the universality of reason will be treated as indicators of a strong affinity with democratic forms of political practice. Not only must there be a belief that reason is relatively evenly distributed in society for democracy to be rational, but that reason must be of a uniform nature. Only under such conditions can those who employ it be drawn to the same conclusions. There must be continuity of thought in order for the collective practices that it supports to have legitimacy.

The issue of ideology manifests another question. What is the relationship of ideology to political practice? More generally, what is the relationship between the beliefs about human identity and historical context? Traditional forms of political analysis have tended to treat the political process as a manifestation of the essential character of human beings. From Plato to Marx, some formulation of the human character has served as the basis for political critique and the establishment of a new direction for political practice. The assumptions of Nietzsche, Foucault, and others generally falling into the school of poststructuralist thought, reverse that relationship. The institutional structure generates an accompanying discourse that supports the exercise of power.

Unity is created through the development and refinement of a common language, shared history, and a standard of behavior, coupled with the technical means to disseminate them as a common symbolic identity. The unity of outcomes, the self-affiliation with a territorial or administrative unit, and the engagement in a common task are the products of a technology of control that lead to an *outcome* that is the commonality of interests, identity, and purpose. It cannot be addressed as something innate, divorced from a process of socialization and the processes by which people gain an understanding of themselves in a wider social context. Ideology is the product of this process and serves as a unifying story of a political culture in which the population participates.

Therefore, democracy contains no truth, no inevitable logic of history, and no correspondence to human essence. It is neither good nor bad. It is simply a system of governance that evolved along with the consolidation of technologies for human administration. It generates its truths out of a system in which the majoritarian sentiments of the demos are translated into collective action. In this regard, it comes with no guarantees of wisdom or humanity, or their opposites. It is a mechanism for generating binding political decisions that guarantee that the public gets the outputs from the decision-making processes that it deserves.

Genealogy and the Study of Domination

This study is interested in the material forces that enhance a particular form of political association. Material conditions generate the potential for the expansion of power. Therefore, the materiality of existence cannot be separated from the forms of domination. We are also interested in the legitimating texts on subjectivity that accompany the distribution of power in a given period. The human being is shaped in the wake of power. Texts on the subject reflect the norms and expectations of the populous in a given period. They also serve to be the focal points of struggle, as a clash of models of subjectivity translate to a struggle over the logic of resource distribution. Such a study requires a broad, interpretive reading of history.

As has been discussed, poststructuralist epistemology opposes language that characterizes history as a teleological quest, containing a linear path to the fulfillment of human essence. History has no plan. Human essence is undefinable. However, there are contextual forces that move history and shape the activities and beliefs of people caught within them. Therefore, no form of domination can be characterized as either "good" or "bad" in any foundational sense. Such a claim would require some metaphysical claims both about the nature of the subject and the character of the social order that do not follow from our assumptions.

How can these methodological constraints be applied to the analysis of domination? Such a task requires moving in a different direction than much of the traditional analysis. In the history of political thought, political prescription has tended to follow, deductively, from some characterization of human nature. For example, in the modern period, democracy has tended to be connected with some notion of human essence, as the manifestation of the human longing for freedom. Further, this tends to be tied to the notion of an unfolding of democratic practice as a measure of social and political development. The assumptions of this study prevent the incorporation of such claims, rejecting them as components of the context out of which they were constructed. Therefore, the question remains, how does one proceed within such epistemological constraints?

In this perspective one must begin with some understanding of the materiality of domination. That is, one must examine the contextual components of a society, in this case broadly viewed as the "West," in order to dissect those elements that will enhance or detract from the conditions that make a particular form of political arrangement possible. To be more specific, the context that gives rise to monarchy is different than that which gives rise to democracy. What follows from this is simple. If the conditions that give rise to a particular form of domination are transformed, the structure of domination will be transformed.

As mentioned above, the procedure used to approach this analysis will be based on the general outline of the poststructuralist epistemology. The methodology we will employ addresses what will be termed the *material dimensions of power*. These constitute a set of interrelated propositions that describe the materiality of power. That is, they will seek to provide a set of variables that are significant in determining both the scope of power and in influencing the particular configurations that domination takes in a particular age.

Dimension One

Domination is a system of power relations in which a person or group can effectively alter the actions of another person or group. This can be carried out either by the threat or use of force, or by the more subtle techniques of socialization, propaganda, and persuasion. In either case, the goal of domination is to bring the behavior of individuals and groups in harmony with the project of the *persuading* agent.

Domination takes many structural forms. These forms will be linked to the historical conditions in which the system of domination is formed. Systems can be centralized, decentralized, on the scale of empires, or local city-states. However, regardless of the form, material conditions ultimately shape the system that is generated.

While it is our intent to avoid any hard, deterministic language or monocausal formulations, what follows from the materialistic approach is the conclusion that material conditions establish the basic environment for the formation of a system of domination. This means that when the conditions of social existence change, there is the likelihood that a transformation of the political institutions will occur. This will produce a corresponding alteration in the construction of the subject. Changing the construction of the subject alters the norms and expectations of what constitutes the definition of *rational* action in any age. This is the political nature of the break or rupture Foucault addressed in his work.

There are two implications of this position that should be made explicit. First, from the perspective of material history, the scope and reach of power will be tied to the material conditions of its manifestations. This sounds logical enough when one considers the reach of military power being limited to its technical capacity. However, our suggestion goes beyond that. As will be argued throughout the work, the organization of the capacity of dissemination is also of major importance, as is the level of administrative competence. These also constitute the material premises of power.

The second implication of the material approach to power is manifested in a rejection of any teleological understanding of history. History contains no plan, no direction, and no inevitable course. History is shaped within the material conditions of its generation.

Such a position is particularly relevant in the study of democracy within a culture that is tied to the modernist view of the subject. This study rejects such a notion. Democracy contains no necessary connection to freedom in either the abstract or practical sense. It is a form of social arrangement in which the decision-making that binds all attains its legitimacy from the fact that there is some mechanism for attaining input from the demos on the direction those binding decisions take. In this sense, Aristotle is correct in the way in which he framed the discussion of democracy. It should be seen and studied only in relation to other forms of domination.

Democracy, therefore, is not synonymous with the idea of free-dom. It is a mass form of regulation and control in a double sense of the word. In democracy, domination has its origins in the mass, its beliefs, attitudes, norms, and values. Its institutions receive their legitimacy from the fact of this connection. Democracy is also a system for dominating the masses. In that sense, democracy can be expected to rise along with mass forms of administration. As do all forms of domination, it creates the institutional reinforcements and ideological attendants that give it its particular character.

As a result of this condition, the rise of democracy should be studied in relation to the ebbing of other forms of domination. As democracy rises, there is a decline in the forms of domination characterized as autocratic or oligopolistic. However, this should not be confused with the decline in domination in a more general sense. Domination, as the control over human bodies and the direction of behavior in the name of power, does not decline within democracy. It simply changes its means of legitimation.

Dimension Two

Power and domination are functions of organization. The organization of masses of people for a common enterprise is the measure and means of power. The ability to aggregate human energy and give it direction in a common endeavor manifests the collective power of individual acts into, what can metaphorically be called, a living machine. Taken in total, the organization of activities on a grand scale has been the key to Western expansion, domination, and technological advancement. This feature of Western civilization has allowed the growth of empires, and in its absence, has led to their decline.

Such an organization requires a highly differentiated administrative apparatus. It requires specialized training and skills. Every successful empire in history has had some form of advanced education for its bureaucracy. Therefore, examining the means, techniques, and scope of administrative units in a political organization will give some indication of the potential capacity of its power.

However, the technical skills are only part of the consideration of organization. Each organization needs some core idea which establishes a sense of duty to the common mission. The legitimating discourse for the sense of a collective calling has changed throughout history. It has taken the form of divine missions, struggles of ethnic identity, cultural hegemony, and national economic interests.

When it comes to the consideration of democracy, democracy is not only compatible with the growth and extension of a centralized form of domination, it actually constitutes a refined means to that end. Democracy is a mechanism for creating and legitimating a shared enterprise, for which the administrative apparatus is the technical means. Therefore, as a mass form of domination, the rise of democracy will be tied to the rise in the technical skills of the masses. In practical terms, this means that democratic domination must have some material basis for growth and development that is grounded in the skills of the population.

Dimension Three

Literacy and education are central material components in determining both the origin of collective power and in shaping the particular configuration of domination that will exist. Some level of educational competence is necessary, even if only manifested in the elite and their advisors in order to create the conditions for the performance of the administration. Further, the level of education among the citizenry seems, in a historical sense, to have a determining outcome on the particular form of domination present in the social order. For example, in Athenian democracy there was widespread education among the limited class of full citizens who participated in politics. In the modern day, the spread of universal education has been directly correlated with the growth of suffrage.

It is our view that education is indirectly tied to increases in democratic participation due to universal education reinforcing one of the pillars of democratic practice: equality. An educated population is not simply more competent in their ability to understand the complexities of the contemporary world, they are also more equal in terms of their ability to engage the common definitions of what constitutes reasonable action. Further, as will be discussed in later chapters, the educational process is a *conditioning* process in which the populous is socialized into the common mission of society. To the extent that they are so conditioned, extending the vote does not constitute a threat to the status quo.

For all of these reasons, the level of literacy will be of great importance in understanding the materiality of power and the ebb and flow of democratic institutions throughout history. Mass education is necessary for the growth of democracy, but it also enhances the growth of centralized forms of domination. It is essential for mass administration, the development of written law, the development of constitutionalism, the emergence of contracts, and the formalization of procedures within bureaucratic organizations. From this perspective it was not a coincidence that the collapse of the Roman Empire was coupled with the breakdown of the educational system and the deterioration of public libraries. When the infrastructure that provided the conditions necessary for mass administration collapsed, the end of the empire was not far behind.

In addition to providing the skills necessary to administer vast territories and peoples, education also serves another function. With the development of semiotics as a subset of linguistics, it is clear that education is also essential in the transmission of a symbolic identity to human beings. Mass society of any sort would simply be impossible without a mass means of disseminating the culture identity that binds a community together. Education is the means by which the mass forms of mobilization necessary to expand centralized power become possible. Only after the socialization of an identity into the public is it possible to use the symbols of that identity for mass forms of mobilization.

Dimension Four

Centralized institutions require some means by which a common set of signs and images can be transferred to a population. This is the process of dissemination. These signs integrate the community and constitute the symbolic identity of the population. They differentiate that population from another.

The process of translating common symbols to an organization requires a technological means of transmission. Dissemination begins with the creation of a common language. However, the oral tradition as a technology of dissemination is limited in its scope. A single person speaking to a crowd will have a limited effect. Such an audience would be small and this would limit the range and appeal of such a process. Writing is a technological revolution in the area of dissemination. As Joyce Marcus stated in *Mesoamerican Writing Systems*, writing must be considered as a tool of political organization, necessary for the development of mass administration.[32] Advances in the technical means of dissemination, from the printing press to the internet, increase the audience that can be reached. This alters the size of the population that can be effected by new narratives of history and new constructions of subjectivity.

The emergence of these new technologies also has an effect on the content of subjectivity more directly. New conceptions of subjectivity, ownership and property rights, levels of individual choice and rationality, are all tied to a structure of the subject that includes the ability of human beings to act as rational agents in the world. This alters the conception of the self, and alters what is possible in the realm of domination and the prospects for democratic institutions.

Dimension Five

The scope of domination will expand to the technical capacity of the system. Every system of domination requires structural components that make the system of domination function. The political system must have some mechanisms for administration; collecting taxes, record keeping, property transfers, dispute resolution, and public projects. However, there are technical constraints on the extent to which those acts of administration can be carried out. Viewed this way, democratic practice can be viewed as tied to the conditions that give rise to the expansion of domination in a more general sense. While not a direct cause of the expanding scope of domination, the same conditions that give rise to expanding power, such as increases in literacy and administrative competence, give rise to the growth of democracy.

The rise of democracy is correlated with these developments as a result of the fact that some of those increases in technical capacity are the same conditions that reinforce the growth of democratic practice. Literacy enhances the administrative competence of the political unit, but also increases the culture of equality. This translates into increasing demands for participation. Therefore, it is not only possible that expanding literacy increases democratic practice, but that it also creates the material condition for the expansion of state power and centralized institutions.

Therefore, democracy should not be viewed as the opposite of expanded centralized power. There is no necessary tension between these two forces. Democratic practice and centralized power are quite compatible. The rise of centralized power is linked to the technical means for the expansion of that power, not to its ideological components or constructions of human identity.

Dimension Six

The construction of an ideology in support of any form of domination results from the material capacity of the system to support it. Ideology emerges to rationalize a particular configuration of power. This is manifested in the aggregate of practices that are part of the institutional order of society. The most significant institutions may change, depending on the historical period, but the list must go beyond just the central political actors. For example, the list of significant organizations must include economic institutions, as matters of production, the system of social distribution, and the dispersion of social wealth in the society will have an impact on the configuration of power more generally. The church, or the presence or absence of voluntary mass organizations, may play varied roles depending on the period. However, the central point is that ideology emerges to formulate the configuration of power into a coherent picture. Ideology is the legitimating discourse, a set of assumptions and connections that make the existing practices part of an integrated story.

Monarchy, democracy, technocracy, plutocracy, and all the other systems of power can only arise within a context containing the material conditions that support them. Plutocracy will not flourish where wealth is widely dispersed. Technocracy does not emerge in an illiterate society. Democracy is not compatible with a feudal system of property arrangements. It is only when material structures are in place that can support the growth of democratic ideology that the practice emerges in the form of a "rational" political practice.

The example of democracy is particularly illustrative on this point. Given the historical nature of democratic practice, its manifestations will have characteristics unique to the context in which it is formulated. For example, even though the Greeks are often asserted to have "invented" democracy, they did not view all human beings as equally deserving of the rights of political participation. Citizenship was an essential component for the involvement in rulership. For the early moderns, property was a central component in the formation of the *contract* basis of legitimation. Hence, property ownership bestowed the rights of participation.

Therefore, even within the democratic form of domination, the character of democratic practice is not uniform. It is tied to the particular configurations of power that are part of the institutional order in which it arises.

Conclusion

These dimensions of materiality are designed to serve as general guidelines for this inquiry into the study of domination in its various forms. From a material perspective, political power is the ability to organize and direct collective action. The rise of political power is tied to the emergence of conditions that enhance the ability of organizational units to create the structured concerted action that exercises domination.

It will be our aim to focus on the material and historical conditions that gave rise to the systems of domination in general through an examination of various periods in the development of power in the Western world. In such an endeavor, it is not possible to account for every historical detail, every event that may have had some influence over the course of history. Hence, this enterprise will be an interpretive one. Our goal is to focus on those events and conditions that altered the discourse of what is possible in the realm of power relations.

In the chapters that follow, we will focus on the material elements of social life that have created the conditions for change. After examining these conditions, we will look at the way in which the transformation of the material elements of social life alters the conceptions of subjectivity present in the culture. Therefore, ideologies will be treated as symptoms rather than as causally significant features of social and political transformation.

Our goal is not to show any *necessary* trends in social and political development. No doubt, certain trends may, nevertheless, appear. Where are those trends embedded? Do they have their origins in the unfolding of history and human essence? If so, then the trends will be read in the most positive of terms. Our natures are becoming both revealed and reified in a kind of Hegelian logic of history. However, if the content of our natures is shaped by emerging conditions, then we must come to a realization. Every generation, within every historical configuration of power, has deluded itself into believing it has stepped outside the historical process in generating the political truths of its age. It is our hope that this work will represent a step away from such self-deception.

Notes

1. Aristotle, *The Politics of Aristotle*, ed. Ernest Barker (Oxford, UK: Oxford University Press, 1977), 115.

2. Aristotle, *The Politics*, 118.

3. Nietzsche, Friedrich, *The Birth of Tragedy and The Genealogy of Morals*, trans. by Francis Golffing (Garden City, NJ: Doubleday and Company, 1956), 45.

4. Nietzsche, Friedrich, "On Truth and Lies in a Non-Moral Sense," in *Nietzsche Selections*, ed. Richard Schacht (New York: Macmillan, 1993), 49.

5. Nietzsche, *Will to Power*, ed. Walter Kaufmann (New York: Vintage, 1968), 267.

6. Nietzsche, *Will to Power*, 267.

7. See Koch, Andrew M., *Knowledge and Social Construction* (Lanham, MD: Lexington Books, 2005).

8. Foucault, Michel, *Power/Knowledge*, ed. Colin Gordon, trans. Colin Gordon, et al. (New York: Pantheon Books, 1980), 114.

9. Nietzsche, "On Truth and Lies," 49.

10. Derrida, Jacques, *Dissemination* (Chicago: University of Chicago Press, 1981), 292.

11. Derrida, *Dissemination*, 355.

12. Derrida, *Dissemination*, 352.

13. Derrida, Jacques, *Writing and Difference* (Chicago: University of Chicago Press, 1978), 289.

14. See Koch, Andrew M. "Power, 'Text,' and Public Policy: The Political Implications of Jacques Derrida's Critique of 'Subjectivity,'" in *Southeastern Political Review* 26:1, 1998.

15. Derrida, *Dissemination*, 314.

16. Foucault, *Power/Knowledge*, 93.

17. Foucault, *Power/Knowledge*, 98.

18. Foucault, *Power/Knowledge*, 117.

19. Nietzsche, *The Birth of Tragedy*, 152.

20. White, Richard, "The Return of the Master: An Interpretation of Nietzsche's *Genealogy of Morals*, *Philosophy and Phenomenological Research*, Vol. 48, No. 4 (Jun., 1988), 684.

21. Nietzsche, Friedrich, *The Birth of Tragedy and The Genealogy of Morals*, trans. Francis Golffing, (Garden City, NJ: Doubleday and Company, 1956), 29.

22. Nietzsche, *Birth of Tragedy*, 26.

23. Dreyfus, Hubert L. and Paul Rabinow, *Michel Foucault: Beyond Structuralism and Hermeneutics* (Chicago: University of Chicago Press, 1983), 106.

24. Shiner, Larry, "Reading Foucault: Anti-Method and the Genealogy of Power-Knowledge," in *History and Theory*, Vol. 21, No. 3 (Oct. 1982), 107, 108.

25. Foucault, Michel, *Power/Knowledge*, ed. Colin Gordon, trans. Colin Gordon, et al. (New York: Pantheon Books, 1980), 117.

26. Foucault, *Power/Knowledge*, 83.

27. Foucault, *Power/Knowledge*, 85.

28. Foucault, *Power/Knowledge*, 83.

29. Foucault, *Power/Knowledge*, 85.

30. Foucault, *Power*, ed. James D. Faubion (New York: The New Press, 2000).

31. Philp, Mark, "Michel Foucault," in *The Return of Grand Theory in the Human Sciences*, ed. Quentin Skinner (Cambridge, UK: Cambridge University Press, 1985), 76, and Dreyfus, *Beyond Structuralism*, 105.

32. Marcus, Joyce, *Mesoamerican Writing Systems* (Princeton, NJ: Princeton University Press, 1992), 3–4.

Chapter Two

Athens and Rome: Dissemination, Identity, and the Rise of Central Power

Introduction

As discussed in Chapter One, the development of a system of power is the product of a set of material and technical conditions that give rise to the centralization of structures for human activity. Political power is the product of collective action. It can be manifested only in a condition in which the population has an understanding of shared history, experience, and values.

Such a set of conditions is not the product of any special status regarding the truth claims of a given group. Rather, collective action is the product of the "belief" in the truth-value of the common identity. Hence, the rise of political communities, empires, and later nation-states, has a common origin in the ability of a collective body to generate and disseminate an identity that incorporates the people within its domain. As a result, the creation of political entities is tied to the technical capacities of the system to both bring people within the sphere of collective power, and indoctrinate them in the identity of the collective.

Therefore, it is necessary to consider the material capacities of the system in order to understand and analyze the conditions that give rise to a particular form of political practice. The force of a particular characterization of the subject is limited by the carrying capacity of the system that seeks its dissemination. A political order must have the material means of dissemination, not simply the content to be disseminated, in order to expand its power and influence.

As a result, skills such as reading, writing, and arithmetic have a dual effect on the political communities in which they are prevalent. Such skills are necessary to the external growth of the administrative apparatus and the expansion of the territory and population governed by a particular political unit. However, these skills are also components that make up part of the structure of subjectivity necessary for the internal ordering of the social and political relations. For example, democracy can arise only where there are basic views of human identity that include human rationality and human equality. Widespread literacy is a necessary condition for the belief in both of those human capacities.

Greece and Rome represent important examples of how these processes interact. The rise and fall of Greece and Rome can be interpreted from the perspective of the material conditions of domination. For example, literacy was important within both contexts as it gave rise to the increased means of centralizing domination. In Greece, literacy fostered a notion of citizenry that extended full political rights to a community of equals, extending the legitimacy of the central institutions. In Rome, literacy increased the technical capacities of empire, as skills in administration and engineering produced the potential for the expansion of population, urbanization, and the growth. These results are the effects of literacy and the transformation in the technical means of integrating people into collective units of administration.

Ancient Greece: Literacy, Collective Identity, and Power

Dissemination: From the Oral Tradition to the Technology of Writing

The majority of ancient Greek societies before the formation of the polis, or city-state, were isolated due to the geography. Greece is on a peninsula and quite mountainous. Groups subsisted on hunting at first, then shepherding and agriculture. Isolated groups were usually tribal with a king, or hegemon, of some fashion. As Thucydides stated, in the beginning of the history of the Greeks there was not a difference between a barbarian and a Greek as "there were not any Greeks yet."

According to Greek fables, a clan led by Hellen and his sons, located in an area in the "northern hills" of Pythia, were summoned by other tribes to assist them. The groups then interacted and came to be labeled as

"Hellenes."[1] Eventually, the term "Hellenes" came to describe the greater population of the Greeks and separated them from what they considered the uncultured and uncivilized "barbarians" who did not speak the Hellenistic language. The conversion of groups to the Hellenistic language brought with it a transition to Hellenistic decorum, beliefs, and perspectives on the world around them.

Out of the conversion of tribes into Hellenistic communities came the idea of a Hellenistic identity. As the customs and beliefs were spread along with the dissemination of the language, a distinction developed between those of "civilized" ancestry and those considered "barbarians." The civilized Hellenistic peoples, who understood each others' language, concepts, and beliefs, were in contrast to the wide spectrum of peoples whom the Greeks regarded as the "unintelligible," uncivilized barbarians with behaviors and customs that were considered by the Hellenes to be inconceivable.[2] The creation of common language and customs created the rudimentary conditions for the centralization of power and collective action. It also created the distinction between those internal to the group and those outside. Hence, a social context was created for the political domination of others.

Before the advent of the Greek alphabet and spread of literacy among the Greek people, Greek society transmitted and disseminated information through the use of memorized epic poetry, sagas, and myths. For example, the bard Homer was a storyteller of epics, such as the *Odyssey*, and at the same time a kind of "tribal encyclopedia."[3] Information was memorized, and therefore only accessible by memorization and recitation of already memorized material. This meant that the socialization of the population took place through the means of oral communication in direct encounters between the teller and the listener. Such conditions limit the scope and range of the socialization process and circumscribe the boundaries of those who could be incorporated into the developing system of Greek power.

With the advent of writing and literacy to Greek society came the ability to transmit knowledge more accurately, more uniformly, and on a more mass scale throughout society.[4] Greek writing is based upon the Greek phonetic alphabet and was introduced to the Greeks in the early part of the eighth century B.C.[5] The Greek alphabet is closely derived from the North Semitic alphabet, as the Greeks had close mercantile contacts with the Phoenicians, who used the North Semitic alphabet.[6] After the alphabet was adopted by the Greeks, they altered the letters, yet still called the letters Phoenician.

The adoption an alphabet by the Greeks was a product of the rational efficiency of the written word. Embracing the Phoenician alphabet was a result of the fact that it is infinitely easier to borrow and adapt a writing system than to invent one.[7] Evidence of the restricted origination of script can be found in anthropological data that supports the hypothesis that the independent origination of writing has occurred in only two locations for certain, ancient Sumer and Mesoamerica.[8] For the Greeks, the development of writing created the conditions for the unity of the various Greek settlements.

The Greek alphabet was comprehensive. It included vowels which allowed for spoken language to be more precisely put in written form. In altering the Phoenetic alphabet to transliterate all spoken words accurately into visual signs, the Greeks were able to include all linguistic sounds into writing, reduce ambiguity in their writing, and restrict the number of written signs or letters to about twenty to forty symbols.[9] In this manner, the Greek alphabet was unique, and the era that followed the conversion of the Phoenetic alphabet to the Greek alphabet was a period of intense creativity in the areas of formalized logic, abstract science, representational art, axiomatic geometry, and philosophy. This correlation between the development of the Greek alphabet and the flourishing of ingenuity cannot be ignored. Robert K. Logan contends that "the alphabet helped create the unique conditions for this development . . . the alphabet stimulated the abstract and rational system of thought that characterized ancient Greek culture and subsequently all of Western civilizations."[10]

The dissemination of writing to the masses was also more widespread in Greek society than in previous ones. With only twenty to forty symbols to memorize, reading and writing the Greek alphabet was more easily taught. Other ancient scripts have hundreds or even thousands of characters to memorize. As a result, the literacy rates and the education levels in ancient Greece were much higher than in other civilizations at the time. Higher literacy and education rates almost certainly led to the following expansion of Greek intellectual ingenuity.[11]

When Greek society began using an alphabet, the dissemination of ideas and record keeping was no longer dependent on stylized, memorized poetry. Therefore, the author was not constricted by a formula or poetic mnemonic devices in preserving their ideas and conceptions about the world. Writing also generated the potential for record keeping and written law. This expanded administrative structures extended Greek culture.

The use of the phonetic alphabet also increased the ability to capture in language increasingly abstract ideas.[12] Abstract notions such as "body," "matter," "essence," "quality," and "quantity" emerged and continue to be used as part of Western societies' vocabulary. Writing, especially phonetic letters, are then double abstractions. A spoken word is broken into phonemes and sounds, and then the sounds are represented by signs and letters.

These abstract constructs contributed to Greek philosophy and thought as it encouraged a rational approach to investigating social and scientific questions. Knowledge constructs in an oral society are asserted in a context that is constituted of occurrences in "real" time and "real" space. Alphabetic literacy allows for the abstraction that leads to analytic statements and pronouncements that claim to be universal in nature and independent from the context in which they originate.

Information is also organized differently in oral societies than in literate societies based on phonetic language systems. Oral traditions encourage a method that aids in the memorization of information. In opposition, a written phonetic alphabet allows information to be organized in a manner that seeks to present material in a logical form.[13] Thus, the phonetic alphabet influenced the rise of Western scientific thought and method as "ideas of cause and effect in the literate West have long been in the form of things in sequence and succession."[14]

Alphabetic literacy, in encouraging abstraction, also enhanced the ability for the Greeks to subdivide knowledge in a rational, methodical manner. A manifestation of this was the division of knowledge into separate disciplines and subjects, such as geometry, ontology, epistemology, logic, ethics, aesthetics, rhetoric, politics, physics, and dialectics. This approach to the organization of knowledge impacted the ways in which knowledge was disseminated, and the ways in which society, politics, and economic action were arranged. These societal structures and their organization, in turn, influenced how the individual human subjects perceived of themselves within society.

Greek literacy, based on a phonetic alphabet, had a profound effect on Greek society, culture, and politics. About five hundred years after the introduction of the alphabet came a "reading public" in Greek society. Many citizens had reading skills and were thus technically competent for the tasks of politics and administration. The availability of written texts increased dramatically during this period, and by the time of Aristotle, access to the written word was widely available for Greek citizens.

Writing allowed for the expansion of Greek culture. It also formalized the process, as the signs, symbols, and meaning of the culture were able to be transmitted in greater detail, creating a fixed and stable history, identity, and way of life through the permanence of the written text. Plato recognized the implications of writing and expressed his concerns through the character of Theuth in the *Phaedrus*, "[Letters,] said Theuth, "will make the Egyptians wiser and give them better memories; it is a specific both for the memory and for the wit." Such is the precondition for the expansion of culture and the dissemination of its content across a wide area of territory.

The ability to engage in abstract processes of thought brought about by the invention of writing transformed the conception of the self present in Greek culture. The individuals in literate Greek society began to perceive of themselves as being increasingly separate from nature and from one's connection to a family, tribe, or clan. Each was a rational creature, able to use the power of reason to investigate nature as an object, and generate knowledge about nature as the product of reason itself. As Robert Logan describes the result:

> They [the Greeks] created the Individual Man. Individualism was born, where alone perhaps it could have been born, in the narrow cradle of the diminutive republic founded by a people endowed with unique social and intellectual gifts.[15]

Prior to the advent of the alphabet, the conception of subjectivity did not contain elements of individual thought and reason. In the epics of Homer, the tribe's welfare was to come before an individual's interests. Furthermore, knowledge was not considered separate from action, nor is there an emphasis on a separation of an individual from one's society. The Greek alphabet gave rise to a construction of the human subject that had individual responsibility: "Men have a moral responsibility which animals do not."[16] Consequently, by the seventh century B. C. E., Greek society developed the concepts of *individual* actors.

The rise of the individual in Greek society also resulted in the emergence of codified, written law to "meet the demands of individuals for greater justice."[17] Written law was publicly enforced *nomas* (public law), as distinguished from *ethos* (private practice and personal ethic).

Individuality and Collective Action

The development of writing, and the increasingly abstract nature of the construction of knowledge, generated a model of subjectivity that reflected the Greek experience. Rational actors came together as parts of communities in which each citizen (as distinct from "irrational barbarians") was assumed to have the necessary skills to participate in the discussion of the matters of the day. However, this is not to suggest that *individual ends* were considered the appropriate outcome of such discourse. The betterment of the community was the proper outcome of public discourse.

Writing allowed for the development of abstract reasoning and the creation of a model of subjectivity in which individuals possess the power of reason. What was needed was a structure of political relations that accounted for both the equality of skills among the citizens and the collective nature of the social enterprise. Out of this condition emerged the earliest foundations of democratic practice.

By the eighth century B.C.E., with the exception of Sparta, tribal kings no longer held power. In some cities the title remained as a religious designation, but a new structure of domination was emerging along with the transition of Greek tribal culture to that of the city-state. Attica, where Athens is located, was about the area of an average-sized county in the United States. Like other communities of the tribal culture in early Greece, production of agricultural commodities was for self-sufficiency. When the population was small, these tribal societies were governed in a traditional fashion, by a Council of Elders (*gerusia*). However, these traditional forms of rule diminished as the population of Greece grew and the *polis* emerged as the new territorial unit.

A growing population required increased food production. The Greek peninsula is surrounded by water and it was logical that as the population grew people turned to trade to increase their livelihood. Learning navigation from the Egyptians and Phoenicians, some Greeks began engaging in piracy and pillaging areas outside of their tribal region. Others departed their original communities to build new societies in uninhabited areas.[18] For example, the tribes of Athens intentionally sent people to establish colonies in order to alleviate the population and economic strain on the region. From these roots, ancient Greek colonization began and would spread to southern Italy, Asia Minor, northern Africa, and islands in the Mediterranean Sea over the course of about 200 years.[19] Contact with non-Hellenic civilizations also occurred, arousing an attraction for foreign trade and commerce from the eighth to the sixth centuries B. C. E.

These developments further eroded the tribal structure of Greek politics. As the society became more urbanized and complex, the society of rational subjects had to consciously strive to create a new structure of political domination that was compatible with the transformed sense of subjectivity. For example, tribal societies do not have a strong focus on matters of private property ownership or the need for currency. There was common ownership of land, with only limited private property. With the erosion of tribal structures came private property, along with social institutions and a belief system in support of this transformation. People no longer intuitively and unquestionably understood their place in their communities; they had to *think* about their role and function in society. Doubt and uncertainty crept into Greek minds and a need for contemplation and consideration of alternative realities appeared.[20]

Out of this condition the concept of the *polis* emerged. The *polis* was a concept that emerged to address a unique set of issues. Greece is a peninsula, broken up by mountains. It also has limited resources.[21] This condition gave rise to the emergence of relatively small tribal groups, and also led to the creation of the small city-states that characterized the *polis*. The Athenian form of direct democracy was only possible due to the city-state being relatively small in population, which allowed all citizens to directly participate in governing themselves.

In ancient Greece, the *polis* was a constitution of the citizens, the *politai*. Full citizens exercised exclusive rule, or "sovereignty," over the state. The procedure and observance of democracy by the citizens of a city-state ruling themselves was logically perceived as the "perfection of the [p]olis."[22] Civil society was not separated from government. They were one and the same. In this context there was no distinction between the public and private spheres of life. Matters of collective and religious life were considered the domain of the political and, therefore, part of the common bonds of social life.

There was also no notion of a separation in legislative, executive, and judicial functions. Governance was a collective activity in which the community participated. Decisions were made by the consensus of the *politai*, not by precedent or a *rule of law*. Such a process could only be carried out within a model of the subject that trusts the rationality of the citizens to arrive at an outcome that is just. In fact, within this model, the outcome must be deemed just, as it was arrived at through the collective reason of the citizenry, without the constraints of tradition or precedent. Also absent are the principles of tolerance, moderation, and respect for dissenting opinions associated with modern democratic values. Justice was defined and applied by the members of the community. The legitimacy and integrity of the process is assured by the structure. All citizens were entitled to participate, according to the belief in *isonomia*, equality of citizens. This argument in favor of equality was necessary in order to justify the citizenry's claim to rule.[23]

Arriving at *justice* required open discourse. To have an open discourse requires a certain degree of freedom of speech, *Parrhesia*, to express opinions and desires within a discourse. All complaints could then be heard and acknowledged and this increased the likelihood that politicians would be well-informed of public sentiment. It is speculated that the Athenian notion of freedom of speech originated as the opportunity of having a person's personal opinions and feelings heard in public political assemblies. Such a view was engrained by the fifth century B. C. E. In Pericles' *Funeral Oration*, made during the Peloponnesian War (431–404 B.C.E.), he voiced the opinion that every citizen in Athens should participate in politics.[24] To participate fully, Pericles asserted that every citizen has the right to one's own individual convictions and should be permitted to express those beliefs.[25]

All of these societal changes, such as the rise of secularism, the growing emphasis on the individual, and the increased travel, trade, and commerce transformed the understanding of political existence. The cosmopolitan nature of Athenian society, in particular, left the citizenry with the view that there were no sweeping, absolute "truths," that must be applied in the world. The Greeks came to realize that what was judged as "good" in one society could be regarded as "bad" in another.[26] Democracy, as a practice of collective decision-making, gains in importance under the conditions where there are no universal principles to be applied through deductive logic. For the Greeks, this resulted in the need for some form of practice to resolve the questions of social existence that had only the reasoning of the citizens as its guide. Democracy emerges as a form of domination to meet this condition.

Athenian democracy was a chaotic process. Direct democracy in decision-making was practical only due to the small-scale nature of the participants. Not only was the city-state small in size, but there were a limited number of full citizens. Nevertheless, in the administration of public life the system of direct democracy produced large organizations for matters of public affairs. There were elected officials that served on political councils, but these councils were on a large-scale, numbering in the hundreds. Members to sit on councils were voted on by lot and were required to attend council meetings, or were fined.

Many decisions were made in a disorderly and untidy manner through public discourse among citizens. Even in a direct democracy on a small-scale, this was a messy and complicated procedure to reach some form of consensus amongst citizens. As situations presented themselves, citizens engaged in discourse to resolve issues. Therefore, a rule by precedence was not followed. This led many of the educated and upper class Athenians to conclude that democracy was a form of mob rule.

Democracy and Class

From its earliest days, Greek democracy made accommodation with class interests. Hence, even as the notion of participation of the citizenry in the collective action of the social order was becoming ingrained in the political culture, it was circumscribed by the extent to which one could be defined as a citizen, with full rights of participation. Unlike the Romans, who would grant citizenship but not institutional access, the Greeks had a more limited view of who could become a full citizen. At the origin of Greek democracy, full participation was bestowed to those with the most pecuniary status. As Athens developed as a trading center, the rights of participation became more dispersed among some of the lower classes.

Equality in democratic Athens manifested itself in equal protection and equal rights regarding the political participation of each citizen. However, to be considered a full citizen and to be granted full political rights, one had to meet social class and material wealth standards. This kept political power and influence in the realm of those with wealth in Athenian society. From the era of Pericles until the end of Athenian democracy, almost all of the political leaders were from aristocratic families.[27]

In the beginning of Athenian democracy, the lawmaker Draco created a Council (*Ecclesia*) made up of members of the aristocratic families in Greek society. Complete political rights were only granted to citizens who sat on the *Ecclesia*. The Council was composed of four hundred and one members, chosen by lot among the wealthy class of full citizens. After Draco's reforms at the end of the seventh century (622 B.C.E.) it was apparent that political power and rights corresponded to an individual's financial condition.[28]

As the importance of commerce and trade grew, the value of money gained significance. Instead of focusing on status based on birth, the emphasis shifted to the amount of wealth a person possessed. The new emphasis on status based on pecuniary standing denoted a shift in the constitution of attributes of status and social hierarchy. At the top parallel to the *Eupatridae* were persons having at least 500 medemni of corn, oil, or wine, the *Pentacosiomedemni*. To be considered a *Knight*, or member of the warrior class, one needed at least 300 medemni. Wealthy farmers were the *Zeugitae* and had incomes of at least 200 medemni. *Thetes* were pedestrian peasants. All of the members of this hierarchy were considered citizens, but the *Thetes* were not given rights of political participation and as a result became restless.[29] Eventually, the *demos* compelled the reforms of Solon in the early sixth century B.C.E., which instituted new social classifications that gave the *Thetes* access to political assemblies.[30]

These new class divisions existed along four main lines. The *Eupatridae* were the landowners with large amounts of property. Below them in the social hierarchy were the *Georgi* who were small farmers or peasants. Traders constituted the *Demiurgi*. They were held to be citizens, but with restricted political rights. At the bottom of the hierarchy were farming laborers and craftsmen who were free, but not considered citizens. The emergence of the popular attitude that considered and prized private property resulted in the *Eupatridae* being at the top of the hierarchy.

The development of private property, and the rise of Athenian wealth more generally, brought with it a class conflict in Athens during the fifth and fourth centuries B.C.E. Classes owning land clashed with the trading ones. Aristocrats by birth disputed with the aristocrats who claimed their position through intellectual capabilities. The monarchy had been ended a long time before, and the institution of democracy had been developing and expanding.

However, after the Peloponnesian War, and the death of Pericles, Athenian democracy began a steady decline. Arthur J. Grant suggests that the "character and constitution of Athens" was ill suited for "government and war." The Peloponnesian War revealed a necessity for a central, strong executive in order to coordinate the security functions for the collective, something that was lacking in the structure of Athenian democracy. Grant claims that as a result of this deficiency Athens lacked a "coherent policy" during the war.[31] Whether or not this thesis is true, it is clear that the structure of Athenian democracy was eroded by the war.

Proponents of democracy also had to face another set of criticisms coming from the class of Athenian aristocrats and intellectuals. Philosophers such as Plato and Thucydides believed that the premise of equality, on which democracy was built, lacked an empirical basis. People are inherently unequal in skills and talents, and a system that treats everyone as equal contains, at its very foundation, the seeds of injustice. This type of equality denied the "noble, wealthy, educated, capable, experienced, and morally superior upper classes" of commanding exclusive rights of political power. Democracy did not "sufficiently reward existing merits."[32]

This was the view of Plato and Aristotle, two of the most well-known dissenters regarding democratic practice. Plato viewed democracy as unprincipled mob-rule. Such a system of political practice will produce outcomes that are considered legal and binding, no matter how unjust, unmerited, and irrational it may be. As Plato states in Book VIII of *The Republic*, democracy is one of the "disorders of the state," along with oligarchy and tyranny.[33]

Plato's unease with democratic procedures was amplified by the trial and execution of his friend and teacher, Socrates. Socrates was executed under the democratic constitution of Athens, not by a totalitarian ruler. It is impossible to state the extent to which this event undermined democratic processes in Athens, but it clearly reinforced the notion that the mob was incapable of thoughtful, deliberative action.

This act also assists in clarifying the tension between Plato and the Sophists. The Sophists represented an intellectual position that was more compatible with the functioning of Greek democracy. From the claim of Protagoras, that "man is the measure of all things," emerges a relativism that is more suited to the ebb and flow of democratic institutions. Transcendent claims to truth are rejected in favor of discourse and persuasion. The art of rhetoric is taught by the Sophist as a manifestation of the open nature of democratic discourse. The sons of the aristocracy were taught by the Sophists in order to enhance their persuasive abilities within Athenian democracy. In this context, Plato's rejection of the Sophists' position should be seen as an attempt to undermine the art of persuasion in political life in favor of a more rigid notion of truth. Such notions of truth led to more hierarchical forms of domination.[34]

In the end, the triumph of Plato's position helped spell the end of Athenian democracy. Its positions are contrary to the openness and participation that were the hallmark of Greek practices under Pericles. The people's will was not to be trusted. The light of "justice" would elude them.

In Athens, democracy was exclusive rather than inclusive, giving rights to a minority of the populace who were considered citizens. But this was a view of democracy that focused on the technology of participation. As Thucydides wrote, Pericles stated in his *Funeral Oration* that in Athens "its administration favors the many instead of the few; that is why it is called a democracy." Pericles' understanding of democracy was not as a *form* of government, but as a *process*.[35]

Subjectivity and Democratic Practice

It is our position that the historical and social conditions shape the content of subjectivity. This is the case in a double sense. First, the content of subjectivity is going to reflect the distribution of political power, the techniques of production, the assigned "naturalness" of the social institutions, and the ethical standards that evolve as reflection of those conditions. Secondly, the discourse on subjectivity must be disseminated in order to gain ascendancy. In order to generate a concept of "Greekness," the historical conditions must be present for the dissemination of such a discourse.

Foucault uses the term "discursive formation" to describe this process. Discursive formation must be understood as "the form of a system of regular dispersion of statements."[36] We must keep in mind that genealogy and the tracing of institutional systems to their origins for Foucault is "a form of history which can account for the constitution of knowledges, discourses, domains of objects, etc. without having to make reference to a subject which is either transcendental in relation to the field of events or runs in its empty sameness throughout the course of history."[37] In the contexts of Greek culture, this means that in order to understand the rise of democracy, and its undoing, it is necessary to examine the conditions that shaped the construction of subjectivity that would allow or hinder democratic practice.

Subjectivity should not be viewed as fixed, or stagnant, due to the constant transformation of the historical conditions that give rise to its construction. The subject is continually altered in the process of history. Therefore, there can be no absolutes when it comes to the structure of subjects, only their repeated adaptation and transformation owing to changing historical conditions. *Truths* regarding the subject are only what the current social conditions deem as acceptable. This is the case as "the least glimmer of truth is conditioned by politics."[38] The concern is then investigating "not only these discourses but also the will that sustains them and the strategic intention that supports them."[39] The construction of subjectivity must be understood by giving an account of "who does the speaking, the positions and viewpoints from which they speak, the institutions which prompt people to speak about it and which store and distribute the things that are said."[40]

In his discussion of the Athenian subject, Foucault argued that to understand its construction the "development of the great instruments of the state, as *institutions* of power" must be taken into account, as well as the "*techniques* of power present at every level of the social body and utilized by very diverse institutions . . . their development, and the forces working to sustain them."[41] This is the case because "...the movements of life and the processes of history interfere with one another . . . political technologies ensued, investing the body, health, modes of subsistence and habitation, living conditions, the whole space of existence."[42] Therefore, in order to understand the construction of subjectivity, the totality of material conditions must be understood as having an effect on the structure of subjectivity itself.

Since the epistemology of Kant, and the methodology of Weber, such an understanding cannot be addressed without some form of "narrowing" by investigators. It is necessary to look to "interpret" what is causally significant and what conditions have an affinity with one another in the rise of a particular practice. In the context of ancient Greece, the adoption of phonetic writing and the rise of literacy among the citizens were essential components in the construction and dissemination of a concept of citizenship that give rise to the rationality of democratic procedures.

In a political sense, the adoption of the phonetic alphabet enhanced the ability of the Greeks to create a centralized apparatus for the administration of public affairs with the creation of written law. In terms of socialization, the expression of a written history created a shared experience that fostered a common identity. That had a binding effect on the society. Without literacy among the citizens, the notion of equality could not emerge, and democracy would lose its foundational support.

Phonetic writing also allowed for the development of abstract thought and the development of the logical tools of inductive and deductive reasoning in the preparation of rational arguments in politics and philosophy, as well as providing the basis for the classificatory schemes of scientific inquiry. Such developments led to a decline of the "old religion" of Athens, particularly in the period after the Persian Wars. This was particularly evident during the time of Pericles, especially among the more educated Athenians.[43] The focus on reason led to an unraveling of the traditional grounding of moral thought within the domain of religious institutions. Previously, Greek morality looked to nature as its model. With the integration of social and political life came an interest in the study of men.[44]

The old traditions and beliefs only made sense in a belief system where "the convictions of men on the greatest questions of life were fixed." [45] However, since the political circumstances had become more uncertain and confused, in the period after the Persian War, there was a need for a new understanding of the condition of social life. An unchanging, absolute code of morality made less and less rational sense to the Athenians as it had "no sufficient instruction for practical life."[46] There was a new focus on the practical matters of politics, with a rise in organization, public works, and the preparation of defense against outside attack. All were concerns of practical matters of political life.

As a result, the "technique" of applying rational argument and discussion to politics emerged in the Periclean era.[47] This "technique" was structured "assum[ing] that argument must be met by argument and that in the end the better case won." Trained, professional teachers taught these debate tactics to young men in society who wished to enter and be successful in politics. Much of these verbal contests were based on logical abstractions and concepts.[48] This was the domain in which the Sophists, as teachers of the techniques of rhetoric, thrived.

Rhetoric is the art of persuasion. It is the ability to generate an empathetic response to one's position using a logical structure in argumentation and a selective use of facts. The sons of the citizens of Athens, the class of nobles that could afford such training, were taught these skills as part of their education. Persuading others, using these techniques, became one of the enduring hallmarks of democratic politics since the time of ancient Greece.

But for the Athenians, the struggle for power among the political class was a struggle among equals vying for power. Such a condition reinforced the notion that politics took place among equals, each of whom possessed the power of reason, and, hence, each of whom was technically proficient to rule. Only with such a view of the subject, does democratic practice have the conditions in which it can grow.

In the time of Pericles there was stress on equality amongst the citizens of Athens. This produced a view of democracy that included the supports for citizen participation in all matters relating to the structure and processes of the social order. This is compatible with openness to ideas and the view that reason could be manifested collectively as equal and rational actors would perceive a *just* outcome of political debate. As previously discussed, this view of subjectivity was compatible with the teaching of the Sophists, as they promoted an idea that emphasized the lack of over-arching truths in social discourse. The result was a stress on rhetoric and persuasion.

The Sophists were comprised of many men who taught numerous subjects, but were not affiliated exclusively to one another and had no common, unifying beliefs. They taught in the fields of metaphysics, rhetoric, grammar, mathematics, music, logic, and politics. However, the most common area of study was the art of rhetoric and dialect, of speaking and arguing, the subjects that were by-products of the advent of the phonetic alphabet in Greek society. Those who mastered these skills would be able to become a prosperous and influential statesman. The goal of political argument was to claim victory, not to discover "truth."[49] It is in the absence of universal truths that democracy, as a technique for arriving at the agenda of collectivized power, has its greatest rationale.

However, this was not the only structure of the subject in ancient Athens. The period after the Peloponnesian War, the death of Pericles, and the aftermath of the plague, was a time of uncertainty in Greek society. This created conditions in which an alternative view of subjectivity emerged.

The challenge to the foundational supports of democracy came from philosophers and writers such a Thucydides, Socrates, and Plato, and Aristotle, who argued against rule by a mass that was not trained in the art of ruling. They concluded that human beings were not equal in their ability to employ inductive reasoning and develop "general terms."[50] Without the wisest rulers, as Plato argued, there can be nothing but trouble for the collective. As Plato states in *The Republic*:

> Unless either philosophers become kings in our states
> or those whom we now call kings and rulers take to
> the pursuit of philosophy seriously and adequately,
> and there is a conjunction of these two things, politi-
> cal power and philosophical intelligence, there can be
> no end of troubles for our states, or, I think, for the
> human race.[51]

Coming after the catastrophes associated with the Peloponnesian War, such a view of the decision-making skills of the masses is understandable. It was under the democratic order that Athens undertook some of its most aggressive military campaigns. But Plato does not identify the problems of collective power with the creation of central structures and mass administration. Instead, the problem is a matter of who gets to direct and control those institutions. Events such as the Peloponnesian War, the execution of Socrates, and the erosion of civil life in Athens, diluted the commitment to the view of subjectivity that made democracy a rational undertaking to the citizens of Athens.

However, whether as a democratic or non-democratic society, the material conditions that led to the expansion of Greek power did not significantly alter. The Greeks were able to expand their influence as a result of the creation of centralized institutional structures made possible by the integrating effects of a common language and culture. The central power of the Greek state mobilized vast numbers of people and engaged them in a common enterprise. This was only possible after the dissemination of a common history and identity among the people.

From this perspective, the Peloponnesian War can be viewed as an inevitable conflict between the Athenian and Spartan over the power to socialize the public into their competing systems of identity. With the advent of phonetic writing came an enhanced ability to spread the identity of the city-states to wider audiences, and secure greater power for the centralized state. Conflict among the forces competing for control over the people, the necessary component of expanded state power, was unavoidable.

The power of a political unit can only expand by bringing increasing numbers of people within the orbit of its socializing technologies. Only in this way can a common identity be spread among the people, generating the homogenization of people into a collective force.[52] Therefore, even in ancient Greece, the struggle among political units had the character of a battle over the rights of socialization and integration, as the ultimate repositories of political power.

The Romans as Inheritors of Hellenistic Society

Nowhere were the lessons of the Greek shortcomings in the management of power learned more effectively than in ancient Rome. Small city-states struggling among each other for the power to disseminate an identity to people is a formula for continual conflict. Rome was interested in assigning one identity, that of Rome, to all the world.

Greeks granted the full rights of political participation to citizens, but managed the system of domination by keeping the number of citizens low in relation to the overall populations. Such a strategy for "direct democracy" could only work in a small community. The Romans altered this formula, granting Roman citizenship to all under Roman domination, but limiting the numbers that had access to the institutions of power. In this way, the socialization in a Roman identity was assured, even while the power to influence collective action was restricted.

Roman Education

The first known Greek colony in Italy, Cumae, was founded in 740 B.C. It was from Cumae that the Romans and the Etruscans derived their Hellenistic alphabets and cultural legacy. The Etruscans were in part

Hellenized, and influenced early Roman development in teaching the Romans their forms of organization, administration, and technological innovation. These basic proficiencies would later prove to be the Roman Republic and Empire's most advantageous assets.

The Romans began their empire by first conquering the Etruscans in 510 B.C. After securing Italy, the Romans went on to conquer the Mediterranean region that included Greece and Carthage. Both through colonization and conquest, the Romans became the heirs to Greek culture. For example, the Romans intertwined their history to that of the Greeks in adopting many of the gods and myths of the Greeks. Romans even made the claim that they were the descendants of the Trojans and the Greeks through the hero Aeneas.

As the Greeks borrowed their alphabet from the Phoenicians, so the Romans borrowed and adjusted their alphabet from the Greek alphabet. The Romans shortened many of the letters of the Greek alphabet to be more succinct; *alpha* was shortened to *A, beta* became *B, gamma* was transformed to *C,* etcetera. Today, the alphabets of the languages of Western Europe are all based on the alphabet of the Romans.

Literature in Rome began near the end of the third century and was simply translations of Greek literature. Roman literature is considered to never have equaled that of the ancient Greeks, due in part to the Romans perceiving literature as not a significant, vital aspect of society. Instead, the Romans considered literature "an adornment of cultivated life."[53] Later, this perception of literature and literacy would aid in the fall of the Roman Empire's administration and domination of the ancient western world.

Roman civilization was more concerned with practical technological innovations such as civil engineering, architecture, urban planning, administration, a written code of laws, and military expertise. This was a civilization that placed a much higher value on practicality; the fine arts were for the most part seen as a superfluous byproduct of society. Notwithstanding this attitude, the Romans utilized the technologies of the alphabet and writing in practical manners. The phonetic alphabet, like the Roman's practical technological undertakings in general, was a systemized, uniform method of organization.[54]

Initially, the instruction given to Roman citizens was by educated Greeks that had been taken as slaves after the Romans conquered Greece. As a result, most teachers did not have much social status in the republican period, as they were members of the slave class. However, due to the disdain toward the conquered Greeks, Greek teachers were finally expelled in 161 B.C. Latinized rhetoric replaced Greek rhetoric in Roman society. The anonymous Latin rhetoric book, *Rhetorica ad Herennium*, was the first complete treatise on Latin rhetoric and is thoroughly a practical guide.[55] The Romans placed a heavy emphasis on the practicality of rhetoric; "All of these faculties we shall attain if we follow up the rules of theory with the diligence of exercise."[56]

Rhetoric and writing were the two main columns on which the Roman educational system was structured. Rhetoric, the art of "oral eloquence," was viewed as having practical applications in social life. *Facilitas,* or facility, was described by Marcus Fabius Quintilianus in 95 C.E. as being a desired product of the educational system by teaching students to "produce appropriate and effective language in any situation."[57] Therefore, the logical system of education that would generate *facilitas* involved a very meticulously constructed process that taught students reading, writing, speech, and listening.[58] The educational system's main goal was to instill "rhetorical efficiency."[59]

Roman education was structured in a familial manner that relied on private tutors and apprenticeships. A young male would first be tutored in the elementary elements of his education in the home, and then would be taken by his father or other family relations to be put under an apprenticeship of an orator or other professional in a prominent position in Roman society. The young apprentice would be expected to shadow his patron by accompanying the patron to law courts and other speaking appearances.[60] As the educational process in Roman society required many material resources and free time, the literate political elites were the aristocracy (the patricians). Commoners, or plebeians, did not have the status or the resources required to undertake the educational process in ancient Rome. Therefore, the entire population of Roman society was not represented in the republic of Rome, and the acronym SPQR (*Senatus Populusque Romanus*, or "the senate and people of Rome") only referred to the political elite of Roman citizens that participated and made decisions in Roman politics.[61]

The importance of this type of education was a reflection of the values and the power hierarchies in Roman society. Roman society, as previously mentioned, was concerned with the usefulness of a thing. Everything had to have a functional purpose in serving society. The utility of a thing was measured on whether it served the purposes and goals of the Roman state. To serve the state was a high honor, and many aristocratic values were judged based on being the "first," the "best," the "greatest" in relation to that contribution.[62] The art of rhetoric was then to be a tool that would prove useful in resolving disputes over who made the greatest contribution.[63] In the arena of politics, the ability to speak well and construct a convincing argument was vital to having influence in Roman society.

Given the goals and structures of Roman education, it was a system designed for upper class males who were interested in the pursuit of wealth and power. Women were essentially closed out of this system, with legal status of women and children close to that of property. They were "subjects" of the head of the house, with little or no autonomy. Even adult sons that had established careers were still seen, in legal terms, as being under their father's authority.[64]

Literacy was essential to the Roman system. As Quintilianus stated, ". . . the roots, in writing are the foundations of eloquence."[65] Such a system assured that the highest levels of power would only be open to the sons of the aristocracy. They were the only groups trained in the reading, writing, and mathematical skills necessary for the administration of power in Roman life.

A system of education was central to the development of the Roman power. During the days of the Republic it was necessary to have an educated class, even if concentrated in the aristocracy, that could make informed decisions for the state. The promise of representative democracy is that by having an educated class of citizens, they will be able to elect those who have the best talents and skills to make those critical decisions of collective power.

However, for the Romans, power and education remained closely affiliated. As republic gave way to empire, education took on an essential role both internal and external to the actual structures of power. To manage the Empire it was essential to have people trained in the skills necessary for the vast engineering projects that linked the Empire, protected its borders, and provided necessary resources to the urban centers. In addition, literacy provided the ability to extend written law and communication over vast territories allowing for the administration of diverse people. Drawing from a talent pool limited to the aristocracy would not produce the optimal outcome, but it was sufficient for the growth of Roman power greater than any previously seen in the West.

Education also provided a means by which the people living in diverse cultures under Roman control could be socialized into the identity of Rome. Writing is a technology for the dissemination of culture. It assists in the rise of centralized forms of domination by socializing people into the culture being spread. By spreading a culture that is "Roman," the population was educated in Roman signs and symbols, altering their understanding of what constitutes the source of their identity. Through this process their allegiance is assured.

Technologies of Collective Power and Administration: Aqueducts and Roads

In the ancient world, the coordination of human activity that is required to generate power occurred through the rise of great, centralized, urban centers. These would be the core of a civilization's culture, the focal point of administrative power, and the place in which the territory's wealth became concentrated. However, every urban environment faces similar problems. The concentration of people into a small space has vulnerabilities. There must be adequate food, water, and sanitation in order for the city to remain viable. The Romans confronted these problems with a series of technological achievements that allowed for the growth and spread of their culture, ideas, and political power. As Strabo wrote "The Romans have provided for three things that the Greeks, on the other hand, neglected: roads, aqueducts, and sewers."[66] These architectural feats also were products of the Roman educational system that had the practical goals of maintaining and extending Roman power.

The Romans were not the inventors of the aqueducts, though they did build aqueducts on a more massive and grander scale.[67] The Roman aqueduct system was composed of arcades and tunnels that spanned approximately 500 kilometers. Not only was water used as a necessity in Rome, but also became a vehicle for recreation. The grandeur of many of the projects was also representative of the expanse of Roman wealth and power. There was a sewage system, public waterspouts, pressurized plumbing on the higher slopes, as well as the massive fountains, public baths, and watered terraces. All relied on the water transported by the system of aqueducts. As with various structures that the Romans built, the aqueducts were functional and, at the same time, as imposing as any other Roman structure.[68]

Aqueducts in the city of Rome began mainly as underground channels that were most likely utilized as a drainage system. As the wealth and power of Rome grew, it underwent a rapid increase in population. Construction of a more complex and imposing system was needed.[69] Roman culture fully supported the construction of civic projects such as the aqueducts. Patronage of such schemes was a sign of loyalty to Rome, as well as a symbol of the state's commitment to the material comforts of the citizens with such projects as public baths.[70]

The aqueducts allowed for the city of Rome to support a massive number of people within its jurisdiction. Seventy percent of the water that was delivered by the aqueducts went to Rome itself, with the rest apportioned outside of the city.[71] Distribution of the Roman aqueducts gave priority to public fountains,[72] a good administrative priority to assure that the needs of the populace city were maintained. The aqueducts proved to be vital in maintaining the order of Rome and of the Empire. Where Rome conquered other territories, it also built aqueducts and other infrastructure, as a goal of imperial Rome was to provide "civil amenities" to the conquered lands.[73] As the Empire grew, the spoils of conquest financed the building of more aqueducts and other public works, throughout the Empire[74] Therefore, as Rome became more powerful, more public services could be administered to a larger number of people.

Public building projects abounded in ancient Rome for both pragmatic and aesthetic objectives. The now famous ruins of temples and triumphal arches are only some examples of the construction feats that the Romans accomplished.[75] But many of the Roman building projects were essential to the growth of the Roman Empire. This was certainly true of the Roman road system.

Roads were the information corridors of their time. They were central to the administration of the vast territories conquered by the Romans, allowing information, culture, laws, and soldiers to travel the breadth of the Empire.[76] It also allowed for the Romans to control the flow of people and goods over land routes.[77]

The Roman road system centered around the nineteen roads that originated and led from Rome.[78] A massive economic structure was central to the Roman state and the roads were an economic lifeline. Not only did the roads provide the infrastructure for trade and transport, but they also provided the means of enhancing Rome's power through taxation and conquest.[79]

The Roman road system was organized, managed, and maintained by the state. Routes that originated from Rome were organized in a unified system.[80] There were no tolls, which made the roads open to all, and included military, commercial, postal, and personal travel.[81] Unification of roads brought the ability for the Romans to not only conquer and integrate other lands, but also to organize, supervise, develop, and control them for their own benefit.[82]

So important were the roads in the centralization of Roman power that the state had strict regulations regarding their construction. The state was also engaged in a process of road improvement as one of its major administrative undertakings. Roman roads were initially unpaved, packed dirt, or gravel. The result of rain and heat on these original roads was mud and dust. In 238 B.C.E., the brothers Lucius and Marcus Publicius funded the first paving of the road *Clivus Publicius* by impressing fines on unlawful lessors of public grazing properties. Paving activity was expanded in 174 B.C.E. [83]

Regular maintenance of the Roman system of roads was delegated under the Republic and in the age of empire. Under the Republic, the four *aediles* of the four regions that divided the city of Rome were responsible for the preservation of roads. These aediles were aided by four specialized functionaries (*quatuorviri viis in urbe purgandis*) who attended to matters concerning the roads, such as sanitation.[84] In an era of empire, most likely in the age of Augustus, *curatores* (*quatuorviri viarium curandarum*) replaced the *aediles*.[85]

The ancient world thought of roads and other architectural achievements as "monuments," meant to serve as a legacy and testimony that would last for generations to come. For instance, the paving stones used in Roman roads were required by Roman law to be "eternal" (*lapidibus perpetuis*). Naming roads after wealthy and powerful families during the Republic (the Valerii, Giulii), and later on after emperors (Augustus, Hadrian), intended to leave an enduring legacy.[86]

But more than monuments, the Roman road structure reached to every location in the Roman Empire. This system allowed travel to be more efficient, and facilitated conquest, defense, administration, and control over the vast region of the largest empire the world had ever seen.[87] Soldiers on foot could move at an average speed of twenty to twenty-four miles a day with one day of rest for every four of marching. On horseback, travel by road was even quicker. An exceptional example of rapid travel on horseback was in 58 B.C.E. when Caesar journeyed eight hundred miles from Rome to Lake Geneva in eight days.[88]

The increased efficiency and speed of travel facilitated communication throughout the Roman Republic, and later the Roman Empire.[89] More rapid communication meant more proficient and effective management and administration of the Roman territories. As the Roman Empire grew, faster communication from the center of power in Rome to the rest of its vast empire became increasingly more vital to the effective control of Rome over its territories.

Class Rule, Domination, and Empire

The Empire was a means to increase the wealth and power that benefited the Roman aristocracy. However, in order for the empire to expand, it required certain material conditions. As previously mentioned, the technology of writing was essential to the spread of both a Roman identity among the provinces, and to the creation of a regulated adminis-

trative apparatus. The ability to organize a central administrative structure that can command the labor of thousands, or millions, of individuals
is critical to the rise of power in the state. Writing is the first technology
that can create such a large aggregate of collective identity and activity.

For Rome, the control over the instruments of the state constituted
effective control over the instruments of dissemination. Such control was
exercised by a political class of elites, educated in reading, writing, and
the art of rhetoric. Having a literate class of rulers was essential to the
growth of the Roman Empire.

Early Roman historical works have not survived. The earliest written history of Roman civilization is from the third century B.C.E. and
was recorded by Roman senators.[90] Not until around the age of Cicero
and Tacitus (*History of Rome from the Death of Augustus* or *The Annals*)
do we have sources that document Roman history. Even these later sur-
viving works are based on the testimony of Roman politicians, official
Roman documents, and description of senatorial debates.[91]

During the period of the Roman Republic, which stretched from the
late sixth century B.C.E. to late in the first century B.C.E., politics was
competitive among the various individuals and elite families. Factions
among these competing interests formed and, along with them, cooperative alliances.[92] These alliances and action were considered bad (*factio*) if
they were in the interests of the individuals.[93] They were considered
good if they benefited the society as a whole.

Politicians who exploited their political power and political alliances for "unjust ends incompatible with the laws and the common
good" were to be judged as corrupt and manipulative of their political
authority.[94] Certain cooperative efforts, such as the triumvirate between
Caesar, Pompey, and Crassus were seen as being *factio* by many, and
viewed as "perversions" of Roman politics and society.[95]

However, in general the norms that guided politics were constructed
by the elite political class with the aim of promoting their own wealth
and power. From the position of power, they were able to create norms
advantageous to themselves and labeled as "depraved" any norms that
were not. This assured that the actions of the political system worked to
the benefit of the elites in society, allowing political action and decision
making to perpetuate the existing hierarchies of power, and to detect dissenters from the norm that may disturb the organization that sustained
the power of the elites.

Such a system of governance could be considered favorable to chaos
and conflict.[96] However, the powerful, established elites usually had
nothing to gain from turmoil in politics. Elites were already benefiting

from the current political and social hierarchies. Too much conflict could undermine that position. Therefore, the texts and information that was disseminated to the public tended to encourage the reinforcement of securely held beliefs and practices. Such textual dissemination would have the added feature of promoting uniformity in thought and behavior on a mass scale among the elites in Roman society.

An example of such a text can be seen in the Roman constitution during the Republican period. Rome's constitution was unwritten. It was a product of, and a reinforcement of, a set of agreed upon norms and principles that aimed at maintaining the procedural functioning of the state. These principles and norms served as a guide for citizens in their decision-making and in the ratification of laws. In this way, the Roman constitution's norms could be implied from the laws enacted in a residual manner.[97]

The constitution of the Roman Republic is just one instance of a societal narrative that was produced by an aristocracy that was designed to further the current conditions and hierarchical structures of domination. Prior to the widespread introduction of writing, Roman legal code, as its constitution, was unwritten. When the law was oral in nature, the priests were solely entrusted with enacting and administrating the laws. During the Republic, laws were put into writing and codified along with the creation of citizen assemblies. As literacy became more widespread, written law created greater accessibility by the citizenry, as well as more continuity in practice across a wider territory. In contrast with the Greeks, the Romans placed a much greater emphasis on written law, allowing for the growth of a rule-governed administrative apparatus along with the growth of the centralized state.

Both Virgil and Cicero stated their robust defense of the Roman legal code. Law was seen as a means to avoid chaos and bring peace to society.[98] As Cicero stated, "We are servants of the law in order that we may be free."[99] As in many other spheres of Roman society, the law was driven by the desire for practicality. The codification of law addressed topics such as the transfer of property rights, entering and fulfilling contractual responsibilities, and relied greatly on precedent. With the dependence on precedent came the need for compellations of the law and legal decisions, spurring the establishment of legal libraries.[100]

While the individual was treated in Roman law as being a distinctive identity,[101] it should not be assumed that the law was somehow antithetical to the concentration of power within Roman society. In fact the opposite is the case. Law is an essential component in the concentration and centralization of power. The law creates uniformity and predictability. It is essential to the consolidation of power within an institution. It coordinates the activities of the population into a common enterprise and synchronizes their movements. Roman law was constructed to create these conditions. For that reason, the power of Rome continued to expand even during the Republic.

Further, the force of law in Roman society did not bring with it an egalitarian social order. The norms of the Roman Republic dictated that power be unequally divided between the nobles and the commoners. Later in the Republic the *plebeians* were able to gain some power, but the *patricii* maintained their far superior position in the social and political hierarchy. Since no salary or direct compensation was given for governmental service, and only the wealthy had the time and resources for education, only the wealthy had the material latitude to participate in the political process.[102] The result was that the law, and its institutional apparatus, had the effect of both concentrating power and assuring that it was concentrated in the hands of the elites.

But even the limited form of participation allowed in the Republic would come to a close. Roman culture had no strict division between civilian and military leadership.[103] Allowing the same individuals to occupy both civilian and military administrative positions produced an outcome that seems almost inevitable. The collapse of the Republic brought Rome's limited democratic practices to an end. Elites had always dominated with the center of Roman political life, but with the rise of Caesar and Imperial Rome the circle of those able to effect political change shrunk even further. It is testimony to the power of Roman administration and organization that the Empire would last another three centuries. The combination of literacy, especially wide-spread among the elite, superior organizational skills, especially in the art of war, and technical capability in the area of civil engineering, all produced a concentration of power that was unrivaled, even as it began its slow process of internal decay.

The legitimacy of such an institution as the Roman Empire could not be found within its institutional processes, many of which were dysfunctional. Legitimacy was found in the idea of "Romanness" itself. To be a citizen of the empire was its own justification, its own rationale for allegiance. Such a condition speaks to the power of dissemination, the ability to transmit an identity and socialize those in far corners of the earth that their interest is found in pursuing the dictates of those in a distant land.

Conclusion

The rise of Greece and Rome is testimony to the power of organization. The people of those regions were socialized into the culture and practices of evolving civilizations, in both cases beginning with the technology of oral communications and later through the technology of writing. With the emergence of writing, one of the essential conditions was present for the emergence of a mass form of domination. Writing is a necessary technology for the organization of mass forms of social administrations, including the centralization of power, the emergence of uniform code of law, and the keeping of permanent records. These elements constitute the preconditions for the rise of the mass form of political domination.

Writing is also an important feature in the dissemination of a collective identity to the population. Common texts, transmitted through a shared language, create a public history and identity. Such an identity is a necessary condition for the creation of a mutual sense of purpose and directing the power of collective action. Without a common identity it is not possible to discipline the population into the service of collective power.

Both Greece and Rome (under the Republican constitution) had elements of democracy embedded within their structures of domination. For the Greeks in the time of Pericles, citizenship embodied a notion of participation in the direction of collective power. To be equally deserving of such participation, it was assumed that the citizenry would have the education and training that was implied by entry into the class of citizens. Equality was not embedded within the expectation of reason, culture, and skills that came with class position. Much the same could be said of Rome, under the Republic. The practice of democracy was circumscribed as a struggle among the aristocracy, with minimal input from the poor, even though they were considered citizens of the state. Democracy as a form of mass politics does not emerge until the modern period.

Within the framework of this study, it could be said that in both Greece and Rome, the limited amounts of democracy practiced conveyed a strong commitment to the idea of reason, but weak commitments to the idea of human equality. Both states functioned in a manner that manifested the idea that reason could shape and alter the world. Each embraced the power of reason in the construction of social, political, and technical ends, albeit different ends in each case. However, in both cases the commitment to equality was weak, too weak to sustain and expand democratic practice. For the Greeks, the community of equals was too small to embrace what today would be considered a democratic ideal.

For the Romans, with the emergence of the Empire there seemed to be very little equality embedded within its institutions.

With Rome's collapse, there is a general disintegration of the institutional order that held Western civilization together. The system of education, the creation of libraries, and the reproduction of the ancient texts that disseminated the traditions from one generation to the next, all fell into ruin. Under these conditions it was impossible for culture of "Romanness" to continue be the locus of human identity. In the rubble of the old empire a new notion of the subject was constructed.

The collapse of the system of education and training meant that an age of illiteracy was being born. In such a circumstance it is not possible to embrace the power of human reason as the source of collective will and power. However, even as the power of reason as part of the make-up of subjectivity was waning in the Western world, the other support for democratic practice was ascending. A new configuration of human equality was being formulated in the evolving nature of a new religious doctrine. Equality, in this new religion, was not based on the expectation of a common educational proficiency or set of skills in the temporal world. Equality was disembodied from the physical world, an attribute that was transcendent in character. All human beings must be considered as subject to the same conditions of existence and judged by the same rules of social order. The grounding of the disciplinary order of centralized power is, thus, transformed and a new structure of domination emerged.

Notes

1. Myres, John L., *The Political Ideas of the Greeks* (New York: The Abingdon Press, 1971), 34.

2. Myres, 36.

3. Logan, Robert K., *The Alphabet Effect: The Impact of the Phonetic Alphabet on the Development of Western Civilization* (New York: St. Martin's Press, 1986), 102.

4. Diamond, Jared, *Guns, Germs, and Steel: The Fates of Human Societies* (New York: W.W. Norton and Company, 1999), 215.

5. Diamond, 227.

6. Logan, 99.

7. Diamond, 217.

8. Diamond, 218–219.

9. Logan, 101.

10. Logan, 100.

11. Logan, 101.

12. Logan, 104.

13. Logan, 105.

14. Logan, 112.

15. Logan, 124.

16. Logan, 124.

17. Logan, 125.

18. Sibley, Mulford Q., *Political Ideas and Ideologies: A History of Political Thought* (New York: Harper and Row Publishers, 1970), 30–31.

19. Myres, 38.

20. Myres, 30–31.

21. Myres, 44.

22. Wood, Ellen Meiksins and Neal Wood, *Class Ideology and Ancient Political Theory: Socrates, Plato, and Aristotle in Social Context* (New York: Oxford University Press, 1978), 13.

23. *Cambridge History of Greek and Roman Political Thought*, eds. Christopher Rowe, et al. (Cambridge, UK: Cambridge University Press, 2000) 18.

24. Robinson, Charles Alexander, Jr., *Athens in the Age of Pericles* (Norman: University of Oklahoma Press, 1959), 102.

25. Robinson, 42-43, and "Pericles on Athenian Democracy—The Funeral Oration (Thucydides 2, 35–46)," in *Sources in Greek Political Thought: From Homer to Polybius*, ed. by Donald Kagan (New York: The Free Press, 1965).

26. Myres, 32.

27. Raaflaub, Kurt A., "Democracy, Oligarchy, and the Concept of the "Free Citizen" in Late Fifth-Century Athens," in *Political Theory*, Vol. 11, No. 4, (Nov., 1983), 518–519.

28. Sibley, 37–38, and *The Cambridge History of Greek and Roman Political Thought*, 44.

29. Sibley, 37–38.

30. Wood, 21–22.

31. Grant, Arthur J., *Greece in the Age of Pericles* (New York: Charles Scribner's Sons, 1893), 291.

32. Raaflaub, 519.

33. *The Portable Plato*, ed. Scott Buchanan (New York: Penguin Books, 1976), 586.

34. See Koch, Andrew M., *Knowledge and Social Construction* (Lanham, MD: Lexington Books, 2005).

35. Sagan, Eli, *The Honey and the Hemlock: Democracy and Paranoia in Ancient Athens and Modern America* (New York: Basic Books, 1991), 63–64.

36. Foucault, *Power/Knowledge,* 63.

37. Foucault, *Power/Knowledge,* 117.

38. Foucault, Michel, *The History of Sexuality, Volume 1: An Introduction,* trans. Robert Hurley (New York: Vintage Books, 1990), 5.

39. Foucault, *The History of Sexuality,* 8.

40. Foucault, *The History of Sexuality,* 11.

41. Foucault, *The History of Sexuality,* 141.

42. Foucault, *The History of Sexuality,* 143–144.

43. Robinson, 18.

44. Robinson, 67.

45. Grant, 300.

46. Grant, 301.

47. Bowra, C.M., *Periclean Athens* (New York: The Dial Press, 1971), 211–212.

48. Bowra, 212.

49. Grant, 301.

50. Robinson, 68.

51. *Philosophy and Power in the Graeco-Roman World,* eds. Gillian Clark and Tessa Rajak (Oxford, UK: Oxford University Press, 2002), 1.

52. Logan, 130–131.

53. Logan, 133.

54. Logan, 134.

55. Murphy, James J., "Roman Writing Instruction as Described by Quintilian," in *A Short History of Writing Instruction: From Ancient Greece to Twentieth-Century America,* ed. by James J. Murphy (Davis, CA: Hermagoras Press, 1990), 24.

56. Murphy, 29.

57. Murphy, 19.

58. Murphy, 19.

59. Murphy, 19.

60. Tacitus, Cornelius P., *A Dialogue on Oratory,* trans. Sir William Peterson (Loeb Classical Library: Harvard University Press, 1946), 105–106.

61. Shotter, David, *The Fall of the Roman Empire* (London: Routledge, 1994), 4.

62. Wiseman, T.P., "Competition and Co-operation," from *Roman Political Life 90 B.C.–A.D. 69,* Exeter Studies in History No. 7, ed. T.P. Wiseman (Exeter, UK: University of Exeter Press, 1985), 3.

63. Wiseman, "Competition and Co-operation," 4.

64. Murphy, 22.

65. Murphy, 19.

66. Staccioli, Romolo Augusto, *The Roads of the Romans* (Los Angeles: Getty Publications, 2003), 7.

67. Gladden, E. N., *A History of Public Administration,* Vol. I (London: Frank Cass and Company Limited, 1972), 128.

68. Aicher, Peter J., *Guide to the Aqueducts of Ancient Rome* (Wauconda, IL: Bolchazy-Carducci Publishers, Inc., 1995), ix.

69. Hodge, A. Trevor, *Roman Aqueducts and Water Supply* (London: Gerald Duckworth and Co., 1992), 274.

70. Aicher, 4.

71. Aicher, 18.

72. Aicher, 19.

73. Aicher, 23.

74. Evans, Harry B., *Water Distribution in Ancient Rome: The Evidence of Frontinus* (Ann Arbor: The University of Michigan Press, 1994), 11, and Aicher, 26.

75. Gladden, 128.

76. Chevallier, Raymond, *Roman Roads*, trans. N.H. Field (Berkeley: University of California Press, 1976), 200.

77. Chevallier, 199.

78. Von Hagen, Victor W., *The Roads that Led to Rome* (Cleveland, OH: The World Publishing Company, 1967), 274.

79. Ward-Perkins, Bryan, *The Fall of Rome and the End of Civilization* (Oxford, UK: Oxford University Press, 2005), 132.

80. Gladden, 128.

81. Staccioli, 5.

82. Staccioli, 7.

83. Staccioli, 17–18.

84. Staccioli, 19.

85. Staccioli, 19–20.

86. Staccioli, 8.

87. Staccioli, 83.

88. Staccioli, 104.

89. Chevallier, 200.

90. Wiseman, T.P., "Introduction," from *Roman Political Life 90 B.C.-A.D. 69*, Exeter Studies in History No. 7, ed. by T.P. Wiseman (Exeter, UK: University of Exeter Press, 1985), 1.

91. Wiseman, "Introduction," 2.

92. Wiseman, "Competition and Co-operation," 13.

93. Wiseman, "Competition and Co-operation," 13–14.

94. Wiseman, "Competition and Co-operation," 14.

95. Wiseman, "Competition and Co-operation," 14.

96. Paterson, Jeremy, "Politics in the Late Republic," in *Roman Political Life 90 B.C.–A.D. 69*, Exeter Studies in History No. 7, ed. by T.P. Wiseman, (Exeter, UK: University of Exeter Press, 1985), 21.

97. Hildinger, Erik, *Swords Against the Senate: The Rise of the Roman Army and the Fall of the Republic* (New York: Da Capo Press, 2002), ix.

98. Logan, 137.

99. Logan, 138.

100. Logan, 138.

101. Logan, 138.

102. Hildinger, x.

103. Shotter, David, *The Fall of the Roman Republic,* 2.

Chapter 3

The Middle Ages: Domination and Administration in an Age of Illiteracy

Introduction

The Greek and Roman cultures were urbanized, with a large portion of the urban citizenry able to read, write, and perform simple mathematical calculations. In the case of Greece, this allowed for a concept of the citizen-administrator to emerge. In Athens, Periclian democracy emerges precisely because the conditions allowed for the rise of a class of equals. Officials could, essentially, be chosen by lot.

Ancient Rome used a class of professional administrators. These were people who were specially trained to the tasks, whether they were record keeping, tax collection, or civil engineering. Such specialization had two major effects. First, it allowed for the growth of the Roman Empire, as the professional civil servant with specialized training could more efficiently address the affairs of state. Second, because of the disconnect between democracy and the functioning of the administrative apparatus brought about by this professional class, it was possible for the Empire to continue to expand, even as the age of the republic gave way to domination by a series of autocrats. Rational administration did not require democracy.

Therefore, for the development of both Greece and Rome, the material conditions for growth and expansion relied heavily on a substantial literate population able to carry out the functions of the state. The organization and refinement of tasks necessary to the manifestation of centralized state power are impossible without at least a moderately literate population. As the oral tradition gives way to writing, it is possible to formalize law and create the centralized apparatus of domination that characterizes the rise and fall of empires in the ancient world.

However, by the third and fourth centuries the conditions that gave rise to the Roman Republic, and then to the Roman Empire, were beginning to wane. The Empire had been overextended. Plunder from the provinces was no longer sufficient to fund both an army and the infrastructure of education and training necessary to replenish the ranks of the central institutions. The Roman system of education was in decline, libraries were in disrepair, and the conditions necessary to maintain the centralized apparatus of the state were in fading. By the time the Empire collapsed, rates of literacy had declined considerably. The weak notions of equality that had sustained Greek democracy only had a rationale with a literate population. The efficiency of the Roman Empire required a literate class of civil servants to administer the territories. A new society, with new forms of domination, had to arise in the place of the centralized apparatus of the Roman Empire.

Within this new apparatus of domination new constructions of human identity would be formed. Central to this new identity was the notion of human equality. However, this new understanding of equality had a different foundation than that found in ancient Greece. Equality did not result from a common set of skills mastered by the population, but from an intrinsic, transcendent, worth resulting from an equal relationship that all shared with the Christian deity. Such an idea is the foundation for the transcendent notions of equality found within Enlightenment humanism at the beginnings of the modern period. However, in medieval times such an idea cannot come to fruition as democratic practice, as the subject is not claimed to be in possession of a faculty of reason with sufficient strength to generate truth claims without the aid of God, His text, and the interpretations of the church hierarchy.

The centralized system of administration characterized by the Roman Empire also gave way to a new, decentralized system of regional monarchies. As the skills necessary to the managing of vast territories declined, the insular feudal estate is born. The material task of administration over a large territory is impossible without an educated, hierarchically organized system of trained staff. As the old system collapsed, rule by written law ceases to be the most efficient form of domination. Written law is replaced by the oral decrees of the newly emerging monarchs and the administration of territories also reverts to a pre-literate mode of organization. Without technology linking people over a vast territory, this organizational arrangement is only compatible with smaller territorial units.

Both the church and the feudal estate are hierarchically organized. They are both products of an age of illiteracy and a construction of the subject that emerged from such a context. The subject does not create, judge, or challenge the existing order. One obeys, or one finds both a church hierarchy and a feudal monarchy engaged in acts of repression. It is important to remember that the oppression of the population is carried out with the systemic legitimacy that is consistent with rule over an illiterate population.

The Collapse of Centralized Administration

Urbs antique ruit, multos dominate per annos.
[The ancient city falls, after dominion of many long years.][1]

The period of decline in the Roman Empire was a transitional period. With the conversion of Emperor Constantine to Christianity, the establishment of Christianity as the official religion of the Roman Empire in 380 C.E., and the disintegration of the Roman system of administration, the early Middle Ages constituted a radical transformation of life for the people of Europe. The centralized system of Roman administration was replaced by a decentralized system of local kingdoms. The institutions of learning that were central to the administration and engineering feats of the Roman Republic were in decline, as were the systems of writing, record keeping, and technologies of dissemination that were central to maintaining the network of administration for the empire. To maintain and expand the Empire it was necessary for Rome to not only spread its military power, but to also disseminate the identity of Romanness. With the decline in the technologies for such socializing practices, the maintenance of the Empire was unsustainable.

It was in this environment that a small cult from the eastern fringe of the Empire began to take hold. With the rise of Christianity the strong connections between nature and social life were replaced with a creed that divorced and discounted the significance of the natural world in an article of faith about a "world to come." A new construction of subjectivity, epistemological models, and technology of administration would transform the world into its image.

Due to its vast territorial reach, the Roman Republic was generally tolerant of fringe religions. All that was required was a willingness of the various sects to pay some public homage to the Roman gods as part of public ceremonies. Christianity's reluctance to engage "in the pagan cult of the divinity of the emperor"[2] generated a reaction by the Roman authorities and made them an easy scapegoat for the internal decay overtaking Rome by the second and third centuries. The Christian aversion to the conformity with Roman law came directly from their religious beliefs. As stated in the Bible, there is only one God. Jesus is quoted as saying, "My kingdom is not of this world."[3] Christians concluded that the earthly life of human beings was a transitory readying for the afterlife. In heaven they would find their permanent haven from any suffering found in the world of the flesh.

However, the rise of Christianity needs to be understood as a symptom of Roman decline rather than its cause. The Empire had been over-extended, over-taxed, and unable to maintain the infrastructure needed to maintain both the extension of administration and military power abroad, and provide the necessary condition for the continuation of a functioning civil apparatus at home. Rome was collapsing from within. Literacy rates were falling. Education in the technical skills necessary to maintain Rome's infrastructure were declining. Two years prior to Christianity becoming the official religion of Rome, in 380 C.E., the Roman libraries were closed.[4]

With the collapse of the civil service, the incentives for learning to read and write evaporated.[5] Employment in the bureaucracy was no longer an option for the urban inhabitants of Rome. In addition, teaching, learning, and the generation of textbooks, were considered pagan activities by the Christian church.[6] When church sentiment was coupled with the lack of material incentives for the learning of reading and writing skills, literacy rates fell to almost nothing among the general population soon after the collapse of the Empire.[7] Except for the few remaining schools in Italy, non-religious public education disappeared throughout the territories of the Empire by the seventh century.[8]

As early as the fifth and sixth centuries, barbarian kingdoms appeared in the shadow of the old empire. Rome had been sacked by the Visigoths in 410 and by the Vandals in 455. The Roman Empire broke into a collection of regional kingdoms, often under the extended families of the old Roman rulers. The regional nature of these kingdoms would become the foundation of the territorial character of ruling monarchies in Western Europe during the Middle Ages. These regions were divided among the Visigoths in Spain, the Franks in Gaul, the Anglo-Saxons and Celts in the British Isles, and the Lombards in Italy.

The creation of these smaller kingdoms further reduced the need for reading and writing. The merchant class that had once traveled the roads and sea-lanes of the Roman Empire were now largely confined to the newly emerging territorial kingdoms. While these kingdoms had need for some form of civil service, the declines in literacy generated a return to pre-literate forms of civil administration. Written documents were still used in civil and legal transactions, but their role was diminished as rituals, and oral forms of communication, took precedence over the written word. For example, in the transfer of land, the written deed took on the character of a symbol in the exchange process. The binding act that transferred land was a ritual in which the seller conveyed a handful of dirt from the property to the new owner in a ritual carried out in front of the members of the community.[9]

These forms of activity demonstrate that the material conditions for a mass form of administration had declined with the fall of Rome. Political and social life had, out of necessity, taken on a character that was more local and personal than that promoted under the skilled training and literacy of the Roman Empire. Allegiance was given to a person rather than written law.[10] Oral pronouncements of rulers took precedent over formal statutes.

The Roman Empire had been very centralized, with a professional class of civil servants managing the affairs of the empire. Writing had a critical role in the dissemination of the commands of the central state apparatus. With the decline in literacy, the power of a centralized state authority waned. It was common for the kings and senior members of the kingdoms to be illiterate. Even the emperor Charlemagne, the promoter of the so-called Carolingian Renaissance, remained illiterate. However, literacy had not completely disappeared. It still existed among the church hierarchy and was central to the rise of the church power.

Christianity and the Technology of Church Domination

When the sacking of Rome occurred by Alaric, it disrupted the confidence and faith shown by those like St. Ambrose. St. Ambrose of Milan, before the fall of the Empire, optimistically thought that the "piety of its rulers," along with the church in a 'divine' partnership, would sustain the rule of the then crumbling Roman Empire. As St. Ambrose perceived both the Empire and the church to be the two sovereignties given a "special power and authority from God," each would serve to ensure the security and welfare of one another in a reciprocal relationship.

Less optimistic positions were held by other Christian scholars, such as Jerome, who perceived the fall of the Empire to be an opportunity for the Christian community and church to triumph in the heavenly kingdom. The magnitude of the destruction around them signaled to many in the Christian community that the apocalypse was upon them. Turning their horror and fright to a form of hopefulness, scores of Christians pointed to prophecies in the Bible that predicted the end of the world. As Jerome wrote during the executions, assassinations, invasions, and battles that marked the final collapse of the Empire, "The Roman world is falling, and yet we are holding up our heads instead of bowing them down!"[11] The coming of the apocalypse meant that all faithful Christians would soon come to reside in the heavenly City of God instead of the ill-fated, sinful, agonizing City of Man.

Literacy and the Technology of Power

Even as the old order of the Roman Empire was collapsing, a new institution was developing the technical capacity to rise in the vacuum of power. The emergence of the Catholic Church as an institution exercising political power results from a set of material conditions that emerged at the end of the Empire. With the fall of Rome, many in the ruling class were displaced. Some of these become members of the emerging church hierarchy.[12] As a result, many of the rituals that were part of the imperial court in Rome became incorporated into the new church. However, this new church hierarchy also possessed another talent. They were the most educated and carried a tradition of literacy into the church. This became essential for the expansion of the church's power throughout the Middle Ages.

As the temporal order was collapsing, the structures of the old Roman bureaucracy were incorporated into the church.[13] The church was hierarchically structured, with power centralized in Rome. Territorial units throughout the old empire were divided up among a lower tier of clergy responsible to Rome. However, the centralization of authority required some technology for the dissemination of commands. Written codes of church law were transmitted from the offices of the church, providing the church with the ability to extend its power of dissemination with the use of writing. As was the case in the days of the empire, written codes had the power to convey commands over vast territories.

Yet even more important to the expansion of church power was the control over the reproduction of texts and the sanctioning of what could enter the domain of discourse. From the fall of the Roman Empire until the invention of moveable type, Europe was dominated by "manuscript technology."[14] Monk's copied manuscripts as part of their religious duties. The church's goal was to multiply God's word in the world. Such a practice had profound effects on the growth of church domination, a reign of power that lasted a thousand years in Europe.

The copying of manuscripts by the church was not just a religious act, but also a political act. The church scribes were assigned the text to be copied by the officials of the church hierarchy.[15] They did not choose them. Nor were they permitted to create new texts. Such an act would have been considered heresy.[16] Considering the length of time needed to copy a manuscript, only a small, select, group of works were copied. Naturally, this meant that the church replicated those works that aided the church in its services, or otherwise supported church practices. Copies of such works were given to clergy throughout the church's domain in order that the words could be read to the illiterate masses, passing on church law and tradition, and securing church power in the process. Thus, a social divide emerged between those who could only converse in the oral tradition and those who could repeat the permanence of the written word. The priests became the purveyors of that which appeared eternal, as they deciphered the written word.

Such a socialization pattern among the masses of illiterate peasants had a powerful impact. It socialized the people into the traditions and practices that reflected the teachings of the church, as institutional norms and values replicated the conditions for the church's maintenance and expansion. Institutional legitimacy is secured through the socialization of the public into its mode of thinking, epistemological model, and its sanctioning of social institutions. In such a context, a challenge to the authority of the church becomes nearly impossible. Even if such thoughts are present among the laity, they are not expressed openly without the charge of heresy, and without the swift and certain punishment of the church. A "free spirit," a literate member of the laity, was always a threat to the church's power. The concept of "heresy" was invented to keep such challenges under control.[17] Thus, by completely controlling the instruments of socialization, the mode of knowledge construction, and the context for socialization, the church enjoyed the power to simultaneously both shape and reflect popular opinion. Such a condition assures the continuation of church domination for a reign of a thousand years.

The Doctrine of Power: The Nicene Creed

Despite the technical capacity of the church to spread its message, there remained a contradiction between church doctrine and church practice. If the church was to be concerned with otherworldly matters, and the purity of human souls, then did this not conflict with the amassing of wealth and power by the institution of the church? Also, if all are to be judged according to the same commandments of God, then are not all equal in the eyes of God? If this is the case, how can the rigid hierarchy of the church be maintained? The church worked out these contradictions early in its development in a document known as the Nicene Creed.

The "Nicene Creed," or the "Niceno-Constantinopolitan Creed," was established by the ancient church at the end of the fourth or the beginning of the fifth century. The Nicene Creed is one of the most extensively employed articles of faith from the ancient church, and is still invoked by the Roman Catholic and Episcopal Churches. It is the "ecumenical creed" in which the church is asserted to be *unam, sanctam, catholicam et apostolicam,* "one, holy, catholic, and apostolic."[18]

The term "catholic" in its earlier use did not simply mean "universal." Catholic meant "identity plus universality," where identity is what differentiates the church from the rest of the humanity.[19] Universality within this definition of "catholic" meant encompassing all of humanity in scope. By its very description in the Nicene Creed, the church contained a sense of identity that was to be separate, different, and holier than the rest of humanity, but was also to embrace all human beings to be under the dominion of the church.

Being "apostolic" is both a social declaration and a theological doctrine. By asserting itself as apostolic, the church alleged that it was able to convey and transmit the will of God to the society of human beings. In the sense of being a theological doctrine, apostolic meant the elementary means of discerning what was legitimate or not within Christian doctrine. The church had to have a claim to being apostolic to be able to serve as the justifiable arbitrator of the catholic Christian community.[20]

The Nicene Creed's statement shaped the social context that allowed the Roman Catholic Church to become such a prominent and influential political and social institution in the Middle Ages. The church was to be of a singular nature, without any other institutional branches or differing interpretations of faith. This generated an institutional structure in which all branches came off of a central institution. Power was centralized at the core. This encouraged a hierarchy to emerge within the church that had a pope at its helm, who was considered the sole and ultimate authority of Christian faith.

The pope was considered holy, or sacred. The term "holy" as it appears in the ancient texts must be understood, in the spiritual sense, as not being equivalent to moral veracity or decency of character. Rather, "holy" as used in the Nicene Creed, meant "chosen by God, because He has predestined it to a glorious inheritance, and because He dwells in it in the Person of the Holy Spirit."[21]

The Nicene Creed is self-affirming. It asserts that the church is singular, holy, universal, and apostolic in nature. As the church recognizes no rival doctrines or institutions, it is the sole leader of the Christian faith. As it is divinely ordained, its pronouncements represent the word of God in this earthly existence. Its word is infallible, beyond question or challenge. To suggest otherwise is to be branded as a heretic.

However, while the Nicene Creed solves the problems of centralizing institutional power and doctrinal hierarchy, it must also be acknowledged to create tension between doctrinal purity and established authority. Christ's declaration in the Bible, "My kingdom is not of this world,"[22] clearly contradicts the contention that the church, which is of this earthly realm, is holy and sanctified.

In the *City of God*, Augustine makes it clear that in his understanding of Christ's teachings, God and Christ do not inhabit the *city of man*. Further, the church's extensive intervention in politics during the Middle Ages conflicts with Jesus' other statements regarding the separation between the activities of this world and the preparation for the next.[23] The intent of the Nicene Creed appears to alter the relation between man and the word of God. It is no longer the infallibility of God's word in the Bible that exists at the core of religion, but the institutional hierarchy of the church that carries the mantle of perfection, even as it dwells in the place of human sin.

As a worldly institution, the church now pursues wealth and property as part of its mission in the *city of man*. The early church's rejection of earthly, material possessions as contrary to God's kingdom, was overturned by the evolving institutional character of the church. The Roman Catholic Church's position after the Nicene Creed was to exploit the material goods of the *city of man* in order to serve the needs and wants of religion. In practice, this meant the expansion of church property and possessions.[24]

In the final analysis, the movement of the church into worldly matters brings internal tensions and contradictions. The earth is not considered the place of salvation, yet the church seeks to expand its presence.

The pursuits of property and power are not the proper domains of the holy, yet the church pursues both with vigor. The Nicene Creed sanctioned these moves and solidified them as part of church doctrine.

Such a move also brought tension in the consideration of human equality. While Christian teaching reflects the equality and universality of all human beings, the establishment of a structural hierarchy asserting infallible powers would run counter to such notions. In addition, the distinction between believers and non-believers affords different levels of rights and expectations within the emerging structure. Those who lie outside the church are not considered part of the community, and are, therefore, not worthy of the same respect as believers.

Still, it is from this narrow notion of equality before God that one of the central pillars of support for democratic practice emerged in the Enlightenment. Equality is asserted as a "natural law." Human beings are considered equal in their rights and responsibilities as members of communities, and even as members of the human race. Universal in its application, Enlightenment Humanism, cannot be divorced from its roots in the Middle Ages.

Saint Augustine and the City of God

In a society dominated by the manuscript as a means of disseminating the truth of human existence, the narrow focus of the church would allow for the reproduction of very few texts. One author, whose works were considered of value by the church was that of St. Augustine. St. Augustine answered questions that the church needed to address. Was Christianity the cause for the fall of Rome? Opponents of the Empire had not defiled Rome during the eight hundred years of pagan rule, and Rome was ravaged under the rule of Christian emperors.[25] What is the role of the church in its engagement of earthly power? How has Christianity assisted men, except in possibly making man's lot even worse?[26] St. Augustine took up these charges. Writing prolifically, Augustine explained the nature of the rise and fall of temporal, earthly kingdoms, and warned other Christians not to be misguided by the ridicules of their opponents that may make villainous claims for Christianity.

Living during and immediately after the disintegration of the Roman Empire in Northern Africa, Augustine sought to reconcile and salvage Christian doctrine in the face of the (converted and Christian) Roman Empire's collapse. Augustine's objective was to resolve early Christian dogma with the political concessions that Christianity was forced to make in order to endure confrontations between faith and secular authority that were occurring in Augustine's historical context.

St. Augustine maintains that Christ's self-sacrifice was for the salvation of *individual* souls, not for the salvation of political establishments, meaning that the Christian community should not be confused as being a corresponding entity to any terrestrial, political state. Hence, the church is separate from any earthly political systems. Augustine posits that even if nations profess to have Christian political governance, their Christianity is merely a façade, an exterior resemblance. There can be no true Christian political rule.[27]

For Augustine, human existence is built upon God as the foundation and the nucleus. The transcendence of God is the reality, and the most vital choice of human beings is then between electing to believe and follow God and his divine law, or to turn away from God and choose the path of sin and transgression. The most important relationship is the one between a human being and God. Every other relationship and determination made by human beings is inferior to the relationship between a human being and their choice of believing and following God and his canon.[28]

Human beings who choose God and focus on the spiritual realm of the Christian afterlife constitute the *civitas Dei*, the City of God. The love of God drives those who dwell in the City of God to choose that path. Their love of God is "a love of God carried even to the point of contempt of self."[29] The City of God ". . . unquestionably surpasses the earthly city, whose citizens . . . are fixed only on material goods and earthly enjoyments."[30]

On earth, the sole form of a legitimate political command is "that of coercive power used to restrain coercive power," which has always characterized the *civitas terrena*, the City of Man. The *civitas terrena*, in turn, should not fear the political intervention from the Christian community.[31] The rationale for this perspective comes from the disparate natures of the characteristics of the City of Man versus the City of God. The impetus of human beings in the world is the "love of self carried even to the point of contempt for God," with value being placed on living "carnally . . . in the things of this world."[32] Augustine cites Jesus on the division of the *civitas terrena* and the Christian brotherhood: "Hear then, ye Jews and Gentiles; hear, O circumcision; hear, O uncircumcision; hear, all ye kingdoms of the earth: I interfere not with your government in the world."[33]

However, Augustine confronts and transforms this doctrine in a way that reinforces the growth of church institutions. His reasoning is simple.

Despite their being "not of this world," Christians are still to sojourn through the terrestrial realm of man. Therefore, they should not live *completely* separate from the earthly world. Christians should not focus on the temporal *city of man*, but rather on becoming "good" Christians in *this* world for the purpose of being able to take pleasure in the life to come after this one in the *city of God*.

In Augustine's work, *City of God*, the assertion is made that:

> God, desiring not only that the human race might be able by their similarity of nature to associate with one another, but also that they might be bound together in harmony and peace by the ties of relationship, was pleased to derive all men from one individual. And He created men with such a nature that the members of the race should not have died, had not the first two (of whom one was created from nothing, and the other out of him) merited this with their disobedience; for by them so great a sin was committed, that by it the human nature was altered for the worse, and was transmitted also to their posterity.[34]

Since human beings' nature is inherently recalcitrant and sinful, human societies are destined to be chaotic and will require coercive force to maintain order. Augustine continues that since "God does not wholly desert those whom He condemns, nor shuts up in His anger, His tender mercies," human beings are controlled by codes of law, which can be guided by the education of God's word, as found in the Bible. Laws and education then "keep guard against the ignorance that besets us" as well as "oppose the assaults of vice" that are innate to human beings. God has given "free will" to human beings in order that they may choose the correct path. Should they stray, laws are to be punitive, "used to restrain the folly of children." Augustine cites, "the birch, the strap, the cane, [as] the schooling which the Scripture says must be given a child."[35] Punishments are to ultimately defeat and overwhelm the inborn ignorance and sinfulness of human beings.

As God is asserted by Augustine to not "desert" mankind, human beings should not attempt to explain fortunate or unfortunate human events as being a consequence of the worship or abandonment of any particular deity or religious system. Further, God's design for human history can never be completely understood. Therefore, human beings cannot interpret God's actions in the temporal world with any accuracy. History and politics are constituted of colossal conflicts of influences and forces that God, and God alone, can understand and fully know. God has not forsaken human beings. He has given us signs of the importance of human struggle in the forms of Christ of the Incarnation and in the Scriptures of the Bible.[36]

The focus of Christianity is the afterlife, not the terrestrial world. From this reasoning, politics and governance is regarded as something to give enough order in society to prevent the truly wicked from fully corrupting the entire society. The political prescription becomes a paternalistic, authoritative, punitive system of rewards and punishments in which the church and the monarchical sovereign rule side by side in a reciprocal relationship.

This relationship between the church and the monarchies in the Middle Ages proved both conflictual and symbiotic. Each depended on the other for some political legitimacy. Two doctrines, in particular, bound the two institutions together. In the assertion that human nature is wicked and sinful, the temporal world of politics necessitated a strongly authoritarian style of rule. Only concentrated power can keep the wicked in check. The monarch is performing a divine function by asserting authority. Therefore, he must be considered to have divine authority.

Also, by maintaining the position that human subjectivity possesses the power of free will, a role for "judgment" and "punishment" is secured in both the religious institutions and the state apparatus. If all could choose to act righteously, then one is accountable for all acts and subject to the appropriate rewards and penalties. Since free will is a transcendent part of human nature, it has both temporal and transcendent implications. Therefore, it is a doctrine that serves both the church and the state.

To Augustine, original sin incurably flawed human beings. Consequently, humans do not possess the ability to reason for themselves, they must rely on God to assist them in the transmission of "truth." Human reason cannot provide the answers to life's riddles, nor can it ascend to touch that which is universal and eternal. The guidance that human beings need must descend to the earth from the heavens. God is the only valid possessor of knowledge and truth. The church transmits the word of God and becomes His messenger.

However, also having origins in the concept of original sin is the idea of human equality. All are born in sin. This makes all human beings the same, even if in the most negative sense. As a result, all human beings are "equal in the eyes of God," as all humans are lacking in the ability to know themselves and the true nature of reality. Within this context it would be irrational heresy for them to believe they could create and transmit their own texts about the nature of life and the world around them.

Therefore, even while seeking to distinguish the sphere of faith from the realm of temporal power, Augustine furthers the legitimacy of church engagement in worldly affairs. Such a position reinforces the church's interest in expanding its power and wealth, also represented in the Nicene Creed. By reproducing and disseminating Augustine's text, the church is able to forward the narrative that expresses a construction of the subject that is compatible with church power and legitimates its worldly role as part of God's agenda. Such a view of human nature is, however, also compatible with the expansion of power more generally and will be used to justify the expansion of state power well into the modern period.

In Augustine, and the formulations of subjectivity in the early Christian church, one can find early formulations of some ideas that will support the growth of the democratic form of domination that will emerge in the Enlightenment. Equality, free will, choice, and accountability all, become elements of subjectivity that emerge with Enlightenment Humanism and support the growth of democratic institutions. However, for Augustine and the early Christian church, equality was not coupled with a strong notion of *reason* as part of the constructed subject. For Augustine and the early Christians, reason cannot ascend to create truth in the world. Without reason as part of the description of human subjectivity, democracy remains irrational.

Saint Thomas Aquinas and the Formation of Society

Strict control over the reproduction and dissemination of text allowed for church power to expand throughout the early Middle Ages. The church invented the notion of "heresy" in order to prevent any alternative narratives from entering the discourse, particularly from the few remaining literate members of the laity. Particularly important to the church was the curb on ancient texts, many of which were destroyed by the church as the teachings of a pagan society. Particularly troubling for the church were the teachings of Aristotle, who taught that through the use of reason, specifically inductive logic, it was possible for human beings to generate new ideas about the physical world.

However, by the thirteenth century several events were taking place that were beginning to erode the church's firm control over the dissemination of texts. Trade had been increasing for a century and the ancient texts housed in Arab libraries began to make their way back into the European theater. Also, the monarchical institution began to expand the power and domain of administration, generating an increased demand for the skills in writing and mathematics central to the keeping of written records. Further, challenges from the Arab world were taking place in theology. The work of the Islamic author Averroses incorporated the concepts of Aristotle and contested church teaching on the limitless nature of God's power by discussing physics.[37] The church responded by disseminating the texts of St. Thomas Aquinas.

Saint Thomas Aquinas endeavored to reconcile the philosophy of the ancient Greek, Aristotle, and Christianity in the thirteenth century. To achieve this, Aquinas had to make the distinction between the metaphysical and the natural theoretical classifications. As Aquinas states, "Grace does not destroy nature, but perfects it."[38] Both the spiritual realm and the earthly realm were created and ruled over by God, but there is a hierarchy between these two spheres. The spiritual domain is superior to the terrestrial, as it determines human beings' final destination in heaven or hell.

In discussing human nature, Aquinas acknowledges that the *Fall of Man*, as discussed in the book of Genesis, signaled the irrevocable imperfection of human beings. However, the *Fall* did not negate the ability of human beings to understand the laws of nature. The *Fall* damaged human beings in their ability to accomplish the obligations of natural law and, therefore, of fulfilling God's will and laws.[39] Due to the *Fall*, human beings' reasoning abilities are not to be trusted. Only God possesses complete knowledge of the spiritual and temporal realms. However, human reason is sufficient to comprehend revelations and messages from God.[40]

This limited power of reason does, however, provide guidance for the political realm. Like Aristotle, Aquinas conceived of the state as being organic in nature. The state was a unified collection of individuals in order to serve the common good. Viewed organically, Aquinas saw Aristotle's characterization of the state paralleling his own view of the Christian community. These organizations are not artificial entities, but living unions of the members that make them up.[41] However, unlike Aristotle, the organic notion of the state in Aquinas followed from the practices of the Roman Catholic Church. The church dealt with its followers mostly en masse, not on an individual basis. A congregation was treated as a collection of followers, where the individual was not considered unless they deviated from the body of worshippers. As Aquinas states:

> Because man living according to virtue is ordained to a higher
> end, which consists in the enjoyment of God . . . there should

be the same for a multitude of men as for one man. The final
end of a congregated multitude, therefore, is not to live according to virtue, but through a virtuous life to arrive at the enjoyment of God.[42]

Aquinas' organic conception of the state, with a belief in the "common good" of the whole, will eventually contribute to the Enlightenment
perceptions of democratic practice. To Aquinas, political legitimacy is
determined by the extent to which institutions pursue the common good.
In the Enlightenment, the masses are not only the object of the common
good, but they are identified with it. The masses are affirmed as both the
focus of the principle of the common good, and the arbiters of what constitutes the content of good practice.

However, while there are some parallels to the Enlightenment, it
should be noted that the origin of the state places Aquinas in a different
context. As Canning argued, many interpret Aquinas as emphasizing the
purpose of a political amalgamation of human beings and not on the historical context in which a political community originated.[43] Unlike the
development of democratic practice in the Enlightenment, the origin of
the principles of government is, for Aquinas, derived from God. Law is
defined by Aquinas as "an ordinance of reason for the common good,
made by Him who has the care of the community, and promulgated."[44]
God is the creator and source of everything in the cosmos, therefore God
is the source of all law in the affairs of human beings.

Aquinas specifies "natural laws" as the morals that are derived from
God's "eternal laws." They are discerned by man through reason. These
natural laws then present human beings with norms that guide and order
human behavior. Things that are determined to be *good* should be pursued once something is recognized as the good. Some good items are
only enjoyed by human beings, such as recognizing and worshipping
God and discovering the truths that God has created. By engaging the
"right reason," Aquinas believed that human beings can arrange a hierarchy and in that manner decide among items if there is a conflict among
different *goods*.[45]

Such a perspective gives considerable more weight to the human
power of reason than is found in Augustine. Reason is a power that allows human beings to discover what is universally prescribed as natural
law and to develop practices that are responses to purely human social
needs. In order to explain this contrast, Aquinas makes a distinction between two forces that guide the discovery of natural laws. He calls them
positive and negative forces. The positive force provides human beings

with a proclivity to do what is natural. The negative force of reason is the inclination to allow a practice that is not strictly prohibited, but is, nevertheless, not strictly prescribed. In other words, something can be added or subtracted from human social practices without breaching natural law if it is not specifically prohibited.[46] Therefore, in Aquinas' theoretical structure, no action by a human being can be recognized as being unnatural unless expressly forbidden.

This principle is particularly important when considering Aquinas' views on kingship, slavery, and property. A master's control over a slave is distinct from the relationship of a prince over a subject. The master/slave relationship has private gain as its intention, while the prince/subject relationship is for the purpose of serving the public good. Therefore, Aquinas treats the association between prince and subject as natural. Where there is a hostile or antagonistic relationship, Aquinas claims that sin has warped the naturalness of the bond.

As for the connection between the master and the slave, Aquinas breaks from his master's teachings. To Aristotle slavery is natural, and hence *rational*, in a case where an individual cannot adequately run their own affairs. For Aquinas, there is a natural equality among all human beings. They are the sons and daughters of God and they are perceived as being equal in their status and judged equally though their acts in the world. As a result of this position, Aquinas viewed slavery as an unnatural condition, one that was perpetrated on earth only because of the sin of personal gain and private greed.[47] In this regard, Aquinas sets the stage for the modern notions of equality, undermining the strict hierarchy associated with feudal institutions.

Regarding private property, Aquinas claimed that it was not natural to the human being. However, as it is not strictly forbidden under God's law, it can be added to nature by human beings. Here he does echo Aristotle's teachings, suggesting that human beings add the notion of private property to natural law because "every man is more careful to procure what is for himself alone than that which is common to many or to all . . ."[48] Aquinas considers human society more able to be organized if each individual has a defined and delineated accountability for tending to material objects. Hence, order is more likely to be maintained in human societies where there is a division of goods based on private property than where there exists communal ownership of goods.[49]

The role of reason in the system outlined by Aquinas is to have significant influence of what comes later in the Enlightenment. Reason allows human beings to have an understanding of natural law. This is accomplished by reason ascending to knowledge of that which stands between human law and God's eternal laws. The notion of natural law became secularized in the Modern Period, as reason became its own teleology in the legitimation of public prescriptions. For example, the right "life, liberty, and property" as natural law pronouncements by Locke were simply asserted as the universal products of reason itself. However, even while stripped of overt theological references, natural law asserted a transcendent truth, disconnected from the vicissitudes of history.

Literacy, Technology, and Feudal Administration

Feudalism and the Monarchical Structure

The fall of the Roman Empire brought a decentralization of power that resulted in small, self-sufficient agricultural centers replacing urban centers as the basic social unit in Europe. Supporting a large population in cities required a technological infrastructure that was no longer capable of being developed and maintained in the manner that had allowed the rise of Rome. The emerging fiefdoms were disconnected from one another. Feudal municipalities were administered by a ruling nobility and a clerical class of peasant workers. Only later in the Middle Ages did towns and burgesses begin to emerge, as trade and commerce increased dramatically with the renewed contact with the Middle East and Asia. This was in large measure a consequence of the Crusades in the eleventh through thirteenth centuries.

Manors consisted of autonomous and self-sufficient communities based on agricultural production carried out by peasants living on the lands of a small aristocratic class. The community consisted of small dwellings surrounding a center of common facilities, such as a mill and a church. Close by would be a castle or manor home of the lord. Framing the manorial village would be cultivated fields, pastures, and forest land.[50]

The feudal system depended upon a contractual relationship between serfs and their lords. The lords provided protection and use of their lands for the peasants, and in return the peasants were expected to labor for the lord and pay taxes in the form of money and goods. Serfs could not leave the manor without permission of the lord, could not participate in outside financial pursuits, and were not allowed to marry without the consent of their lord. A serf was considered part of the land, as they were socially, economically, and politically bound to it.[51]

From the perspective of the church, the hierarchical and oppressive nature of such a system imposed on God's children was a reflection of the injustices found in an earthly existence. Toil, temptations, and servitude reflected the evil nature of life in the City of Man. This view generated some tension between the church and secular authorities. Nevertheless, both institutions benefited from their distinct roles. Two parallel structures emerged. As a general rule, each reinforced the other.

Through the lens of church doctrine, after the *Fall* human beings were forced to toil in order to sustain themselves in the world. Owing to the fact that human nature is flawed by original sin, the emergence of oppressive institutions that produce human misery reflected the natural order of existence. Greed is natural to the fallen subject, and power is the consequence of human interaction.

Therefore, the oppressive conditions of medieval society were explained by the church as a natural consequence of the human condition. While all may be judged by equal criteria in the eyes of God, it is also natural that one lives with strife, subjection, and exploitation. In this sense, the church enabled the very system that Christian teaching condemns. Institutional structures of power were deemed necessary in organizing society to save men from each other and their wanton, selfish avarice, desires and carnal longings.[52] In this manner, the church was able to consider all human beings "equal" before God, while at the same time giving feudalism legitimacy in treating human beings unequally by exploiting human labor in a structural hierarchy. In addition, human beings in the medieval era were taught by the Roman Catholic Church to focus on the spiritual City of God in which they would reside for eternity. Of course, such a fate awaited them only if they were *good* Christians and endured the challenges of the temporal world in a Christ-like manner. Hence, the more a human being suffered, the more they were deserving of rewards in the afterlife. This produced a condition in which people would tolerate any number of terrible conditions in society.

Although the relationship between the church and medieval monarchs was largely one of symbiosis, the monarchy was always wary of the effects excommunication would have on the legitimacy of temporal power. As early as the fifth century in the Visigoth kingdom, the practice of clerics anointing kings became entrenched. This ritual linked church and state together, and solidified the church's position as a temporal authority. This trend continued throughout the medieval period.[53] Later in 800 C.E., Charlemagne was made "Emperor of the Romans" (*imperator Romanorum*), the first Holy Roman Emperor, when Pope Leo III crowned him as he was arising from praying during Christmas Mass.[54]

The pope, the spiritual leader of God on earth, *made* the emperor, linking and enmeshing the worldly City of Man with the holy City of God as manifested in the terrestrial world.

Despite these connections, tension existed between the two institutions. During the Crusades the church moved directly into the realm of secular politics. Clergy in the Roman Catholic Church cannot commit murder against other human beings under canon law. However, the papacy of the church could order secular rulers to kill in particular instances, an assertion that conspicuously manifested itself under Pope Innocent IV. This precedent determined the bloody trend in the eleventh through the thirteenth centuries of the papacy. In addition, supporters of the church required military expeditions for causes that were deemed "necessary" by the pontiff. The Crusades were not only to be waged in lands that were under the authority of the church, but "throughout Christendom." Those individuals who refused to serve in the Crusades could be excommunicated from the church and have their property seized.

In addition to the church's acts in the temporal world during the Crusades, the church also intervened in disputes among the monarchs of Europe.[55] Popes viewed themselves as higher than the laws and codes of secular rulers, a notion in part derived from the universal view of the church that was held by the clergy. This added to the tension between the church and secular authorities in the Middle Ages, with both desiring to be the ultimate sovereigns.

The problem needed to be reconciled. Were human beings to yield to the spiritual authority of the church or to the secular powers of the state in forming guiding decisions for society? Were human beings fully of the material world of men, of the spiritual realm of God, or of both? And if human beings are of *both* spheres of dominion, how are decisions in the political affairs of human beings in the world to be conducted?

To answer these questions requires a new model of the human subject in which this tension is resolved. Only when human beings are asserted to have a power that transcends the dictates of both church and state powers can the notions of individuality, conscience, and autonomy begin to enter political discourse. This emerges in the Renaissance and carries forward the emergence of democratic practice in the modern period.

The Renaissance: The Triumph of Secular Power

By the twelfth century Europe was undergoing a change. Throughout the Middle Ages, "spare children" were assigned to the church for training in the church schools as a means of entering the church hierarchy.[56] However, by the eleventh century the church was no longer able to place many of the nobility's sons into the senior status positions within the church. In addition, urban centers were reemerging, as the movement of people in the Crusades reawakened an interest in trade and commerce with distant lands. The monarchical institutions had the primary responsibilities for the administration of these new activities. This development created a demand for a new class of civil servants and record keepers with skills that had not been taught in the cathedral schools.[57] By the twelfth century, monastery trained clerics were losing out in the competition for positions in the growing civil service sector of the monarchies in favor of those trained by private tutors.[58]

This development led to a rise in the teaching and learning of skills that were more associated with the ancient traditions. The teaching of rhetoric returned along with the skills of reading and writing. As the church began to lose its exclusive control over education, its ability to filter all the texts that were disseminated also began to erode. The power to control the rules that govern the production of truth claims would also recede with the coming of the Renaissance. Human activity would no longer be circumscribed by the application of the principles given in the Bible and interpreted by the church hierarchy. This would eventually culminate in new methods of inquiry and a new representation of human subjectivity. This new representation would eventually change the social and political order and bring the development of new forms of social domination. The early stages of such a development can be seen in the early Renaissance.

Marsiglio of Padua and the Power of the Civil State

Marsiglio of Padua was born sometime between 1275 and 1280, and died sometime in 1342 or 1343. He was from Florence and began his academic career in medicine and the natural sciences. In the time of Marsiglio, the city-state of Florence was still a republic, not having yet been surrendered to the rule of a single family. Due to the changing economic trends of the era, marked by increased trade, the formation of trade guilds, and the resulting increase in urban population following the Cru-

sades, political experiments were conducted in the structure of the Flor-
entine constitution. This was due, in part, to the increased political power
of the guilds, allowing them to pressure for structural changes to the constitution. Resulting from their demands, the Signoria, the primary political association of the time, was formed of Priors chosen from the various
guilds.

Marsiglio turned from his study of natural science and medicine to
discovering the source and origin of social and political discord. In particular, he identified The Roman Catholic Church as a principle source of
conflict. Marsiglio's believed that the church's hierarchical organization,
including its clergy, was the "primary obstacle" in obtaining social and
political harmony.[59] During Marsiglio's life, church authorities argued
for more rights to intrude in the social domains, while clerics also
claimed "immunity" from civic restraints. These entitlements by Church
officials were perceived as a threat to the political authority of the civil
state, and resulted in persistent conflict between the church clerics and
civil authorities. This jeopardized the legitimacy of civil institutions.[60]
One consequence of the dispute between the clerics and the civil administrators was civil legislation in opposition to church officials.

Marsiglio of Padua's personal observations of political events influenced his political thought, which included a favorable position towards
political reform to combat clerical corruption, privilege, and wealth, with
confidence that the emperor could be the instrument of political rejuve-
nation.[61] In Marsiglio's most famous work, *Defensor pacis* (*Defender of
Peace*, 1324), he condemns the church's interference in temporal political matters as well as the clergy's assertions to possess disciplinary and
coercive powers. At the same time, Marsiglio supports the sovereign
state's claims to being the legitimate authority over religious and civil
law in the earthly realm. Marsiglio's argument opposes the clergy's
claims to autonomy that exceeds the state's civil and political mandates.
Such a claim also negates the papal contentions to having "special pre-
rogatives."[62]

The Roman Catholic Church's claim that their power is superior to
the sovereign temporal states was, to Marsiglio, usurping the states' authority under the guise of "holy" canon law. He asserted that church
power "should be exposed and subordinated to the legitimate authority of
the state."[63] In this manner, the state, not the church, was to ultimately
have jurisdiction over the earthly territory of men.

Middle Ages were dominated by a feudal structure, but with the rise
of trade and commerce, towns were reemerging as centers of economic
and cultural activity. The feudal system had a greater affinity with the

rural self-sufficiency of the landed estate. In the urban areas, the balance was tipping away from the church authorities and the ideas of Marsiglio helped define a new conception of the state and the people that made it up.

Drawing on Aristotle and the ancient Greek's organic perception of society, Marsiglio compares the state to an organism in equilibrium:

> . . . the state is like an animate nature or animal. For just as an animal well disposed in accordance with nature is composed of certain proportioned parts ordered to one another and communicating their functions mutually and for the whole, so too the state is constituted of certain such parts when it is well disposed and established in accordance with reason. The relation, therefore, of the state and its parts to tranquility will be seen to be similar to the relation of the animal and its parts to health.[64]

The functioning of the parts operates according to "reason." By asserting the power of reason in the operations of the social order, Marsiglio is opening up the realm of social and political relations to direct human control. Such a control will not necessarily be a reflection of all that is "sinful," but can produce the administration of collective good, along the lines outlined by Aristotle. To Marsiglio, the discord in society is caused, in part, by the Roman Catholic Church and its agents. It is a "disease" that secular government would have to "cure" in order for a community of human beings to function harmoniously. Such a cure can only be carried out by the application of human reason.

The question then becomes who is to have the ultimate authority over the laws in the temporal City of Man, the Roman Catholic Church or the monarchies of Europe. If human beings in a state are part of an organic whole, then is it rational for a pope or a king to make singular, directing decisions that guide the whole of a society. They are performing their function as leaders within the organic union of which they are a part.

Marsiglio is setting the stage for what will develop in the Renaissance. *Reason* allows the earthly domain to be ruled by human beings. This doctrine enhances the legitimacy of the secular authority and fosters a new understanding of the technology of administration. With the Renaissance came the notion of the nation-state, with a new understanding of the state's powers and new relationships between the state and its populace, the church, and the empire.[65]

Conclusion

With the collapse of the Roman Empire, the ability of the central state apparatus to reign over human affairs was severely eroded. The system of state education disintegrated, the libraries were abandoned, and the conditions of urban life that were integrated as part of Roman civilization decayed. The decline in literacy rates among the population left the administration of the state lacking the material conditions necessary for the maintenance of the central structure of the empire.

Within the vacuum created by the collapse of the Roman state were the conditions for the rise of a new institutional order, directed by a new paradigm of knowledge, and which produced a new centralized system of domination. Many of the clergy were literate. After the creation of official church doctrine by the Nicene Creed, the centralization of church power could be established through the process of disseminating the official teachings of the church. As the church retained a virtual monopoly on the technology of manuscript reproduction it was able to control the discourse on subjectivity, power, behavior, and punishment. As the population was conditioned by the message, the church generated the legitimacy it needed among the community of believers. The centralization of power, administration, and church doctrine, all essentially related, would not have been possible without the control over the means of dissemination: the manuscript.

The power to control discourse is the most effective form of political power. This is the case because it circumscribes the limits of possible actions. In an epistemological order in which the church controls the rules that govern truth production, the validation of truth claims reference the conditions that enhance church power. Truth is measured against the words contained in sacred texts, and *properly* interpreted by church hierarchy. The human task is to apply deductive logic in the application of those truths in the world. To generate new truths is to raise a question about future possibilities and the potentials of human reason. Domination can be maintained within this model only if the subject's ability to reason is viewed as limited, and where the social task is to focus on something other than temporal reality.

Only with the return of secular education, and an interest in the ancient texts banned by the church, could an alternative construction of the subject and his/her powers be conceived. With this development the church begins to lose its direct control over social and political life as alternative models for the validation of truth claims open up new avenues for discourse. Religion begins its decent into the domain of the irrational.

The development of the printing press transforms the book from a sacred object to a commodity. However, this development has an even more profound effect on the possibilities for the construction of subjectivity. With the possibility of reproducing more texts on a mass scale, the subject can be assigned the power of generating new texts. The subject can be the *creator* of words. By increasing the texts available for dissemination, the new technology increases the models of subjectivity in circulation. This transformation effectively ends the church's control over dissemination (a development that the church continued to struggle against for several centuries). Both the reformation and the rise of modernity depended on the book and the press.

Despite the domination brought to the masses by despotic monarchs and the church hierarchy, the Middle Ages developed a doctrine that would be influential for the development of modern political practices and the development of democratic institutions. Even though both the monarchical institutions and the church were hierarchically structured, the church promoted a doctrine that asserted the transcendental equality of all subjects. One was equal before the judgment of a higher power. The modern system of jurisprudence would not be possible without such a belief among the populous.

This notion of transcendent equality also develops into the doctrine of natural law in the modern period. Once reason is introduced into the construction of subjectivity, it is a small step to the position that all have the faculty of reason in equal enough quantity to discern that which constitutes the appropriate ethical conditions for all. When, in the Enlightenment the idea began to emerge that human reason possessed the power to ascend to truth and knowledge, and that this potential was not dictated by either birth or theological position, the institutional structures that depended on these hierarchies began to fade. Only then can the foundational premises for modern democratic practice emerge.

If all are equal in their position before God, it is a small step to claim equality in political birthright. Further, if each is asserted to be relatively equal in general faculties such as the power of reason, then consultation, consent, and planning for collective action take on a new impetus. The idea of a contract among consenting participants requires the idea of equality. Serfs and lord do not have a relationship in which both parties are formally free. Freedom of choice requires a construction of subjectivity in which the power of choice has a rational context. Only beings capable of thinking, planning, and controlling their actions can be afforded such a power. Reason and equality come together to make such a subject the center of a new politics. Such a view of subjectivity begins in the Renaissance and comes to fruition in the modern age.

Notes

1. Virgil, *Aeneid*, 2.363, trans. Robert Fagles (New York: Viking, 2006).
2. Canning, Joseph. *A History of Medieval Political Thought: 300-1450*. (London: Routledge, 1996), 3.
3. The Bible, Matthew 22:21.
4. Thompson, James Westfall, *The Literacy of the Laity in the Middle Ages* (New York: Burt Franklin, 1963), 2.
5. Logan, Robert, *The Alphabet Effect: The Impact of the Phonetic Alphabet on the Development of Western Civilization* (New York: Morrow, 1986), 166.
6. Thompson, 2.
7. Logan, 171.
8. Thompson, 2.
9. Biller, Peter and Anne Hudson, *Heresy and Literacy, 1000-1530* (Cambridge, UK: Cambridge University Press, 1994), 105.
10. Logan 165.
11. Pelikan, Jaroslav, *The Excellent Empire: The Fall of Rome and the Triumph of the Church* (San Francisco: Harper and Row, 1987), 44.
12. Logan, 164.
13. Logan, 164.
14. Troll, Denise, "The Illiterate Mode of Written Communication: The Work of the Medieval Scribe" in *Oral and Written Communications: Historical Approaches*, ed. Richard Leo Enos (Newbury Park, CA: Sage Publications, 1990), 97.
15. Troll, 103.
16. Troll, 116.
17. Swanson, R. N., "Literacy, Heresy, History and Orthodoxy: Perspectives and Permutations for the Later Middle Ages" in *Heresy and Literacy, 1000-1530*, ed. Peter Biller and Anne Hudson (Cambridge, UK: Cambridge University Press, 1994), 281.
18. Jensen, 18.
19. Pelikan, 23.
20. Pelikan, 25.
21. Pelikan, 21.
22. The Bible, Matthew 22:21.
23. Stevenson, William R. Jr., *Christian Love and Just War: Moral Paradox and Political Life in St. Augustine and His Modern Interpreters* (Macon, GA: Mercer University Press, 1987), 13.
24. Stevenson, 19.

25. *The Political Writings of St. Augustine*, ed. Henry Paolucci (Washington, D.C.: Regnery Publishing, Inc., 1962).

26. *The Political Writings of St. Augustine.*

27. *The Political Writings of St. Augustine.*

28. Stevenson, 12–13.

29. Stevenson, 13.

30. Stevenson, 13.

31. *The Political Writings of St. Augustine.*

32. Stevenson, 13.

33. Stevenson, 13.

34. Augustine, *City of God,* XIV, 1, trans. Marcus Dods (New York: Random House, 1950).

35. Augustine, "The City of God," in *Classics in Political Philosophy*, ed. Jene M. Porter (Scarborough, Ontario: Prentice Hall, 1989) 139.

36. Augustine, *City of God.*

37. Logan, 173–174.

38. Aquinas, Saint Thomas, *Summa Theologiae*, Ia, Q. 8, Art. 2 (New York: Benziger Bros., 1947–1948).

39. Canning, 129.

40. Sibley, 233.

41. Canning, 129.

42. Canning, 129–130.

43. Canning, 130.

44. Aquinas, *Summa Theologiae,* II-I, Q. 2, Art. 90.

45. Aquinas, *Summa Theologiae,* II-I, Q. 94, Art. 4.

46. Aquinas, *Summa Theologiae,* II-I, Q. 94, Art. 4.

47. Aquinas, *Summa Theologiae,* II-I, Q. 94, Art. 4.

48. Aquinas, *Summa Theologiae,* II-I, Q. 94, Art. 4.

49. Sibley, 245.

50. Jensen, De Lamar, *Renaissance Europe: Age of Recovery and Reconciliation* (Lexington, KY: D.C. Heath and Company, 1981), 8.

51. Jensen, 10.

52. Carlyle, Alexander J., "The Sources of Medieval Political Theory and Its Connection with Medieval Politics" in *The American Historical Review*, Vol. 19, No. 1, 1913, 3.

53. Carlyle, 27.

54. Carlyle, 67.

55. Sibley, 227.

56. Ward, John O., "Rhetoric, Truth, and Literacy in the Renaissance of the Twelfth Century" in *Oral and Written Communication*, ed. Richard Leo Enos (Newbury Park, CA: Sage Publications, 1990), 133.

57. Ward, *Oral and Written Communication,* 136.

58. Ward, *Oral and Written Communication,* 138.

59. Reeves, Marjorie, "Marsiglio of Padua and Dante Alighieri" in *Trends in Medieval Political Thought*, ed. Beryl Smalley (New York: Barnes and Noble, Inc., 1965), 87–88.

60. Reeves, 88.

61. Reeves, 88.

62. Jensen, 197.

63. Jensen, 197.

64. Marsiglio de Padua, *The Defensor Pacis*, I, ii, trans. A. Gewirth (Toronto: University of Toronto Press, 1956).

65. Jensen, 273 and Thompson, 2.

Chapter 4

The Birth of the Nation-State and the Rise of Humanism

Introduction

At the end of the Middle Ages a variety of social forces were manifesting the conditions for a reconfiguration of the structures of power that had been in place for a thousand years. During the Middle Ages, collective power resided in two parallel institutions, the church and the monarchy. Literacy, a common language, a certain level of administrative competence, and the ability to exert influence over the rival monarchies, had given the church great power over the fragmented political order of medieval Europe. But toward the end of the Middle Ages the conditions for maintaining this form of collective power were beginning to change.

As F.J.C. Hearnshaw characterizes the perception of the individual in society during the Middle Ages:

> The central *social* problem of the period was the emancipation
> of the slave, the elevation of the serf, the edification of the
> freeman, and in general the establishment of conditions which
> would render possible the liberation and the self-realization of
> the individual soul.[1]

This project was tied to the material conditions of the Middle Ages. Educational opportunities for the mass of the population were severely limited. What little was available was tied to instruction in church doctrine and the identity of religious communities and ecclesiastical ideals. Medieval economics were directed toward production for self-sufficiency within the institutional order of landed aristocrats. This produced a political climate in which conflicts were often religious in nature and centered around the control of territories for the spread of competing religious creeds.

With the coming of the Renaissance the material conditions within Europe were transformed, creating the conditions for a new structure of domination: the modern nation-state. Central to the rise of the nation-state were developments that transformed the conceptualization of political possibilities. We will focus on three major changes that fostered a rethinking of the structures of domination and the emergence of the modern form of politics. These are: the invention of the printing press, the rise of the bourgeoisie, and the Peace of Westphalia.

Why these three? Each represents an amalgamation of broader trends that are taking place in society at the beginning of the Renaissance. These changes are interrelated and, collectively, transformed the means of conceptualizing what was possible in political discourse. The printing press was a new technology that allowed for the dissemination of alternative conceptions of life and subjectivity that could compete with the dominance of church doctrine. It is essential for the reopening of the discourse about the nature of physical reality and the importance of civilization as a cumulative process of exploration and discovery. For this reason, the church sought to exert strict control over the dissemination of these alternative texts.

The emergence of the bourgeoisie transformed the patterns of production, altering the conditions of social life. The feudal estate now had to compete with the growing urban centers, altering everything from family structures to the ideological residue of the exchange process. The exchange economy required both the equality of exchange partners and the consideration of rationality in the exchange process. The constructed subject that was a product of political socialization in the Middle Ages was no longer compatible with the new practices.

Finally, the Peace of Westphalia in 1648 transformed the structure of administration and introduced a formal model of territoriality into the political structures. Such a development led to the rise of the nation-state as the new unit of domination. The role of the universal church declined as the notion of sovereignty became embedded solely within the territorial state. The pattern of socialization generated by the territoriality of power led to the rise of modern nationalism and the identification of populations in the West with the newly emerging state structures.

Subjectivity as constructed in the early modern period becomes more compatible with the development of democratic theory and practice. Middle Age Christianity had stressed the doctrine of transcendent *equality* into Western ideology. In the Renaissance the belief in the transformative power of human *reason*, a component of Greek civilization, returns to the Western world. Reason can ascend to know truth. A belief in the universality of reason becomes one of the foundational assumptions of the Enlightenment and parallels the development of the scientific method. These two beliefs are the central ideological pillars upon which the rationale for democratic practice is constructed.

Tied to the rise of an ideology with components of equality and reason is the appearance of individualism. Individualism is the logical complement to a construction of subjectivity that contends that human beings are rational and capable of expressing that reason as equal participants in political and social processes. This eliminated the special status of divine princes or church hierarchy.

With this ideology, knowledge and truth became the domain of the common people, altering the relationship between power and the production of knowledge. Therefore, science, reason, equality, and democracy are intimately connected in the emergence of the Renaissance. As a result, in the Renaissance and the early modern period, democratic practice becomes the measure of legitimacy in the exercise of power.

The emergence of a new structure of power, coupled with the accompanying ideology of legitimation, led to the view that this new structure had a permanence that previous constructions lacked. As reason was used to unlock the secrets of nature, so it could be used to unlock a fixed moral and social order. This early formulation of modernity, therefore, could generate a universal morality, a *natural law*, that constituted an end of history in the ethical sense. Reason could ascend and grasp what is fixed and universal. Universal morality would characterize the measure of reason itself. Such a view still dominates some political discourse, even in the twenty-first century.

Technologies of Dissemination and Subjectivity: The Printing Press

We should note the force, effect, and consequences of inventions which are nowhere more conspicuous than in those three which were unknown to the ancients, namely printing, gun-

*powder, and the compass. For these three have changed the
appearance and state of the whole world.*[2]

The Renaissance brought with it many new technological innovations.
One of the most influential was the advent of moveable printing in the
middle of the fifteenth century. Typography, as devised in the fifteenth
century, was a revolutionary technology. Since the twelfth century printing had been carried out by using hand carved wooden blocks. The printing technology of the fifteenth century was carried out by means of replaceable and reusable letters embedded within printing plates. Each
letter or character was cut into metal individually, allowing for the letters
or characters to be placed next to one another in any sequence on a plate
for printing, using ink pressed against a page of paper. The process that
led to the invention of moveable type printing was not completed by one
individual. There were many contributors, such as Johann Gutenberg in
Germany and Laurens Janszoon Coster in Holland, as well as individuals
who developed printer's ink, quality paper, and the construction of the
printing press.[3] Regardless of who is responsible for moveable-type
printing, such an invention had a far reaching impact on society and
transformed the way in which human beings conceive of themselves and
their own powers of reason.

Before moveable type printing, the time required to reproduce a text
made the cost of mass production in printing impractical. This led to a
condition in which the availability of books was severely limited. Printing was a difficult process, and the dominant social and political position
of the church meant that it held sway over what texts were printed and
circulated among the population. The printing of the Bible and other
Christian religious texts held a priority over the printing of other materials.

Limiting printing almost entirely to the Bible and other religious
texts reinforced the dominance of the church in society. The church
maintained a monopoly over social, political, and moral discourse
through control over the methods and material of dissemination within
the society. To challenge the validity of church claims was, therefore, a
threat to the entire established social order that had been created by the
socialization processes in place.

However, with the advent of the more versatile moveable type came
the reproduction of numerous texts other than the Bible. The Bible then
had challengers to its primacy in society. Instead of the one text purvey-
ing its truth, there were multiple texts with multiple competing truths in a
marketplace of ideas. These competing texts reflected and reinforced the

market competition that was emerging in the nascent capitalist economy of the Renaissance and the individuality that was surfacing as the underpinnings of political practice.

The availability of new texts provided an impetus for two other developments: the rise of literacy rates and the emergence of the scientific method. In order to partake in these new texts, people had to learn reading skills. Interference by the church created an underground market for books, with early book dealers often engaged in nefarious and clandestine activities to get the most sought-after books of the day.

Multiple texts also aided in the growth of modern scientific thought, as it allowed individuals to explore their own ideas, compare them to others', and spread that knowledge to a wider audience.[4] As this was a form of communication for the public, printing was carried out in the vernaculars of many different regions, not only in Latin. As a consequence, literacy rose during this time period.[5] Moveable type allowed for the introduction and proliferation of numerous printed texts. Multiple texts meant that many human beings had the ability to write, express their own individual thoughts, and disseminate those texts widely in society. These texts created a challenge to the textual exclusivity of the Bible and church doctrine as the source of truth in society. The focus shifted from the church and the *city of God* to the individual human being. Renaissance Europe brought a renewed emphasis to the temporal earthly realm that had not been experienced in the West since ancient times. As Jacob Burckhardt stated in his work, *The Civilization of the Renaissance in Italy*:

> In the Middle Ages both sides of human consciousness – that which was turned within as that which was turned without – lay dreaming or half awake beneath a common veil. The veil was woven on faith, illusion and childish prepossession, through which the world and history were seen clad in strange hues. . . . In Italy this veil first melted into air; an *objective* treatment and consideration of the state and of all things of this world became possible. The *subjective* side at the same time asserted itself with corresponding emphasis; man became a spiritual *individual*, and recognized himself as such.[6]

The transformation of the conception of the human subject during the Renaissance meant a rebirth and rediscovery of the "self as subject," as an individual actor in the world.[7]

In this evolving context a new construction of human identity emerged that reflected the transformative possibilities brought about by the changing material conditions. This doctrine was *Humanism*. Humanism resulted from a blend of forces that reflect the unique character of the age in which it was born. Humanism asserts that human individuals, possessing the power of reason, are able to generate knowledge about the world that is meaningful in charting the course of human history. This stress on reason can be found in the ancient texts of Greece and Rome, and were part of the rebirth of classical ideas in the Renaissance.

The Rise of Capitalism and the Autonomous Subject

The economic foundation in the Middle Ages was based on the feudal order, small, self-sufficient agricultural centers that were separate from one another. Late in the Medieval era, in the eleventh and twelfth centuries, renewed contact with the Middle East and Asia due to the Crusades resulted in an increase in trade and commerce. This development led to towns and burgesses emerging as trade centers. Especially in the Mediterranean region, trade between the East and the West became quite lively. Demand for foreign goods increased, giving merchants and traders more incentive to expand commerce, as they were able to produce more profits from their ventures. Also emerging were additional marine centers of trade in the Baltic and North Sea region. Trade centers soon became connected by both water and land routes. The increasing trade and commerce resulted in commercial exchange becoming a more fundamental aspect of European economic life. This would eventually lead to the development of modern industrial capitalism.

Other contributing factors in the growth of towns came from growth of the population and the increases in agricultural production. Agricultural production became more efficient, in part due to refinements in the metal plow. This helped produce a small amount of food surplus. This led to both an increase in the European population and the rise of commerce among the expanding population centers.[8]

Italy led the expansion of trade and commerce due to its geographical advantage. Italian merchants in coastal commercial centers became an integral link in the trade between the East and West. These towns were the center of commercial capitalism, growing in size as the demand for traded goods increased in Europe. The emergence of a new mechanism for generating wealth produced a new class of urban traders in Europe with the power to affect social and political conditions. The class of landed aristocrats found itself in competition with this the new merchant class.

This undermined the traditional hierarchies that were part of the medieval social structure. Medieval social classes consisted essentially of the nobility, the clergy, and the peasants. The merchants did not fit neatly into this class system. The merchants as a "middle" social class were, therefore, alienated from the nobility, the clergy, and the peasantry. The nobles perceived the merchant class as uncultured and spurned them. The clergy distrusted those in the merchant class due to the latter not having to depend on the clergy as a source of legitimization for their wealth, success, and power. Finally, the peasants were resentful of the merchants as they were not members of the nobility, but had risen above the status of peasantry.

The formation and organization of merchant guilds allowed for the implementation of monopolizing control of the commercial and marketing interests and activities within towns. These guilds regulated the conduct that guided business transactions as contractual agreements, a foundational requirement of capitalist economics. Guilds, oftentimes, were the dominating forces in town governance organizations, which allowed their interests to be fulfilled and protected.

Another aid to the merchant class was that, despite the animosity accrued from across the social spectrum, the merchants were able to gather support from many of the European monarchs. As possessors of wealth, the new bourgeoisie could be useful to the ruling princes. The monarchs made alliances with the merchant class as they had much to gain from those that possessed money and resources.[9]

Craft guilds also emerged alongside merchant guilds, which allowed for regulation and supervision of the production process. Specialization in the production of goods among craftsmen appeared with the emergence of towns due to the availability of a supply of raw materials made possible by the increase in trade. An average craft shop had a craftsman as the operator of the shop, with apprentices as assistants who learned from the master. In the shop, raw materials could be either manufactured into semi-finished or fully completed objects.

There were more craft guilds than merchant guilds, as there was a craft guild for each separate step of production in a craft activity. The production quality, price of the produced goods, the quantity and quality of admission in becoming a master craftsman within each specialized trade were all regulated by the governing rules that the craft guilds created. However, these regulations were not inflexible. Instead, the guild system responded promptly to alterations in economic conditions by achieving some sort of consensus. In working to achieve their regulations and guiding rules through consensus among their members, guilds operated in a somewhat self-governing manner. These basic democratic practices in guild organizations allowed some in the emerging middle class of merchants and artisans to be able to define themselves as subjects that had some measure of self-determinism in making guiding decisions in an organized manner. Such a development would be influential in the emergence of democratic political structures.

Guilds of any type had a tendency towards exclusivity and economic production on an individual level. The regulations that guilds adopted were protective measures that encouraged monopolies among those who held guild membership. Protections implemented by guilds were meant to prevent over-saturation within trades. Some tactics included raising the admission fees of guild members, extending apprenticeship periods, and demanding that candidates must have enough capital to found their own business establishment.[10]

A division of labor existed during this time period in the production process and encouraged the specialization of industry. Each craft shop was engaged in one aspect of the production in which they were experts in the field. For example, wool would be spun, then woven by weavers, then would be sent to fullers, and finally finishers would produce the final cloth product.[11] This division of labor was in part a matter of efficiency in small-scale manufacturing, but also reflected the dispersal of power across the guild structure.

The merchant class's position in society was outside of the traditional structures in a medieval political economy. Therefore, they were instrumental in the changing economic and social conditions in the Renaissance. With the coming of this "middle class" came the rise of a burgeoning capitalist economic system. Capitalism emphasizes the individual and their role as individual economic actors within the system. In contrast to the Middle Ages, the rational calculation of individual actors in forming contracts and generating economic structures extended and reinforced the notion that individuals possess the power of reason in ordering their affairs.

A rational model of the subject required a reorientation of the relationship between the political sovereign and the population. Monarchs that had reigned with absolute power were not conducive to the emergence of a private economy focused on the production of private wealth and capital. Capitalism relies on the ability of individuals to be able to associate with one another as freely as possible in the economic market to maximize their individual interests.

Within a capitalist economic market, the ability to protect property and transactions from arbitrary and capricious interference by the government was essential. Market economies require the conditions for orderly calculation. They also require respect for the bond established by the formation of a contract.

In the emerging private exchange economy the use of contracts became integral in societal relations.[12] A contract was considered a binding agreement between parties, and was an essential component in a capitalist economy. Buyers and sellers must have contractual arrangements to be able to conduct business within a market. This is dependent on free exchange between individuals operating in a private sphere of activity.

As the domain of private economic activity expanded it required the development of practices to further the rational efficiencies of the private economy. This necessitated the evolution of the banking system to include: deposit transfers, bills of exchange, insurance, and double-entry bookkeeping. Deposit transfers allowed making a payment for purchases without a direct transfer of money from one agent to another. Once a price in the exchange had been negotiated between buyer and seller the parties would inform a banker who would transfer the funds from one account to another. Bills of exchange were similar to deposit transfers, but parties could exchange money without being in the same location. Exchanges could then be conducted over large areas between agents.[13]

Insurance also developed during this period as a means to protect property investments, money, and goods. Engaging in commerce involved risks. In order to offset these risks, an investor would pay a small premium in order to be protected in the transaction. In this way the exchange process could be enhanced, as the buyer would be protected if something went amiss.[14]

Finally, adopting double-entry bookkeeping permitted those engaged in business transactions to be able to keep a record of their financial situation. Each business transaction within this method is recorded by entries in at least two accounts. To balance these accounts, the debit value total should be equal to the total value of the credit accounts. The method was not utilized widely until the Renaissance, and is evidence that commercial exchange in the capitalist model was burgeoning in the time period.[15]

Banking as an institution served as an intermediary between parties engaged in business arrangements, while concomitantly allowing money to be stored and amassed in central, urban locations. This development was essential for the later rise of the large-scale industrial enterprises of the nineteenth century. Only with the centralization of capital and the creation of a banking system could the industrial form of capitalism emerge.

However, the emergence of modern banking is only a component of an emerging form of collective life. In the Renaissance a repatterning of institutional existence begins that will dominate the modern period. The rise of modern banking is the result of power concentrating in new urban commercial centers. The centralization of production within the guilds, the establishment of guild administrations, the organization of training and rules for guild members all need to be viewed as part of the process of creating rational efficiency. The organization of this new economy requires the creation of formal structures across a wide spectrum of human activity. Rules of conduct, patterns of activity, and structures of association are all manifestations of the centralization of power in the promotion of the rational efficiencies of administration. Taken together, these economic organizations help to create central institutional relationships between the emerging notion of individual presence in the world and the structures of power that govern the patterns of institutional life.

From Economic to Political Contracts

The formal freedom necessary for the production of an exchange contract created a new conception of subjectivity. The exchange contract takes place between formally free, autonomous parties that enter into an agreement for their mutual benefit. Each is able to consider what is in his or her best interest. The social contract emerges as a political corollary.

The assumptions that informed the medieval conceptions of subjectivity are incompatible with the beliefs that inform modern state practices. In the Middle Ages subjects are considered devoid of both the capacities of rational calculation and the legal equality necessary for the development of a private exchange economy. Therefore, as the system of exchange manifests wealth and power, the assumptions regarding the nature of the subject must be transformed in order to accommodate these institutional transformations.

An exchange economy requires the assumptions that the parties entering into the trading process are rational, in that they can make a calculation as to whether or not the exchange will be beneficial. Without such an assumption, the internal logic of the capitalist system fails to align with the practice of exchange. Such a calculation is private in character and reinforces both the rational character of subjectivity and the individualistic ontology of the human being.

Exchange also requires the formal equality of the parties subject to the transaction. Each must be free to enter into the transaction or not, depending on their personal decision. It is, therefore, necessary that the law be adjusted to create the formal equality among all that would potentially engage in the exchange of goods. The maximum efficiency of the exchange economy demands nothing less. Therefore, the rise of the capitalist system of economics requires a reformulation of human identity. Such a transformative understanding of human identity must produce a transformation of the legal and political structures in which power is manifest. The new institutional order is based on the idea of voluntary agreements made among the equal and rational members of the society.

Politically, a social contract was defined as an agreement made between the governed and the sovereign institutions regarding the relations of power between them. Such an agreement can only be entered into by beings that are fully rational, in that they can calculate the conditions of their own advantage. Furthermore, the notion of the social contract was premised on the belief that the individual is the central constituent of society. Only the individual has ontological status, the thinking nature of being that allows for such judgments. The contract is external and artificial, arrived at only as a condition of individual autonomy. Within this framework, the social contract is viewed as a constructed and artificial means of organizing the power relations between the individual and the collective.

Even though individuals agree to the conditions of government's domination over them, force is still seen as necessary in making the social agreements and arrangements compulsory.[16] The exercise of force by the political association is only legitimate if it takes place after such an agreement of free individuals. Such a position is developed by John Locke, and other social contract theorists and will be discussed later.

Without the advent of capitalist economics, and the contract as fundamental institutional arrangements, liberal democratic practice based on the social contract would have not have developed in the way that it did. The idea of a social contract between the ruler and the ruled, especially within the context of private property, created the notion that the government should protect property rights as part of a *natural law*. The rights contained in the liberal construction of natural law protect the evolving conception of subjectivity that places emphasis on the rational, free subject as the center of social life. Therefore, political power operates with some constraints as pertains to a person's private realm of existence and property.[17]

However, two points must be remembered in this discussion. The Renaissance is a phase in the evolution of Western institutions that represents a radical transformation of the institutional order and the notions of subjectivity that are reinforced by those institutions. The Renaissance was only the beginning of the process, which extended into the modern period. The rise of the liberal order in the West was tied to the increases in literacy, the rise of the scientific method, the expansion of urban wealth and the development of a new class structure that required institutional accommodation. The creation of institutions that promoted a concept of the personal and the private were manifestations of this transformation. Modern democracy has its roots in these material changes.

Further, the emergence of liberal democracy in the West should not be seen as diluting the power of central institutions, but as a mechanism to enhance the compelling nature of their prescriptions. Liberal democracy emerges as a legitimating mechanism, compatible with the new structure of subjectivity, for the emerging centralized nation-state. Individuals, expressing some level of choice within the institutional framework, generate an integrating effect on the dispersed communities within the newly formed states. Individual interests, in theory, are harmonized within the democratic institutions, and this allows for the further expansion of the collective and centralized institutions of political power.

The Peace of Westphalia and the Rise of the Nation-State

The nation-state as an institution began to emerge during the Renaissance as well, and was also an expression of the individualism that was being forged in the new social and political context. A state and its political structures were not merely perceived as the mode by which men were organized to traverse through the temporal city of man. The state began to be perceived as a *work of art*, an inspired product of reason itself that produced social conditions in the terrestrial realm.[18]

The Thirty Years War (1618-1648) and the subsequent Peace of Westphalia are considered by many to mark the end of the great wars of religion, where the divisions between areas loyal to Catholicism battled with those splintering off from the Roman Catholic Church in the Protestant Reformation.[19] Ending the Thirty Years War, and the following reconciliation with the Peace of Westphalia, addressed the problem of Germany at the end of the Middle Ages. Germany was a "ragged remnant of the mediaeval Holy Roman Empire, a congeries of principalities, dukedoms, counties, baronies, free cities, and what not . . . ."[20] These various local territorial divisions, in what would eventually become the modern nation-state of Germany, amounted to approximately three hundred and fifty entities that were only loose associations, a "federation of quasi-independent" territories.[21] The many territories in this region were locally bound together by token loyalty to the elected Holy Roman Emperor and also by a vague acknowledgement of some kind of authority that the assembly of the Imperial Diet was perceived to have.[22]

The Thirty Years War in central Europe not only brought mass destruction in the area, but marked the decline of the influence that the Holy Roman Empire had enjoyed for the duration of the Middle Ages. Attempts were begun to fill the vacuum left by the previous power of the Empire and the church. The Peace of Westphalia that resolved the Thirty Years War was a mainly secular attempt to fix territorial borders. It established hereditary sovereigns within the territories and gave them exclusive power over the affairs of the state. This effectively ended the religious power struggles between the states over religious matters, as Calvinism was recognized as an acceptable choice of religion within the territories of the Holy Roman Empire. German rules could now decide their territory's religious preference as well as their foreign relations policies.[23]

A change was taking place during the Renaissance that bestowed increasing importance to the governing procedures in the terrestrial world of human beings. The newly formed nation-state structure focused power within institutions that were internal to the state, with exclusive claims to sovereignty. States were viewed as autonomous entities, able to control both their internal practices and their external relations.

This further loosened the hold of the church over the actions of human beings and reinforced the idea that human reason can order the affairs of people and create the institutions that serve their material interests. Human beings can administer their environment by creating the conditions that promote their security and well-being while also providing just outcomes for the inevitable conflicts that arise through human association. This is carried out by the externalization and application of formal reason in the creation of institutional structures. When coupled with the increasing literacy among the populations, the conditions for the expansion of the state, the centralization of institutional existence, and the collectivization of power find a new impetus.

Administration in the Early Modern State

With the drastic alterations in the economic system and other material conditions departing from those of the Middle Ages came changes in administrative organizations during the Renaissance. The dominance of the church in secular matters gave way to its retreat under the nation-state system. The Protestant Reformation led to religious division within the Western world. States and territories that did split with the Church were then faced with the task of filling the administrative gap left by the church. Another undertaking of European states that effected administration during this time period was overseas exploration and expansion.[24]

The structure of government administration at the beginning of the Renaissance was fundamentally the same "personal administration" style that had existed in the Middle Ages. Personal administration was based upon a relationship between a minister and a king. As the Renaissance evolved, there was an increasing emphasis on the minister's responsibilities and influence. The complexities of urban trade, transportation, sanitation, and communications required the expansion of government's administrative role. To manage this situation, state administrative structures instated permanent administrative institutions that employed bureaucrats with specialized skill sets. The king, if the state was to have a functioning bureaucracy, would fill these posts with men that were efficient and · competent. In doing so, the state was able to maintain continuous attention on any and all matters of the state without the king having to be distracted by the daily workings of the state administrative apparatus.[25]

Rulers in Europe during this period also gave more administrative capacity to the already established advisory councils. England and France represent two examples of this trend. However, due to the extensive overseas holdings of Spain the authority and activity of the advisory councils was expanded to an even greater degree.[26] The amount of power the ruler allocated to their chief ministers and advisory councils differed from ruler to ruler. Some rulers depended on these positions greatly, while others did not. King Henry VIII was predisposed to allowing his minister to do most of the administration activities of the English state. Others, such as Philip II of Spain, oversaw and personally contributed in almost every administrative duty, despite the expansive nature of his realm with its overseas conquests.[27]

The need for expanded administrative competence generated the rise of a rational bureaucratic model of administration. It was simply not possible to administer the vast territories of the nation-state and the complexities of internal and external relations without a class of trained administrators. This centralization of political power had one of its earliest proponents in Thomas Cromwell. In England, Cromwell recognized the need of the state to have an administrative structure that included subordinate bureaucratic offices that would function properly and efficiently operate despite who held the presiding offices. This moved away from the personal model of rule that characterized the Middle Ages and early Renaissance.

Cromwell established a structure in which professional, impartial bureaucratic experts would give stability to the operation of the state. While there were still elements of the feudal system in Cromwell's administrative apparatus, it moved in the direction of a centralized and rationally organized bureaucratic structure. Salaried offices in state bureaucracies would fully develop later.[28]

The advent of the printing press aided and altered the nature of administration significantly. Printing extended the administrative capacity of the state[29] as records could be organized, filed, and disseminated more easily. Therefore, more information was available for the administration of the territory, such as budgets, imports, exports, and population movements. This allowed for a more extensive and thorough bureaucratic structure in the modern era, especially through the establishment of written recorded law. Written laws allowed for the creation of a uniform code of laws, regulated by a central authority, that had not existed in the Middle Ages.

The rationalization of the bureaucracy and the greater reach of written law allowed for the extension and centralization of state power. Power was taken away from smaller regional authorities and placed more into the hands of a central governing authority. The impact on the European states was an expansion of administration, a central governing bureaucracy, and an increasing reliance on the gathering and use of statistics in the administration of national territory. This eventually led state governments to begin to conduct censuses, with the United States being the first Western state to do so in 1790.[30]

This expansion of centralized power by the states also manifested an ideological rationale for the expansion of governmental power into the economic sphere. This ideology was known as mercantilism. Mercantilism is a mainly economic concept that defines a relationship between the political and the economic spheres of activity. It is an economic model that is "symptomatic of the growing state system."[31] From the perspective of mercantilism, wealth is the foundation of centralized state power. To achieve wealth state action must be organized in a manner that promotes a surplus of imports over exports.[32] This involved obtaining colonial possessions in order to exploit the raw materials that could be extracted and imported to the mother country. For example, the colonies of Spain in Latin America provided Spain with an astonishing amount of gold and silver. Such a system could emerge only after the successful centralization of power and administration had taken place within a territory. The coordination of economic, administrative, and military activities required the rational organization of state power and the collective exercise of that power.

The centralization of state power was both the cause and effect of mercantilist practices. Mercantilist practices required the integration of various state activities into a coordinated movement of human beings and material resources. In turn, these activities expanded the rationale for the further collectivization of power and coordinate state ventures. In theory, this model of economics is replaced by the liberal model by the nineteenth century. However, in practice the appropriation of territories by the Western power continued to expand well into the nineteenth century with the goal of expanding their economic and political power. Thus, the mercantilist model has lurked in the shadows of the nation-state systems since its inception.

The New Subject and the Ideology of the State

Humanism and Political Power: Machiavelli

In its broadest meaning, *Humanism*, as it emerged in the Renaissance, meant an emphasis on studies that focused on the classical texts (*studia humanitatis*) rather than on the sacred studies of the Roman Catholic Church (*studia divinitatis*). *Studia humanitatis* centered more on the temporal world and the interactions between human beings.[33] Humanism is, therefore, the study of human beings attempting to understand themselves and their place in society.[34] More specifically, Humanism regards the individual human being as the starting point and the focus of this understanding. Emerging out of the material transformation coming at the end of the Middle Ages, Humanism constitutes a major break from the focus on ecclesiastical communities and the purity of religious texts.

The thought of Niccolo di Bernardo Machiavelli (1469-1527), while not fully consistent among his various works, is revealing of the philosophical shift from the Middle Ages to the Renaissance.[35] For instance, Machiavelli maintains in both *The Prince* and the *Discourses* that order in human society can be produced by the utilization of human reason and wills.[36] Machiavelli embarks on an explanation of society and politics based on an assumption of human nature, that human beings are mostly self-interested, callous, and individualistic. In beginning with this particular assumption of human nature, Machiavelli's question is: Considering the essence of human nature, how can societies espouse and politically act out moral values that conflict with this definition of the human subject?

Machiavelli states in *The Prince* that in his analysis "I depart radically from the procedures of others" as his purpose is to "write something useful for anyone who understands it . . . [by] . . . search[ing] after the effectual truth of the matter rather than its imagined one."[37] A problem that Machiavelli perceived in other philosophers is their having:

> . . . imagined for themselves republics and principalities that have never been seen nor known to exist in reality; for there is such a gap between how one lives and how one ought to live that anyone who abandons what is done for what ought to be done learns his ruin rather than his preservation."[38]

To illustrate and prove his conclusions, Machiavelli heavily employs the use of historical examples; social and political *realities* are used as examples of triumphs and failings of past political organizations and rulers.[39]

The methods utilized by Machiavelli are not to be mistaken for being based on scientific methods and principles. However, his methodologies are based on observing and analyzing social and political phenomena, and drawing conclusions from what he identified as the realities of the social realm. Thus, Machiavelli undertook what could be generally described as a "scientific" undertaking, using the empirical examples from history to draw out an inductively formulated proposition. Regardless of the extent to which Machiavelli is perceived to be "scientific" in his methods, his approach sought to bring reason and observation to bear on the social and political questions of his day.

The objective in Machiavelli's work is not to simply be descriptive, but to apply the lessons learned from the realities of history to provide a better understanding of human essence. Once that essence is identified, the organization of human endeavors can be rationally organized based on those principles. This approach has profound consequences for politics.

Machiavelli concluded from his observations that human beings are self-interested. As such, they will always strive to act in a fashion that will achieve their goals. For Machiavelli, the *ends* of political action is the acquisition and maintenance of power, both of which require the stability of the political organization and the preservation of social order. To attain these ends, a ruler must possess and exercise qualities that will accomplish the stability of the state, and ultimately of their rule.[40] In this regard, the actions of political leaders are determined by pragmatic necessity.

Machiavelli asserted that to achieve their ends, political rulers may have to engage in immoral behaviors.[41] By extension, individual, personal, and conventional morality that is generated by society to guide moral conduct cannot be applied to political life. Politics and political goals can oftentimes be incompatible with conventional morality.[42] If, in reality, human beings are selfish and corrupt, then political rulers cannot be virtuous either. The Prince must behave according to reality and not strive to uphold and follow a transcendent morality that is disconnected from the world as it actually is. For example, when discussing if rulers can break promises, Machiavelli concludes that "because [men] are bad and do not keep their promises to you, you likewise do not have to keep yours to them."[43]

The perspective of politics that Machiavelli portrays represents a transformation in how human beings in Western society understood themselves and their position in society. Instead of concentrating on the afterlife and the City of God, Machiavelli deliberately analyzes human affairs and concentrates on the temporal world. Furthermore, he does so by drawing a conclusion concerning human nature based upon his observations. The center of his philosophy is the human subject, not a *truth* that has its source in an abstract text.

But Machiavelli was more than a figure in the formulation of Western Humanism. He also was one of the figures that began a discourse on the centralization of political power in state affairs. Machiavelli justifies the concentration of power and its legitimation through the acts of rulers. The consolidation of state power is not questioned, but asserted as a given among the endeavors of human beings.

Rational Self-Interest: Thomas Hobbes

If Machiavelli represented the shift in society from the Middle Ages to the Renaissance, than the philosophy of Thomas Hobbes (1588-1679) corresponds to the beginnings of an approach that is more associated with the emergence of the modern tradition. Hobbes is more rational and scientific in his approach, claiming that one is able to arrive at valid knowledge, a "science of politics independent of rhetorical arts."[44] Science is a method, "a way of searching out the truth"[45] through some type of empirically observed evidence that derives from sensory perceptions of the material world.[46] However, the conclusions drawn from taking a scientific approach "can always be followed with greater or lesser intelligence."[47] Therefore, human reasoning can be right or wrong in its conclusions. The importance of following a scientific methodology is that human beings are more likely to come to a "true" knowledge and a comprehension of the items of inquiry.[48]

In the West, scientific analysis is perceived as being composed of observing and collecting empirical data and inferring explanations of phenomena. To Hobbes, scientific analysis also had the goal of being practical. Human beings were to utilize their reasoning capacity to engage in scientific inquiry that would ultimately lead to the discovery of "truths" that had the ability to make human society "more comfortable." In referring to the gains brought by examining various forms of mathematics and sciences, such as geometry and physics, Hobbes states "How much good is acquired by men from these is more easily understood than said."[49]

Hobbes' philosophy embodied the belief in human reasoning ability that began to emerge in the Renaissance, a belief which had been denied in the Middle Ages. "True reason, is no less a part of human nature than any other faculty or affection."[50] Reason drives and guides human beings towards "follow[ing] particular arguments."[51] In Hobbes' *The Elements*, he states that "reason teacheth us" in regards to questions of the world, including those that involve the nature and significance of the government and of the state.[52]

Hobbes, in his theoretical framework, attempted to create a coherent theory of politics that is based upon premises that are dependable and scientific in nature.[53] From the use and practice of a scientific methodology, combined with a faith in human reasoning capacity, Hobbes concluded that if an examiner observes empirical phenomena and follows "necessary and demonstrable rules," it is possible to produce reliable conclusions. Therefore, it is possible to uncover the conditions that lead to peaceful and harmonious government.[54]

In addition to arguing that human nature possesses rational components, Hobbes also stressed human equality. Hobbes' doctrine of equality has its foundation in nature. He asserted that the "Reason of man is no less of the nature of man than passions, and is the same in all men."[55] "Nature hath made men so equal, in the faculties of the body, and mind. ."[56]

As we have argued, rationality and equality are central pillars in the development of democratic ideology and practice. But Hobbes does not always appear as a democrat, as he saw the world and its inhabitants engaged in a relentless power struggle. In the state of nature, human beings live amongst insecurity where they are exposed to and are defenseless against the unpredictable nature of fate. The state of nature is perpetually in chaos where human beings are forever in a fight for survival and power.[57]

However, it is from our ability to reason that we seek a covenant that will promote our continued existence. To better survive, human beings, who by nature are equally rational actors, strike covenants, or contracts, amongst themselves in a society. These contracts provide for a more ordered existence where survival is more certain. Therefore, Hobbes regarded "That men performe their Covenants made: without which, Covenants are in vain, and but Empty words; and the Right of all men to all things remaining, wee are still in the condition of Warre."[58]

Men keep covenants for two reasons. They fear what will happen if the covenant breaks down, and they fear the coercive power of the government that reason has ordered established. As Hobbes states:

> But because Covenants of mutuall trust, where there is a feare of not performance on either part . . . are invalid . . . Therefore before the names of Just, and Unjust can have place, there must be some coercive Power, to compel men equally to the performance of their Covenants, by the terrour of some punishment, greater than the benefit they expect by the breach of their Covenant; and to make good that Propriety, which by mutuall Contract men acquire, in recompence of the universall Right they abandon: and such power there is none before the erection of a Common-wealth.[59]

Therefore, Hobbes constructed a governance system based upon the assumption of human nature being driven by a rational fear of chaos, uncertainty, and death. In order to prevent this, a social contract is struck among human beings and government is formed. The government is bound to provide order and security for the populace, while the people agree to abide by the government's laws or be subject to the government's use of coercive force. In *De Cive,* Hobbes asserts:

> That Man is a Creature born fit for Society . . . and on this foundation they so build up the Doctrine of Civill Society, as if for the preservation of Peace, and the Government of Man-Kind there were nothing else necessary, then that Men should agree to make certaine Covenants and Conditions together, which themselves should then call Lawes.[60]

For Hobbes, governmental authority is so essential to the survival of the species that all other powers and activities within the state are to be subject to its powers. Religion is to be regulated to protect the integration of the population under common rituals and moral rules. Property is also to be regulated, as it has no existence outside of the conditions that make its protection possible. In the absence of the state, there are no property rights. All property associations are ultimately decided on by the sovereign state.[61] It is acceptable and expected that the state interferes in the realm of private property in society as "private property is in fact the creation of the state."[62]

In seeking to survive, human beings will seek to acquire goods. However, the condition of the world is scarcity. Many human beings will want or need the same material goods. The result can bring people into conflict. Hence, out of this dynamic is the propensity among human beings "to prepare for war, and to make war if necessary, rather than to seek peace."[63]

Hobbes does not see his characterization of human nature as a product of the historical contingencies of his time, so the content is fixed and stagnant. Nevertheless, he produced a powerful case for the expansion and centralization of power. This results from a simple logic. The more people and territory brought under the rule of a sovereign power the more people are engaged in the rational covenant that provides peace. The fewer neighbors there are that are not under a common rule, the less likely the competitive war of all against all will break out. Therefore, Hobbes extends the logic of centralized administration and collective power.

The structure of legitimation has moved away from the doctrine of the universal church, and now rests in the logic of the expanding power of secular authority. Hobbes' theory is grounded in a construction of the human subject that assumes an equal distribution of human reasoning. This allows for the formation of social contracts between a government and a populace based on a faith in "human choice and will" rather than based upon a belief in "divine reason."[64]

The assumptions made by Hobbes regarding human reason, equality, and a society of laws under a central power provide an early formulation of the ideological underpinning of modern democratic practice. In Hobbes' framework, only in civil society can a governing authority make decisions and laws that restrict the actions of human beings. No laws can be made until human beings decide "upon the Person that shall make it."[65] Therefore, the state and its governing laws do not exist until human beings can agree on what or who constitutes it. The assemblage of society to concur "upon the Person" implies a degree of reason that is a principle of democratic practice.

Hobbes' opinion of democracy is none too favorable. In comparison to aristocracy and monarchy, democracy is the most unstable to Hobbes. Democratic regimes are at a higher risk of disintegrating due to the various interests struggling against each other. In addition, Hobbes believed that democracy was not very different from aristocracy or monarchy in the final analysis, as democracy would inevitably and inescapably become ruled by the few as a result of the power-seeking nature of human beings.[66]

Despite these objections to democracy, Hobbes helped in the processes of instituting democratic practice in the Western world and while formulating a logic that expressed the rationality of centralized institutions of collective power. Governments are abstract constructions of rules and procedures generated and expanded out of necessity. The legitimacy of these organizations is secured by reason itself.

The Modern Roots of Collective Power: John Locke

The philosophy of John Locke (1632-1704), in contrast to Hobbes, is an explicit defense of democratic practice. This position is developed out of the assumptions Locke made regarding knowledge, human nature, property, and the natural order of society. These assumptions capture both the spirit of the age in which Locke wrote, but also the scope of collective structures within the nation state.

Locke's epistemology is essential to the understanding of the emergent political philosophy for two interconnected reasons. Locke's assertion that all knowledge begins with sensation connects his political propositions to empirical reality, history, and societal practices. Human beings possess reason and are able to evaluate the world through the senses as they are "the proper and sole Judges of these things."[67]

However, such an epistemological position leads to conclusions that reinforce the logic of democratic practice. If the world is a place in which universal knowledge is not given to human beings, or it does not descend from heaven, then much of the human quest derives from the process of seeking answers to questions through the construction of means and methods to that end. The logic of democracy emerges as a political mechanism to answer the question of how collective action should be directed in the absence of transcendent knowledge.[68] While Locke's notion of natural law still retains a transcendent character, his majoritarian political prescription does not require it for the purposes of legitimacy. Democratic procedures produce an answer that is politically legitimate, even if it lacks the mantle of a universal principle.

Locke's empirical assumptions also inform his view of subjectivity. Empirical observations produce assumptions concerning what constitutes the "nature" of the human subject. This definition of the subject is used by Locke as the foundational premise for his political prescriptions. In other words, Locke uses "external experience" in drawing a universal conclusion about what defines a human being.[69] Locke concludes from these observations that human beings possess the faculty of reason.

Human beings in the absence of a formal political structure are seen as residing in a "state of nature," which is "a state of perfect freedom to order their actions, and dispose of their possessions and persons, as they see fit, within the bounds of the law of nature, without asking leave, or depending upon the will of any other man."[70] The state of nature implies that human beings are inherently equal, with no one having more rights than another. In addition, human beings are all born with the "same advantages of nature," which include an essentially equal ability to use their senses and their reasoning capabilities.[71]

This reasoning ability allows human beings to ascend to moral knowledge. One such *natural law* asserts that human beings have an intrinsic right to life, liberty, and property. Each possesses these rights, as they are born with equal worth as reasoning creatures. These three rights are inherent and associated with one another. Each human being "has a 'property' in his own 'person'" that "nobody has any right to but himself."[72] In addition, material properties, such as commodities, are made into private property through the act of individual labor. The labor carried out by the body converts the raw material of the physical world into private property.[73]

In Locke's state of nature, human beings are inherently "free, equal, and independent."[74] However, reason allows individuals to discover their safety and convenience is enhanced by political association. Human beings "join and unite into a community for their comfortable, safe, and peaceable living, one amongst another, in a secure enjoyment of their properties, and a greater security against any that are not of it."[75] Reason allows for these equal individuals to create an artificial construction, the constitution of the state, to achieve those objectives.

Due to the fact that this agreement is entered into by free and equal participants, legitimacy of the institutional order must come from the consent of the participants. The community that is under the auspices of the government is considered "one body politic" and is to make decisions in society where "the majority have a right to act and conclude the rest."[76] The "will and determination of the majority" is manifested in the consent to be governed. It must direct how the majority are governed. It must also provide guidance through the political process to the laws under which the majority is governed. Should the government seek to end the influence of the majority, the people have a right to withdraw their support from the government they have created. Therefore, for Locke democratic political practice is the key to generating institutional legitimacy. In theory, the will of the masses generates the legitimate authority of collective power.[77]

Therefore, Locke's contribution to democratic theory does not reside with his notion of natural law, but in the view that the constitution is an abstract and artificial product of human reason, the legitimacy of which is embedded in its majoritarian procedures for directing the collective power of the public. Through this mechanism the activities of states can manifest the support necessary for the consolidation and expansion of the central power. Such a practice makes the socialization of the masses a necessary condition for the expansion of state power. Only through the integration of society's members into a mission, with a sense of identity and purpose, will the disciplinary actions of the state be accepted.

The Power of Collective Reason: Jean-Jacques Rousseau

While representing the social contract tradition, Jean-Jacques Rousseau departed from the individualistic philosophies of Hobbes and Locke. The origins of human reasoning derive from different sources according to Rousseau. While human beings have some reasoning capacity, the "methods of rationality" are insufficient for the "truly 'human' understanding of the nature of the human sciences."[78]

Therefore, Rousseau concluded that to understand the human subject, human beings must first be understood in their "original nature." Only then is it possible to understand the potentials of their "present nature." Advances in human societies remove human beings increasingly from the primitive condition in which their true nature can be observed.

> . . . [T]he more we accumulate new knowledge, the more we deprive ourselves of the means of acquiring the most important of all; and it is, in a manner, by the mere dint of studying man that we have lost the power of knowing him.[79]

Rousseau asserted that human beings existed as non-rational actors before the emergence of rational society in the course of human history.[80] Science and the scientific method cannot "teach us merely to consider men such as they have made themselves" in regards to human nature.[81] "Natural men" and "later men" are different from one another because "later men" were men "as they have made themselves," not how nature created them. The human being is something that is constructed by the social system. The "later man," the "modern" human being, resulted from the corruption of "natural man."[82] As human beings amass new knowledge and remove themselves further from their original, "natural" state, the less they have the ability to truly know themselves.

This social determinism constitutes a boundary for both human knowledge and human freedom. Hence Rousseau's meaning when he states that "Man was born free, and everywhere he is in chains."[83] The individual is transformed out of the original state and placed in a complex of social relations in which the individual is constructed by the necessities of the institutional order. Therefore, in society there can be no fixed definition of the human subject as human beings living in society have undergone a drastic alteration from their "pre-rational and pre-social beginnings."[84]

It is important to Rousseau to discover what composes the human being in their "original nature" in order to determine what human beings and societies are capable of.[85] What we call *reason* is a learned reflection of society, so it is possible for human beings to "grow toward[s] other ways of reasoning, of being moral, of being social."[86] Human societies are mutable and subject to change throughout history. There are no universal "laws," only the dictates of "necessity" and what human beings perceive as "useful" to them in a specific context at a certain time. Human beings are slaves to "the bonds of necessity."[87] While science can come to recognize the eternal laws of nature, science *cannot* instruct human beings as to how they should organize the political realm. In contrast to the absolute, immutable laws of nature, the laws of human beings are alterable and usually made by the "rule of self-interest."

After forming social and political structures, human beings are destined to inhabit a "less natural" world.[88] But, "[l]iberty is not to be found in any form of government. . . ."[89] Human beings are born free and independent in their natural state, and as such, there is not any "natural authority" that subjugates them.[90] Due to this there is a tendency toward rebellion against capricious authority and government in order to reclaim the lost "natural liberty."

But Rousseau did not leave the matter there. He asserted that there is a need to organize a political association in order to provide well-being and security for the population. The question is, what is the means of organizing this structure that will be the most *just*. Therefore, even though government will inevitably bring a reduction of their natural freedom, it is still necessary to construct one. The question is how to make a government that is legitimate in holding authority over human societies?[91]

Rousseau's answer to this question is a form of social contract, a government "founded on covenants."[92] Human beings must voluntarily agree to construct a social association, as it is not part of the natural order. A social organization that is based on the consent and the decisions of the populace is also predicated on each person's desire to preserve themselves, as an extension of their self-interests.[93]

Steering decisions of a government are then not to be willed by an individual or one individual interest, but by the collective body politic. The legitimacy of the government and its decisions are derived from the masses, who are considered the "sovereign body." In this context, the law cannot be absolute, but is subject to change as the sentiments of the culture change. The populous must consent to laws, and can alter the laws or even the social contract itself.[94] The "general will" must guide the society. If not, the outcome is civil war.

What is striking about the presentation made by Rousseau is that even while he asserts the existence of an original human character, his political formulation is not one that could be expected to take the human being back to that condition. Instead, Rousseau created a dynamic for moving away from the original condition of the human character, while producing a structure by which that movement was legitimated. Society adjusts to the necessities of existence, reformulating laws as a way of moving forward. The "original nature" of the human being is lost in the past.

The movement forward is a movement toward greater structural integration and expansion. Democracy is a vehicle for that movement. Therefore, while Rousseau's notion of the "general will" reflects an understanding of democratic practice that is less individualistic than that of Locke, it does develop an equally powerful rationale for the consolidation of power through a democratic form of legitimation.

Conclusion: Capitalism, Contracts, and National Power

In the early modern period a confluence of forces brought about the material circumstances for the consolidation of power in the Western world. These forces comprised an integrated set of mutually reinforcing conditions that generated a variety of social and political transformations, from urbanization to the total reconstitution of political structures. All of these forces led in the direction of greater concentrations of wealth, power, and people in the process of Western development.

Increasing trade stimulated urbanization, centralized banking, and the need for centralized administration of concentrated populations. Private production meant the rise of individualistic ideologies, but within an emerging unit of national association. The printing press helped break down the church-constructed notion of subjectivity replacing them with a rationally oriented notion of human nature. This rational model of the human being required the construction of political institutions that were in harmony with a society constituted of equal and rational citizens of the state. The idea of the contract between participants becomes the dominant framework for social exchange. National sovereignty emerges as the underlying presupposition of collective power. Democracy emerges as its vehicle.

These social changes reinforced the linear formulation of history that was a product of the religious doctrine found in the Middle Ages. Transformation is associated with forward progress, thus embedding an uncritical ethos to the processes of Western development. Science was seen as the means to solve the technical problems of concentrated unions, and the externalization of reason within the institution structures were argued to be a reflection of human reason back on itself in the processes of history. The *state of nature* must be left behind, rejected rather than incorporated into the present, as the primitive must be rejected in favor of the *humanizing* elements of collective power and rational discipline.[95] The evolution of the law is defined by its expansion. The path towards the concentration of power is set as the path of civilization itself.

In this period of Western history, democratic practice assists in the consolidation of national power. It legitimates both the expansion of governmental activity from the center, and the extension of that power to the limits of the territorial unit. It is the political force that legitimates the collectivization of power in the modern age.

Notes

1. Hearnshaw, F.J.C., "Introductory: The Social and Political Problems of the Sixteenth and Seventeenth Centuries," in *The Social and Political Ideas of Some Great Thinkers of the Sixteenth and Seventeenth Centuries: A Series of Lectures Delivered at King's College University of London During the Session 1925-26*, ed. F.J.C. Hearnshaw (Port Washington, WA: Kennikat Press, Inc., 1967), 9.

2. Eisenstein, Elizabeth, "The Emergence of Print Culture in the West: 'Defining the Initial Shift,'" in *The Renaissance in Europe: A Reader*, ed. Keith Whitlock (New Haven, CT: Yale University Press, 2000), 55.

3. Jensen, 183.

4. Eisenstein, 71.

5. Eisenstein, 68.

6. Martin, John, "Inventing Sincerity, Refashioning Prudence: The Discovery of the Individual in Renaissance Europe," in *American Historical Review*, 102 (5) December 1997, 1309.

7. Martin, 1326.

8. Jensen, 12.

9. Jensen, 12.

10. Lucki, Emil, *History of the Renaissance: Book I Economy and Society* (Salt Lake City: University of Utah Press, 1963), 63-64.

11. Miskimin, Harry A., *The Economy of Early Renaissance Europe, 1300-1460* (Cambridge, UK: Cambridge University Press, 1975), 82.

12. Miskimin, 15.

13. Lucki, 49.

14. Lucki, 51.

15. Lucki, 52-53.

16. Sibley, 293.

17. Miskimin, 80.

18. Martin, 1311.

19. Pagden, Anthony, "Prologue: Europe and the World Around," in *Early Modern Europe: An Oxford History*, ed. Euan Cameron (Oxford, UK: Oxford University Press, 1999), 24, and Hearnshaw, 19.

20. Hearnshaw, 19.

21. Pagden, 24.

22. Hearnshaw, 19.

23. Black, Jeremy, "Warfare, Crisis, and Absolution," in *Early Modern Europe: An Oxford History*, ed. Euan Cameron (Oxford: Oxford University Press, 1999), 215-217.

24. Gladden, E.N., *A History of Public Administration*, Vol. II (London: Frank Cass, 1972), 85.

25. Gladden, 85.

26. Gladden, 85.

27. Gladden, 86.

28. Gladden, 86.

29. Gladden, 86.

30. Gladden, 141.

31. Gladden, 141–142.

32. Gladden, 142.

33. Coates, Wilson H., Hayden V. White, and J. Salwyn Schapiro, *The Emergence of Liberal Humanism: An Intellectual History of Western Europe,* Vol. I (New York: McGraw-Hill Book Co., 1966), 4.

34. Coates, 7.

35. Savigear, Peter, "Niccolo Machiavelli: *The Prince* and the *Discourses*," in *The Political Classics: A Guide to the Essential Texts from Plato to Rousseau,*" ed. Murray Forsyth and Maurice Keens-Soper (Oxford, UK: Oxford University Press, 1992), 97.

36. Coates, 28.

37. Machiavelli, *The Prince*, Ch. XV, trans. and ed. Thomas G. Bergin (New York: Appleton-Century-Crofts, 1947).

38. Machiavelli, *The Prince*, Ch. XV.

39. See Machiavelli, the *Discourses* and the *Prince*.

40. Machiavelli, *The Prince*, Ch. XV.

41. Machiavelli, *The Prince*, Ch. XVI-XVIII.

42. Machiavelli, *The Prince,* Ch. XVIII.

43. Machiavelli, *The Prince,* Ch. XVIII.

44. Skinner, Quentin, *Reason and Rhetoric in the Philosophy of Hobbes* (Cambridge, UK: Cambridge University Press, 1996), 294.

45. Skinner, 294.

46. Skinner, 295.

47. Skinner, 294.

48. Skinner, 294.

49. Martinich, A.P., *Thomas Hobbes* (New York: St. Martin's Press, 1997), 110.

50. Bobbio, Norberto, *Thomas Hobbes and the Natural Law Tradition,* trans. Daniela Gobetti (Chicago: The University of Chicago Press, 1993), 44.

51. Skinner, 300.

52. Skinner, 300.

53. Skinner, 299.

54. Skinner, 301.

55. Bobbio, 44.

56. Hobbes, Thomas, *Leviathan, or The Matter, Forme, and Power of a Common-wealth Ecclesiasticall and Civill,* Ch. XIII (New York: W.W. Norton and Company, Inc., 1997), 68.

57. Herbert, Gary B., *Thomas Hobbes: The Unity of Scientific and Moral Wisdom* (Vancouver: University of Columbia Press, 1989), 129.

58. Hobbes, *Leviathan,* Ch. XV, 79.

59. Hobbes, *Leviathan,* Ch. XV, 79-80.

60. Hobbes, Thomas, *De Cive, The English Version, Entitled in the First Edition Philosophicall Rudiments Concerning Government and Society,* Ch. I (Oxford, UK: Clarendon Press, 1983), 42.

61. Lopata, Benjamin, "Property Theory in Hobbes," *Political Theory,* Vol. 1, No. 2, (May 1973), 204.

62. Lopata, 207.

63. Bobbio, 39.

64. Saxonhouse, Arlene W., "Hobbes and the Beginnings of Modern Political Thought," in *Three Discourses: A Critical Modern Edition of Newly Identified Work of the Young Hobbes,* ed. Noel B. Reynolds and Arlene W. Saxonhouse (Chicago: The University of Chicago Press, 1995), 124.

65. Green, Arnold W., *Hobbes and Human Nature* (New Brunswick, NJ: Transaction Publishers, 1993), 81.

66. Green, 81.

67. Ayers, M.R., "The Foundations of Knowledge and the Logic of Substance: The Structure of Locke's General Philosophy," in *Locke's Philosophy: Content and Context,* ed. G.A.J. Rogers (Oxford: Clarendon Press, 1994), 49.

68. Koch, *Knowledge and Social Construction* (Lanham, MD: Lexington Books, 2005), 130.

69. Koch, Andrew M., *Knowledge and Social Construction,* 11-12.

70. Locke, John, *Concerning Civil Government, Second Essay,* Chapter II, in *Great Books of the Western World,* Vol. 35, ed. Robert Maynard Hutchins (Chicago: Encyclopaedia Britannica, Inc., 1952), 25.

71. Locke, *Concerning Civil Government, Second Essay,* 25.

72. Locke, *Concerning Civil Government, Second Essay,* Ch. V, 30.

73. Locke, *Concerning Civil Government, Second Essay,* Ch. V, 30.

74. Locke, John, "Natural Rights and Government by Consent," in *Political Philosophy,* ed. Alan Gewirth (New York: The Macmillan Company, 1965), 51.

75. Locke, "Natural Rights and Government by Consent," 51.

76. Locke, "Natural Rights and Government by Consent," 51.

77. Locke, *Concerning Civil Government, Second Essay,* 55-59.

78. Chambliss, J.J., *Imagination and Reason in Plato, Aristotle, Vico, Rousseau, and Keats: An Essay on the Philosophy of Experience,* (The Hague: Matinus Nijhoff, 1974), 46.

79. Rousseau, Jean-Jacques, *The Social Discourse on the Origin and Foundation of Inequality Among Mankind,* ed. Lester G. Crocker (New York: Washington Square Press, 1967), 167–168.

80. Chambliss, 47.

81. Rousseau, *The Social Discourse,* 171.

82. Chambliss, 48.

83. Chambliss, 48.

84. Velkley, Richard L., *Being After Rousseau: Philosophy and Culture in Question* (Chicago: The University of Chicago Press, 2002), 31.

85. Chambliss, 47.

86. Chambliss, 51.

87. Rousseau, Jean-Jacques, *Emile*, trans. Barbara Foxley (London: J.M. Dent and Sons, 1911), 130, 436.

88. Chambliss, 55, 56.

89. Rousseau, *Emile*, 437.

90. Keens-Soper, Maurice, "Rousseau: The Social Contract," in *The Political Classics*, ed. Murray Forsyth and Maurice Keens-Soper (Oxford, UK: Oxford University Press, 1992), 174.

91. Keens-Soper, 174.

92. Keens-Soper, 175.

93. Jennings, Jeremy, "Rousseau, Social Contract and the Modern Leviathan," in *The Social Contract from Hobbes to Rawls*, eds. David Boucher and Paul Kelly (London: Routledge, 1994), 121, and Cohen, Joshua, "Reflections on Rousseau: Autonomy and Democracy," in *The Social Contract Theorists: Critical Essays on Hobbes, Locke, and Rousseau,* ed. Christopher W. Morris (Lanham, MD: Rowman & Littlefield Publishers, 1999), 192, and Keens-Soper, 175.

94. Keens-Soper, 179.

95. Bobbio, 10.

Chapter Five

Democracy, Industrial Production, and the Rise of the National Power

Introduction

What began in the Renaissance and the early modern period as an emerging logic of the centralized state, and the mechanisms for its legitimation, is transformed and extended as developments in technology, production, and forms of administration alter the material conditions of domination in the late eighteenth and nineteenth centuries. Eighteenth century political philosophers explained the logic of the central state, and elaborated mechanisms by which such logic can be managed for both the advantage of the individual and collective. However, this logic was the product of a small, localized system of production in which the practical outcomes were largely within the domain of a small, educated, urban class that was either directly or indirectly associated with the growing class of bourgeois entrepreneurs.

By the eighteenth century there are material changes in the structure of European society that will eventually generate a revolutionary influence over the prospects for the centralization of power, as national power, in the Western states. By the end of the 1700's the early forms of mechanical production that relied on water power are being replaced by steam engines. Mass production begins to transform the material conditions of life for the former agricultural workers who are now in the process of becoming an urban, industrial working class. The printing press, so essential to the emergence of the Renaissance, was transformed from an instrument for the production of books into a technology that could disseminate information of present events for the growing members of an urban literate society.

However, it is not until the middle of the nineteenth century that the nexus of mass production, rising literacy, and technologies of mass dissemination combine to produce the centralized nation-states that characterize much of the late nineteenth and early twentieth centuries. This transformation is facilitated by both the rise of a professional class of administrators and the spread of nationalist ideologies. These forces change the power structures within the Western states.

These technologies produced an integrating effect on society. The spread of literacy, books, and newspapers help generate a national identity essential to the legitimacy of central institutions. This shared sense of nationhood produces the conditions in which a notion of national distinctiveness is sufficiently strong among the public that they accept the concentration of power and tolerate its configuration. While a strong sense of identity had existed in England, France, and other places prior to the nineteenth century, it is with the combining of the material instruments for mass society that full integration and mobilization on a national level becomes possible.

A confluence of social forces generated the legitimacy of these emerging state structures. The massification of production within national borders further assisted in the creation of a national network of consumption. Such a network required the creation of a national bureaucracy to protect the system of production and distribution. Mass education emerged as a technology for the creation of a shared identity. Developing in Europe and the United States in the later half of the nineteenth century, mass education had the effect of further solidifying the sense of national identity among the population. Common history and a sense of collective mission are instilled in the population, generating conformity of purpose and ideas.

Finally, the process of generating a mass form of political association required a mechanism of legitimation. The Enlightenment had destroyed the foundational support for monarchy. A new form of political structure was required which could accommodate both the integration of large numbers of the population, spread out over large territories, and generate legitimacy for the decisions made at the center of the power structures. Democracy solves these problems.

Democratic practice is expanded along with the massification of public life more generally. Democracy is used as a legitimating mechanism for the expansion of centralized state power. It requires technologies for the mass dissemination of information, the creation of mass forms of political participation, and enough of a sense of common culture instilled within the population that the differing social interests will, at minimum, still allow for a common set of rules to govern the struggle over resources and power. In the modern period, these forces do not reach fruition until the nineteenth century, and hence, this is a period in history in which the Western world experiences an expansion of democratic practice. In the process, the procedures of democratic practice become rationally organized at the core of the nation-state.

This chapter will explore the confluence of these forces and their connection to the rise of state power and the growth of democratic institutions. It is our contention that the growth of national ideologies and the rise of the centralized institutions were linked to the material transformation of Western culture. Mass literacy, mass production, mass forms of administration, and mass democracy emerge as the essential material conditions of an age characterized by the expansion of centralized power. It is our view that rather than being seen as an impediment to the concentration of power, democracy should be seen as its vehicle in late industrial society.

Literacy and Identity

As was discussed in previous chapters, literacy is essential to the creation of administrative structures. At a bare minimum, it is necessary to have a literate class that can be called upon to keep records, distribute laws, and register deeds and other legal documents. State power is both legitimated and enhance by these functions. As was argued in Chapter Two, the break-up of the Roman Empire can at least be partially attributed to the collapse of the educational system that provided the skills necessary for the maintenance of these functions.

The Renaissance witnessed a return of literacy among a small class of urban elites. This produced conditions for the rise of a new state apparatus that was not tied to the church, but instead had its interests tied to a new, urban, entrepreneurial class of producers and traders. Rudimentary forms of democracy emerged with its power base in this new class, shifting power from the landed aristocrats of the Middle Ages to a class of owners producing goods for exchange. Capitalism emerged along with its political manifestation, liberalism. However, the liberal political model is not yet tied to mass political participation. In Europe and the United States rights of political participation are the domain of property owners. It is not until the nineteenth century that property ownership wanes as a precondition for rights of political participation.

The nineteenth century also witnessed a very large rise in literacy rates in Europe and the United States. According to Rebecca Powell, such a development follows a moral imperative. The argument of Powell, and others, is that the objective of a pluralistic society can be enhanced by education in reading, writing, and critical thinking skills in which the individual develops as a political participant in the society at large.[1] The works of John Dewey[2] and Benjamin Barber[3] have also asserted the link between literacy and the rise of pluralistic democracy. Both have argued that to have an open, pluralistic society, it is necessary to have democracy. In order to have democracy, the principles and ideals of pluralism must be embedded within the agenda of the educational system. This is contrasted with measuring the value of education through the attainment of vocational goals or the attainment of certain sets of skills.

It is not our intention to suggest that such claims are false, although the assertion of a moral imperative of democratic principles does seem to conflate the notion of Enlightenment Humanism with the practice of democratic politics. Nevertheless, wider literacy produces greater legitimacy through enhanced political participation, if institutional legitimacy is the goal of the political process. However, it is our position that the political implications of broader literacy rates at the hands of state-sponsored education has political effects far beyond the measures of individual efficacy within the institutions of state power. Increasing literacy rates were essential to the rise of nationalism and the dissemination of national identities in the industrial states of the West. They were also essential to the growth of the bureaucratic institutions within the state. Thus, rising literacy rates were part of the material foundation for the growth and concentration of power represented by the modern nation-state.

Prior to the nineteenth century, only a few Scandinavian countries had invested in national literacy. In 1800, literacy rates among males in England and France were around fifty percent. For females in France literacy rates were around thirty percent, and in England they were around forty percent. Even as late as the 1850's literacy rates in Spain, Russia, and Italy were about forty percent for males.[4] In the United States, literacy rates varied greatly between the North and the South in the first half of the nineteenth century. In the 1840's school enrollment in the Northern states for males and females of school age was forty-seven percent, while in the South the figure is only fourteen percent.[5]

However, by the 1860s the countries of Europe, along with the United States, were beginning to take a stronger interest in the literacy of their populations. In Europe, there was general consensus around the goal of "homogenizing" literacy skills.[6] This resulted in an increase in literacy in all the European countries, with literacy rising to seventy percent of the male population in France by 1870, and around seventy-three percent of males in Britain.[7] In the United States, by 1870 the number of males and females attending school had grown to seventy-five percent in the North and forty percent in the South.[8]

Such a material transformation of the society produced multiple effects. Rising literacy rates enhanced the growth of science and technology, as more people were engaged in the pursuit of knowledge and its applications. Organizational strategies for the employment of a literate population generated advances in the productivity of labor and the growth of large corporate entities. Such developments also brought about a condition in which workers were fettered to the pace of machine production, the division of labor, and fixed hours of employment.[9] Rising literacy rates also brought about an increased ability for the organization and dissemination of varied interests and concerns, whether expressed individually or collectively through the generation of mass forms of media. There can be no doubt that such developments enhanced the ability of people to organize and articulate their interests to a wide audience, thus producing the potential to generate a sympathetic response by democratic political institutions.

However, it must also be noted that the educational process does not occur in a vacuum. One does not teach literacy skills in a context that is devoid of content, both cultural and political. This point is articulated by Eugen Weber in his book *Peasants into Frenchman*. Weber argues that by the 1880s elementary education was both free and compulsory. However, its main function was to teach patriotism.[10] Textbooks were used to socialize a sense of national identity. Through the generation of an identity tied to fixed territorial boundaries, the territorial integrity of the state was instilled as something to be defended. Thus, the process of education became an essential tool in establishing a sense of common history and sentiment, giving rise to both the emergence of strongly nationalistic ideologies in the late nineteenth and twentieth centuries and the willingness among the public to submit to an increasingly centralized form of political administration.

The other way in which the state's commitment to literacy enhanced the centralization of power was through the creation of the "literacy project" which became a vehicle for the creation of new state agencies and new avenues of intervention. As David Vincent describes the situation, from the nineteenth century onward there is "interdependence" between the state bureaucracy and the promotion of literacy.[11] In 1864 the government of France launched a study of literacy, which became the basis for greater state intervention. In Russia, the study of literacy became the justification for the spread of government activity in the society more generally.[12]

Therefore, literacy should not be seen in isolation from the other material components of social life. Too often, literacy is simply treated as an addendum to, or culmination of, the Humanism project. It is treated as the transference of skills to a transcendent subject, as if those subjects exist in isolation from the other material conditions of existence. It is then asserted that these transcendent subjects are, through the educational skills they have learned, able to rise above the immediacy of needs, interests, and contextual patterns.

However, literacy is a social phenomenon, linked to other activities in social existence. Its political implications need to be seen in this larger domain. Literacy generates other potentialities beyond its association with the assertion of the individual's power. It is also linked to the rise of state power, as it is an essential component in the rise of democracy and the centralization of the instruments of control.

Printing and the Mass Dissemination of Interests

Francis Bacon stated in the 1600s that printing had altered "the appearance and state of the world."[13] Printing is a mass form of material production that enhanced the ability of states to administer territories. The technology of the printing press also facilitated the dissemination of information and communication on a massive scale. Literacy rates rose along with a means of organizing human beings. The printing press, as with other forms of mass communication, has an affinity with the centralization of power in human societies.

Printing and mass forms of dissemination develop "increasingly rapid communications" and allowed for an ever-growing number of human beings to perceive of themselves differently in relation to each other and to the structures of power in society.[14] The ability to communicate in a mass way, even with the relatively slow processes of education and socialization, allows for a sense of shared identity among people. A shared identity translates into a common perception about the world and the issues that must be confronted on a daily basis. It allows for the creation of cultural boundaries to accompany the territorial boundaries found in Europe after the Peace of Westphalia.

Therefore, the rise of mechanical forms of printing must be seen in relation to literacy, capitalism, and the rise of nationalism. Printing's affinity with literacy is self-evident. Without a populous that is able to read, the demand for books will remain low. However, with the rise of printing, the creation of more and varied texts, the impetus for reading, and the technical means to do so, are more available. Therefore, printing emerges as a business in the sixteenth century as a more educated urban class of merchant begins to create a demand. The publication of materials in the local vernacular furthers the development of a market for books and other printed material.

When the printing industry began in the sixteenth century, each printing of a volume was modest, usually between one hundred fifty to two hundred copies. However, as literacy increased, the demand of the market rose and within the sixteenth century a printing of a single edition would yield one thousand to one thousand five hundred copies, a number that was maintained for the most part for the remainder of the century.[15] However, such increases were not without political concerns among the ruling elites about the rise of literacy and the dissemination of uncensored texts. For instance, in England an order was made towards the Stationers' Company in 1588 that "ordinary editions" of books, with the exception of the Bible and other choice religious and educational volumes, be limited to one thousand five hundred copies "in order to protect the workmen."[16] This order was made despite the demand for books being much higher than it had been even fifty years previously.[17]

Information, and its dissemination on a mass scale, was not as easily regulated by the existing power structure; the Roman Catholic Church and the various aristocratic classes in Europe. Printing was an endeavor of the capitalist middle class, a group whose interest was in meeting an increasing demand in the market. As power shifted toward the rising middle class, the "business" of printing began to develop and take root. The growth of a literate urban class coupled with the technology of printing created a demand for printed documents of all sorts, especially those relating to legal and property matters. This phenomenon began in the Enlightenment and only was augmented in the coming emergence of the modern period.[18]

In political terms, printing texts in local languages had a dual effect. On the one hand this loosened the hold of the church, as the power of Latin declined in favor of local languages. At the same time, the creation of a body of texts in local languages had the effect of solidifying national identities. People identified themselves as belonging to a unique linguistic community, a common set of readers and speakers.[19]

By the dawn of the eighteenth century, printing technology existed throughout Europe, and very few regions were lacking a printing press.[20] The themes and content of the books printed also diverged greatly from the formally acceptable religious and sterile educational texts. Books sold included fiction novels and collections of poetry, oftentimes with erotic motifs, and sometimes complete with illustrations. Obviously, these new thematic compositions were not approved of by the church, and sometimes were disseminated under the watch of local secular officials. However, such works were in demand, and the market responded.

By the nineteenth century a rising demand from an increasingly literate public stimulated a large demand for new books. Faster and more efficient printing presses were developed. As a result, more books were available to the public at lower prices.[21]

However, the rise of printing has a dual character. The modern era brought with it a public that became more literate and more varied in their reading tastes.[22] Printing enhances the rise of literacy, providing the public with more information, more generalized knowledge about the world, and greater access to material needed to make informed judgments about the conditions of political life. Such developments enhance the logic of democracy and the potential to create political structures that generate legitimacy on a mass scale. In that sense, it is a necessary technology for the rise of centralized power within the industrial age.

Literacy is also a vehicle for socialization, the spread of common identities and nationalist sentiments. In the nineteenth century such a development is particularly influential, as nationalism is identified with modernity itself. Printing is also necessary to the rise of centralized structures of administration, as it allows for the expansion of public and private bureaucracies and the creation of greater efficiencies in the discipline and control of human activities.

As is the case with the rise of literacy more generally, our point is not to suggest that the rise of printing should be seen as a negative development in the history of human civilization. However, it should be understood both as arising out of specific material circumstances, and as having an impact on activities of social and political existence. Only by viewing the interactions of these various elements can we see the environment that gives rise to the conditions of domination.

Liberal Economics and the Rise of National Power

The focus of this work is on the changing conditions which give rise to the transformation of social control. In a democracy this occurs through an intermediary step in which the construction of human identity is transformed through a revolution in how people perceive themselves, their social relations, and the way they think about the "naturalness" of their patterns of social and political existence. In this context, the rise of liberalism, as a pattern of beliefs about property, social relations, and distributive notions of justice, cannot be ignored.

However, it is often assumed that because liberalism has a strong emphasis on the individual that it does not favor the development of strong patterns of central authority. Such a position ignores the historical origins of liberalism. It is both an ideology and an institutional structure for the development of a capitalist form of economic relations. As such, liberal institutions developed along with the techniques of production, trade, and commerce that evolved after European feudalism.

Viewed this way, the transformation of production, from human and animal forms of energy to mechanical production, brought with it a corresponding development of the instruments for the effective exercise of power within the new environment. Capitalism is a system of production that is based on exchange, which requires an administrative context that furthers the processes of exchange. Further, capitalism requires the creation of *capital*, the machinery and assets used in the production of good for the exchange process. This requirement of capitalism also generates the need for conditions favorable to the process of capital accumulation. From the eighteenth to the twentieth century, the institutional structures in Europe and the United States evolved to accommodate these requirements of industrial capitalism. This could only be accomplished by extending the reach of the institutions of state power.

Thus, two factors need to be examined; the transformation of production from small scale economic units to the development of the mass production enterprise, and the transformation of state administrative structures that served to further the process of production. Both of these developments need to be seen as mutually reinforcing processes in the growth of centralized systems of power. The emergence of mass production is a significant technological condition for the emergence of mass society and the consolidation of national power. In turn, the transformation of the administrative processes for the advancement of mass production reinforces the rationale behind national institutions.

The Rise of Mass Production

European production prior to 1700 was animated by a mix of human, animal, wind, and water power.[23] Mechanical production had developed as early as the sixteenth century, with the use of wind and water power as a substitute for human energy in some enterprises. In Holland, wind energy was used to generate power in saw mills, and in England water was used as a means to generate power for the textile industry.[24]

However, by the eighteenth century transformations in technology were beginning to manifest changes in the character of production. In 1712 the first effective steam engine was developed and used to pump water out of a coal mine in Dudley, England.[25] This was followed by improvements to the steam engine and its use in the textile mills across England. This led to an increase in the productivity of the mills.

Despite these advances, industrial development was limited by the processes for making iron and steel. In the Middle Ages, iron had been made in small furnaces using charcoal as a fuel. The techniques for converting iron to steel were known, but the costly and time consuming processes for the conversion meant that steel was produced only in small batches. Starting in the eighteenth century coal increasingly replaced the use of charcoal in iron furnaces, promoting the growth of the iron industry in areas where there was an abundance of coal and iron ore. In Britain this took place in Wales and Yorkshire, in France the iron industry developed in Le Creusot, and in Germany this occurred in the Ruhr Valley. In the United States the production of iron was concentrated in Western Pennsylvania around the city of Pittsburgh.

During the eighteenth and the first half of the nineteenth centuries there was a steady growth in the demand for iron. This was pushed, in part, by the further development of the steam engine and its application to new forms of production and transportation. For example, the steam engine was applied to the processes of agriculture, generating an economy of scale in the agricultural sector. However, it was the growth of the railroad industry that was the largest commercial push to the iron and steel industries.

In an economy which is structured around the process of *exchange*, a technological infrastructure that facilitates the expansion of the exchange process will generate the greatest potential for growth. To that end, the railroad was an essential component. This explains why the state was so heavily involved in the development of the railroad in both Europe and the United States. By 1856, the United Kingdom was already transporting 64 million metric tons of goods by rail. In that same year, France was transporting 12.9 million metric tons. However, by 1894 rail transport in Britain and France had grown to 325 and 99 million metric tons respectively.[26] As economic imperatives drove the process of industrialization, it also produced the by-product of cultural integration while reinforcing national identity.

The development of commerce in the latter half of the nineteenth century was made possible by a series of technological breakthroughs that would create the conditions for the rise of mass forms of production. In 1856 Henry Bessemer invented the Bessemer steel process. This technique made it possible to produce large amounts of steel quickly and cheaply. This transformed the steel industry and lead to a massive expansion of the industry. In the United States alone, steel production jumped from 42,000 tons in 1870 to 1.2 million tons in 1880.[27] In France, the amount of Bessemer steel produced between 1863 and 1869 jumped from 1,826 to 52,400 tons.[28] By the beginning of the twentieth century both Germany and the United States had overtaken Britain in the production of steel products.[29]

Industrialization transformed the employment patterns in the West. For example, in the 1880s Germany had approximately the same numbers of people engaged in agriculture and industry. However, by 1907 there was twice the numbers employed in the factories as in agriculture.[30] In the United States, by 1900 there were still more people engaged in agriculture, but the gap had closed significantly, with 7.1 million people employed in manufacturing, and 10.9 million in agriculture.[31]

The development of the Bessemer process was essential to the growth of the railroads, but it also had a significant impact on social life. Not only did the demand for steel increase the scale of industrial production in that industry, but it also enhanced the conditions for urbanization in Europe and the United States. Mass production in the steel industry provided the technical means for the concentration of greater numbers in the growing cities. The percentage of workers engaged in agricultural production declined, even as the railroads produced the potential for profits in the agricultural sector. Between 1840 and 1910, New York City had grown from 349,000 to 4.7 million residents. Chicago had grown from a population of 4,000 to 2.1 million.[32]

Similar developments were taking place in Europe. In England, Birmingham had grown from 28,000 in 1760 to 840,000 in 1910. Dortmund, Germany grew from 4,400 residents in 1816 to 214,000 in 1910.[33]

The period also witnessed other critical technological developments that would facilitate the creation of national grids for a new form of energy, electricity. By the 1880s Thomas Edison was taking Michael Faraday's work on electricity and developing it as a reliable source of power. This led to advances in electric motors by the end of the century. Also at the end of the nineteenth century the early work by N. A. Otto in 1876 on the internal combustion engine had been transformed by Gottlieb Daimler and Karl Benz into the automobile.

This is obviously not an exhaustive list of all the technological changes that occurred in the nineteenth century. However, they are some of the most important ones, developments that were essential to the rise of mass production and the mass, consumer-oriented system of consumption that developed from the nineteenth century onward. It would be impossible for changes of this magnitude not to transform the conditions of social life in their wake. Urban society, with centralized systems of production, distribution, and consumption generate the need for centralized forms of administration, both in the economic system and in the political structures that evolve.

Structural Accommodation to Mass Production

The transformation of production from relatively small scale operations to massive factories were driven by three interrelated factors. First, the commodities that were produced were ones that were compatible with the mass forms of production. It was possible to carry out these new production processes on a scale that had not previously been imagined.

Secondly, the market mechanisms operating for industrial commodities generally favored an economy of scale. It was possible to produce goods at a lower unit cost with a larger factory. Declining unit costs in production allowed for the growth in demand for industrial products.

Finally, market forces required that companies invest in equipment. This meant that companies that did not invest in the high output equipment were likely to be left behind and succumb to an unforgiving market. The purchase of capital goods, however, was expensive, even as machine production was emerging as a necessity. The production of machines themselves had also become a huge business, with the production of machinery as the major industrial output in the United States by 1900.[34]

The investment in capital goods required a context in which economic power was consolidated. What emerged from this historical condition was the oligopolistic organization of production. Such a structural transformation required an adjustment in the political climate.

As early as the 1850s, Napoleon III had taken steps in France to encouraged industrial growth, constructing public works, establishing a credit bank, and by adopting generally liberal commercial policies.[35] Germany established the Reichsbank in 1875 along with a number of joint-stock credit banks to make loans to the industrial sector. In Germany, the banks even took blocks of shares in the industries to encourage confidence among the public in the viability of the new firms.[36]

By the end of the nineteenth century a series of government activities had been engaged that furthered the consolidation of economic power. In Europe, governments established new standards for weights and measures, increased patent protection, centralized banking, and issued paper money.[37] In addition, changes to the legal codes had been made that assigned additional rights to property. Freedom to engage in contracts, freedom to use and dispose of property, and rights of property ownership were encoded in common law throughout Europe.[38]

In the United States, a process of assigning formal rights to property had been embedded in the Constitution. However, those rights were expanded at the end of the nineteenth century. In 1878, Thomas Cooley argued in the *Princeton Law Review* that the Fourteenth Amendment to the Constitution should be applied to property, effectively limiting government interference in the private economy. This view was the dominant position on the Supreme Court in the United States by the end of the century.

The consolidation of wealth within the structure of heavy industrial production generated private wealth on a scale that rivaled the landed aristocracy of medieval Europe. Individual families in Europe and the United States began to amass huge fortunes. The creation of a new class of economic barons also produced an accompanying ideology called Social Darwinism. Influenced by the British author, Herbert Spencer, the proponents of Social Darwinism argued that the consolidation of wealth in private hands was both necessary for the growth of human productive potentials and a benefit to the species, as it produced a measure of who was successful in the evolutional struggle.

Such a position was countered with alternative ideologies from the perspective of the other social classes. In Europe, the socialist parties emerged to represent the interests of industrial workers. The groups generally sought the nationalization of private production while maintaining the concentration of capital. It should be noted, as was argued by Max Weber, that the success of such an agenda does not necessary lead to more rights and power for the individual, but can be seen as part of a transition toward greater consolidation of state power.[39] In the United States, the Populists and Progressives pushed for legislation that would prevent the consolidation of capital and disperse it among a larger segment of the population. However, the effects in both Europe and the United States of socialism were largely limited to the protection, enfranchisement, and income prospects of the work force. As laudable as such developments were, they had little impact on the overall structure and concentration of wealth and power.

In Europe, industrial families such as the Krupps were amassing an industrial fortune. In the United States, Andrew Carnegie, the Duponts, and others were generating mass fortunes in largely oligopolistic markets. However, this period of rapid industrial growth generated an overexpansion of production. In the United States this produced a severe economic contraction lasting from 1873 to 1879. As a result, a new structure emerged to better manage the competition among firms so that such economic events could be mitigated in the future. This was the industrial trust.

Structurally, the trust was a product of the heavy industrial age. It could not be organized in a circumstance of widely dispersed, small-scale production. Trusts were created as a means to bring oligopolies in a given sector together under an umbrella organization in which they joined forces and managed production, with each receiving a pro-rated share of the profits. The first of these trusts to be formed in the United States was Standard Oil, created in 1882. However, the use of the trust model was not limited to the United States. In Germany, cartels of industrial producers were created to ease cut-throat competition in various sectors of the economy. In the case of Germany these cartels were often initiated and sponsored by the commercial banks, given that German banks were often share holders in affected companies.[40] In France, the cartel model was also used, but not as extensively as in Germany. By 1910, the mines in France's largest coal field were controlled by a cartel. At that time there were nine cartels in the iron, steel and engineering industries.[41]

In the United States, the creation of trusts was attacked by the Populists and Progressives of the era. This resulted in the Sherman Anti-Trust legislation of 1890. However, such legislation did little to stem the tide of concentrated wealth. Holding companies and mergers ensued, further consolidating wealth. From 1898 to 1902 there was an explosion of mergers. In this short period, 2653 large firms disappeared through mergers.[42] The American Can Company combined 120 smaller firms into one large conglomerate, controlling 80% of the can industry. US Steel was formed in 1901, combining Carnegie Steel with the National and Federal Steel companies, along with 170 small firms.[43]

The concentration of economic power became an enduring structure within the liberal economic states of the West. However, this process should not be seen in isolation from the other centralizing forces of power in the modern era. The concentration of wealth existed in a mutually reinforcing relationship with urbanization, enhanced national power, the massification of labor, and the rise of mass forms of political participation. While not the exclusive cause for the collectivization of social and political life, the generation of the technologies for mass production had an influence in all these other areas.

The consolidation of economic power needs to be seen as part of the centralization of power more generally. The fact that the economic and political institutions are structurally distinct in a liberal state model is not the overarching factor in the assessment of macro-level structural adjustments. The transformation and consolidation of economic power was a significant contributor to the centralization of power more generally. The conditions for the rise of mass production required political adjustment to accommodate the emerging processes.

Opposition to this consolidation of power through the political process was largely marginalized, structurally bypassed, or suppressed by the dictates of the political economy. European socialists and American Progressives had some marginal impact on the conditions of labor, but were quite ineffective in transforming the structure of wealth and its effects on the process of centralization in the state and economy.

The Institutionalization of Social Life and the Formation of Sub-national Identities

The development of an economy based on exchange within fixed regions required the rapid integration of national territory. The power of the state required the development of national resources, the ability to enter those resources in the exchange process, and a population that identified itself with the integrity of the country and its culture. All of these components of centralized state power were enhanced by the processes of industrialization.

The growth of the railroads had integrated the territorial land-masses of the nation-state system, promoting the movement of goods on a scale that had never been seen. This fostered the growth of common, national languages over regional dialects. Education furthered this process, standardizing both the technical aspects of grammar and the curriculum that promoted national integration. Such developments were furthered by the production of books and newspapers within the language that would reach the widest audience, thus promoting the standardization of language as its byproduct.

These material technical developments led to the creation of two contending social forces. On the one hand, the economic and nationalistic forces of identity construction were moving society in the direction of greater integration. Standardization of institutional practices among an urbanized, industrial, and nationalistic work force were the natural outcomes of this process. On the other hand, there were social forces generating more specific forms of sub-national identity, owing to the division of labor, class stratification, the specialization of educational disciplines, and the formation of a professional class among the bourgeoisie.

By the mid-nineteenth century, professional organizations began to be formed, such as the American Medical Association (1847) and the American Bar Association (1878). These bodies are specifically tied to professional activities of the members and are, in a sense, extensions of the European guild structures begun in the Middle Ages. Nevertheless, they constitute part of the general process of centralization and nationalization occurring across the developing economy.

However, the largest of these groups were the labor unions. Labor unions were prohibited by law in Europe until the nineteenth century.[44] Their illegality was largely based on the claim that they constituted organizations that inhibited the free movement of products and labor. In 1824 British law declared that unions must be "tolerated," but this amounted to far less than the legal rights sought by the unions. It was not until 1865 that British law was altered to accommodate unions as collective bargaining agents for workers on matters of wages and working conditions.[45] By 1871 they were given full legal status. In France, a ministerial declaration established minimal recognition for unions in 1868, but full legal status was not granted until 1884.

In Germany trade unions were illegal under Bismarck. Despite this fact, German labor unions had a decidedly political character. Union elements formed the Social Democratic Party in 1863. However, the party was characterized as a subversive organization by the government until it received full legal status in 1890. The Labour Party in Britain was not founded until 1900, as the various trade unions began to organize themselves politically and select candidates for parliamentary elections.

Legal recognition swelled the ranks of union membership among the industrializing economies of Europe and the United States. From 1870 to 1912, labor union membership in Britain rose from 142,000 to 3.2 million. In Germany, from 1890 to 1912 membership went from 277,000 to 3.7 million. In France, membership grew from 402,000 to 1 million in the years between 1890 to 1912. In the United States, from 1897 until 1912 the ranks of trade unions swelled from 444,000 to 2.5 million members.[46]

While all of the major trade-union groups were created and operated on a national level, there was one organization promoting the interests of labor that sought to represent workers on an international level. In 1864 the first meeting of the International Working Men's Association took place in St. Martin's Hall in London. This organization, which would later be known as the Communist Party, sought to internationalize the organization of labor interest into a political force that would master the increasing concentration of wealth through the collective ownership of the forces of production.

The emergence of sub-national organizations that reflected the interests and concerns of professional and working class groups must be understood in the context of rising material conditions favoring the centralization of power more generally. The rise of producer, professional, and labor organizations would not have been possible on the national level without the centralization of the instruments that made their organizations feasible. The concentration of capital, the development of the railroads, the refinements in printing and communications technology, and the *efficient* organization of labor in large-scale manufacturing, were all material instruments of centralization. Even the emergence of labor unions and the Communist Party need to be seen in this light.

As World War I demonstrated, these sub-national organizations are of secondary importance when compared with the integrative effects of nationalism. They are byproducts of newly emerging material conditions in the nineteenth century. The urban setting produces an amalgamation of the various components of industrial culture: laborers, intellectuals, professionals, state officials, and moneyed interests. It produces the material conditions for the consolidation of interests, as the emergence of political structures with greater access points requires greater political organization.

The Structural Transformation of the State: The Concentration of National Power

In most works that deal with both politics and administrative structures, the governmental institutions are given primacy in the order of discussion. Such a strategy creates the false impression that governments emerge as the first order of business without regard for the either the historical context or the tasks to be performed. It implies that administrative structure is an offshoot of government rather than vice versa.

This impression generates two mistaken views of the relationship between government policy, and the structures that are the repository of power. First, this position implies that the process of creating structures of power is driven by ideologies and principles that are themselves immune from the historical conditions which gave rise to them. It suggests that the structures are the expressions of transcendent reason coupled with universal ideals, which manifest administrative structures as the residue of a historical and teleological process. As such, government and public policy are only secondarily impacted by the material demands of economic conditions, military power, and technological circumstances. While not completely immune to history, the ideal has greater impact than the real.

The second false impression left by such an approach distorts the role and function of democratic practices. It promotes the view that democracy is the counterweight to power, as its principles are embedded within the primary institutions of governmental power themselves. Democracy is the soft, humanitarian check to the exigencies of order and efficiency promoted by the struggle for wealth and power. Such an attitude masks the larger trend toward the centralization of power within the modern state. As Max Weber observed over a century ago, the tendencies in the state are for the expansion of power into ever greater domains of public and private activity. The structures of government transform themselves and adjust to the needs generated from the environment for greater efficiency, standardization, control, and order. Each of these represents the necessary conditions for the expansion of power, as measured by GDP growth rates, and relative military positions in the world system.

In this light, democracy's position is both limited and circumscribed. Democracy should not be seen as a check on the growth and centralization of power. It is rather a mechanism, the very structure of which is designed to legitimate the expansion and centralization of power while seeking to limit the potential for cruelty and terror made possible by the concentration of power itself.

Military Competition, Colonialism, and State Power

During the latter half of the nineteenth century the material conditions for the expansion of state power existed in most of the Western countries. Literacy rates were rising, along with socializing instruments of national identities. Industrialization had linked the internal territories of European countries, bringing both economic expansion and reinforcing the territorial components of nationalism. However, industrialization had also fostered an intense form of competition, particularly among the countries of Europe.

Whether this competition was driven by the pursuit of raw power, or the will of industrial capitalists is a matter of ideological perspective. However, what remains clear is that during this period intense rivalries developed, with each of the states possessing the means and the will to carry out the competitive struggle. Domestically, the major states of Europe began an intense military build up. Industrialization, generally, had produced the raw materials for new and better military hardware. As has already been discussed, the massive increases in steel production made possible the development of warships and battlefield equipment that would have been impossible to produce a generation earlier. The development of new engines also meant that such weapons could now be mobile.

Military expenditures rose dramatically. From 1875 to 1913 the military budget of Britain rose from 133 to 385 million dollars. In

France, military expenditures rose from 137 to 277 million dollars in roughly the same period. Germany increased its military spending in the years between 1881 and 1914 from 106 to 352 million dollars.[47]

As the spending on developing new military equipment was taking place domestically, the rivalry for wealth and power was also extended overseas. By the 1880s steam ships were coming into widespread use, increasing the cargo that could be taken to and from the European theater. This development created the conditions for an expansion into new territories by the European powers, as they scrambled to take more overseas colonies toward the end of the nineteenth century. Ten percent of Africa was under direct foreign domination in 1876. By 1900, that figure rose to ninety percent.[48] During this time the European powers also expanded their control over Asia and Polynesia. Such an expansion of activity could not be carried out without an expansion of the state's administrative apparatus.

The Growth of the Bureaucratic State

In his work, *Economy and Society*, Max Weber asserted that one measure of modernity in society is its level of professional bureaucratization.[49] This is true both in the political apparatus of the state and in the modern organization of industry. It is Weber's assertion that the bureaucracy is the true repository of power in the modern state.[50] Power is exercised through administration.

Weber's position on the concentration of power in the bureaucracy is contradicted by Herman Finer. Finer asserted that Weber ignored the structure of modern government, a structure that places power within the legislative branch of government.[51] However, structure and practice need to be understood as distinct matters. Further, if legislation is, as Ralph Waldo Emerson describes it, an "afterthought," then there is far more credibility to Weber's claim than Finer acknowledges. It is our contention that the historical facts move us closer to Weber's assertion.

By the middle of the nineteenth century two forces were converging to generate not only a quantitative change in the approach to administration and power, but also a qualitative change in the conceptualization of politics, power, and the administrative structure of organizations. Going back to the Middle Ages the administrative power of the state had been limited by several factors. First, the scope of integration had been limited by factors such a geographic space and the limitations of transport and communications. Second, the administration of the territory was carried out by a small staff, often selected through a patronage process in which leaders repaid loyal supporters with positions in the administrative apparatus of the government. These two factors had the effect of keeping central authorities relatively weak, and the scope of administrative action relatively limited.

However, by the mid-nineteenth century the conditions that had supported weak central states had begun to change significantly. The latter half of the nineteenth century was a time of both the rapid growth in the size of governmental institutions and an expansion in the scope of governmental policy. In the period between 1841 and 1911, civil service employees in Britain increased from 17,000 to 644,000. In Germany, by 1911 there were 1,159,000 civil servants. In France, the number increased from 90,000 in 1841 to 699,000 in 1911. Similar increases were also occurring in the United States, moving from 23,000 civil servants in 1841 to 370,000 in 1911.[52]

What caused this expansion? Clearly, the needs of industry for the building and management of infrastructure were a major component in this transformation. However, the assertion that the interests of industry were the sole source of this centralization of power overlooks the interests of the state in a competitive nation-state environment. Government and industry both needed the centralization of administration, and the broad reach of national policy, in order to create the conditions for the expansion of their agendas: profits and power. The mutual affinity between these two forces generated the transformation of political institutions and administrative structures.

Industry, commerce, communications, political integration, and national power all required the growth of an administrative apparatus. National power was dependent upon the growth of industrial production. Integration was necessary for both the centralization of state power within its territorial boundaries, and for the legal framework necessary for the enhancement and stability of commercial calculations. Transportation and communications technologies furthered integration along with the movement of commodities within an exchange based economy. This affinity between state and industrial interests generated a powerful incentive for the expansion of the public sector.

The growth of these functions by the central administration of the state inspired Herman Finer's characterization of modern bureaucracy:

> Nothing like such regulation of human activity has been attempted outside ancient theocracies . . . The record is written on the roads, the gutters, and the buildings, and spells what the

> state has done ... The annual thousands of rules and orders, the
> detailed and present plan of activity of all modern states,
> reveal how the state concentrates upon each individual and
> weaves his every impulse into the myriad-thread warp of its
> existence . . . The state is everywhere, it leaves hardly a gap.[53]

Such growth in the scope of the centralized state would not be possible without the professionalization of the bureaucracy. Max Weber described the modern state bureaucracy as the most efficient form of administration.[54] This is the case because the modern bureaucrat is selected through a competitive process, specially trained, and owes allegiance to the rules that govern the administrative unit rather than individual political agents.

The professionalization of the modern bureaucracy has its origins in the Prussian state as early as the seventeenth century under William of Brandenburg.[55] In the eighteenth century, Prussia began an examination process and specialized training for members of the state administration. However, by the 1740s the centralization of power resulted in a police state which lasted until the invasion by Napoleon. After 1815 the civil service continued to be of a high caliber and became a model for the creation of bureaucracies across Europe.

After unification in the 1870s, the civil service took on an increasing role in furthering the logic of industrialization through the promotion of policies that increased commercial efficiency. Training in economics and finance was added to the curriculum for civil servants, and legislation that would free industry from regulation was promoted as the best means to spur the growth of economic and political power by the central government.[56]

Similar activity was taking place in Britain, France, and the United States. In 1853 Britain began a reorganization of its civil service, introducing competitive exams for the posts in the Indian Civil Service. However, the local constituencies within the civil service resisted the complete elimination of patronage until 1870.[57] In the 1870s, due largely to the increasing demand brought about by industrialization, Britain formalized its testing processes for civil service positions. However, it should be noted here that Britain focused less on specialized training for its civil service positions than the other states in Europe, instead looking for people with broad training in what would be considered *liberal arts* today. Such an education was a luxury only afforded to the wealthy, thus retaining a class privilege within the British civil service.[58]

France had been a centralized nation since the fifteenth century. Monarchical power had been extended to the various regions through the stationing of administrative representatives of the crown in various regions. Until the time of the French Revolution, these positions were either purchased or inherited.[59] Napoleon established a more professional body of civil servants, further centralizing the administrative structures in France. By 1834 France had created five institutes to advise the central government on policy matters. These institutes focused on matters ranging from politics and morals to art and science.[60]

However, during the restoration of the monarchy, elements of this system were undermined. It is not until 1882, largely with pressure from the emerging needs of the industrializing economy, that France adopted the modern rules for its civil service. These include rules for training and recruitment, appointments based on civil service exams, and technical training.

The United States had a relatively small civil service sector until the middle of the nineteenth century. In 1821 the United States had only 8,000 civil servants working for the national government. This small number is due largely to the fact that until the Civil War, the United States was largely an agriculturally based economy with a federalist governmental structure. The civil service was widely viewed as a place where party loyalists could be rewarded, as the positions in the civil service constituted the *capital* that could be distributed among the victorious party.

This system of patronage began eroding in the nineteenth century. In 1820, the Tenure in Office Act was passed in order to improve accountability among civil service workers that had responsibilities for handling money. In 1853, the Salary Act created a structure within the civil service, establishing four different pay grades and setting up some professional standards for appointments.[61] However, it is not until passage of the Civil Service Act in 1883, commonly known as the Pendleton Act, that open competition and competitive exams for civil service positions were fully instituted.

A similar process occurred in the four major industrial states discussed in this section. Due to the pressures coming from the entrepreneurial sector, and the concerns of the central governments over the competition for power, there was tremendous pressure for rapid growth. These conditions required the most efficient structures possible. This need fostered the development of a professional bureaucracy in which trained personnel scientifically gathered data, organized institutions, and implemented policies in order for the centralized institutions of power to maximize their ends.

These developments began the age of rational "scientific management," or Taylorism. Knowledge is gathered, codified, and embedded within the structures of the state apparatus. Through the efficiency of organization, technical details can be mastered and put to use in the promotion of economic and national power. In what Weber called the "rational-legal" form of administration, agents of the state generate rules by which information can be gathered, codified, and used for the efficient management of the government. At this stage in development, efficiency of organization and orderly obedience to central authority become substantive values within the state.

Whether called Taylorism, "scientific management," or the rational-legal form of organization, the process these terms describe is similar. Society generates a technical infrastructure in service of the components of power. In the nineteenth century this resulted in an extension of centralized institutions to enhance the regularity and calculability of investment capital, at the same time the regulation of capital itself was being dismantled under a liberal strategy of growth and development.

It is this process that led Weber to despair. He claimed that both national bureaucracies and factory production were determining the character of his age.[62] Bureaucracy and the machine were fabricating the shell of bondage.[63] The result of technically superior administration would be better structures of domination.[64]

The Commercial Imperative: International Integration

Though the activities of the nineteenth century were largely directed toward the integration and promotion of power within the nation-state, the development of an exchange economy, coupled with new means of transport, would lead to the growth of commercial exchanges across borders. The problems generated by such a development were numerous. Matters involving the exchange of currencies, the standardization of weights and measure, the problems of localized tolls and tariffs, and the management of rivers and roadways, were all matters that involved two or more nations coming to some agreement on the structure for the exchange of goods.

Prior to 1786, the two most economically advanced nations in Europe, England and France, had no commercial treaty between them. The period of heavy industrialization had not yet taken hold, and the small scale of water power and early steam-driven machinery had not yet produced the saturation of domestic markets. In 1800 French external trade amounted to 323 million francs in imports and 272 million francs in exports. The United Kingdom during the same period imported 62 million pounds of commodities, while exporting 38 million pounds worth of goods.

However, by 1900 external trade had increased significantly. France was importing almost 4.6 billion francs worth of commodities, while exporting 4.1 billion francs worth of goods. In the United Kingdom a similar pattern of growth can be observed. In 1900 the United Kingdom imported goods worth 523 million pounds while exporting 291 million pounds worth of commodities.[65] Other countries in Europe saw comparable patterns of growth.

The increasing volume of trade generated the need for new agreements among the trading partners. Many of these transactions were carried out by bilateral agreements among the specific nations involved. By 1914 most of the powers in Europe had at least one commercial treaty with the other powers in Europe in order to manage the conditions of trade.[66]

However, such developments also produced demands for more generalized treaties across the span of the continent. The international logic of the capitalist economic system created the need for standards and organizational strategies that transcended the limits of the nation-state system. Thus, the number of transnational organizations grew from 7 in 1857 to 108 in 1910.[67] These organizations included the International Rivers Commissions, which controlled the Danube and the Rhine, the Latin Monetary Union, the International Postal Union, and the International Bureau of Weights and Measures.

These organizations are a prelude to what will develop in the twentieth century in the period after World War II. International trade requires the expansion of power, and the transfer of certain elements of sovereignty to newly created, centralized institutions for the management of trade and commerce. This will be explored in greater detail in the next chapter.

Mass Democracy and the Legitimacy of Central Power in the Nation-State

Legitimacy is the most central ideological component of democratic theory. However, legitimacy is not an easy concept to define. It does not constitute a specific structure or practice, as it cannot be separated from a "belief" or "feeling" that is present among the population. Therefore, it is not identical with democratic institutions, per se, as people who believe in the divine right of kings are likely to believe a monarchical system of governance is "legitimate." What can be said about legitimacy is that it is a psychological condition, a general sense that the institutional structures are "appropriate," "fairly structured" in that they will produce an outcome that the majority will agree is arrived at through a logical and rational process. This belief must be sufficiently strong to hold the collective institution together, even if the specific policy enacted is not one that is universally popular.

Suffrage and Political Consolidation

Early liberal doctrine tied the legitimacy of institutional decision making with the expansion of suffrage within democratic institutions. However, there was a problem. The rise of liberal theory, and its notion of consent as the foundation of political legitimacy, was connected to the emergence of a politically powerful bourgeoisie. The bourgeoisie was a propertied class. Thus, even while their interests clashed with those of the landed aristocracy, they were, nevertheless, proponents of property as a condition of political enfranchisement. As a result, even with the triumph of liberal ideology by the eighteenth century, the universal principles it espoused were not widely embraced until the middle to late nineteenth century.

Both the aristocracy and the bourgeoisie feared the expansion of power among the propertiless. This was founded on a simple idea; that those without property would, given sufficient political power, take the holdings of those with property using the legitimate institutions of government.[68] In England, this meant the poor were denied the right to vote. The Reform Bill of 1832 expanded some suffrage rights, but the poor were not fully enfranchised until 1867.[69] In the German states, with the exception of Prusssia, universal suffrage was granted after 1848. In France, suffrage was also expanded in 1848. However, even with the expanded voting rights the French population chose another Bonaparte who established himself as emperor within three years, rather than a socialist or even a strong republican.[70] Even in 1871, with the constitution of the Third Republic promoting representative government, conservatives negotiated over the prospects of returning the monarchy.[71] In the United States, the individual states controlled voting criteria. By the 1840s, most of the rules requiring property ownership for voting had been eliminated in the individual states.

As the Western states were moving in the direction of heavy industrial production, and its enormous concentrations of wealth and power, suffrage is extended to the masses of the population. While this did have the effect of creating some political movements committed to the expropriation of property by the poor, in the form of the creation of socialist and communist political parties, these parties did not have the effect of overthrowing the social order and the structure of wealth.[72] Such an outcome would seem to contradict the idea that democratic institutions in civil society produce conditions in which all will pursue their own self-interest. However, such a conclusion misinterprets the subtle side of power.

By the middle of the nineteenth century the effects of national integration had taken hold in Europe. The slow process of integrating the poor into the democratic processes actually generated a conservative outcome. In reality, the poor were not much of a threat to the emerging centralized economic and political institutions. Much of Europe was still agricultural, with the rural population conditioned by centuries of feudal oversight. In France, an alliance developed between the industrialists and the rural population to protect the rights of property.[73] In Germany, a similar situation developed with the elites of heavy industry forming an alliance with the Junkers and other feudal elements of the landed aristocracy.[74]

Thus, even while the structural conditions of class are being transformed, and the possibilities for a class-based structure of political power are emerging, structural transformation along property lines does not occur. Is this the result of "false-consciousness," nationalistic propaganda, strongly traditional elements of socialization such as the church, or some other mechanism? It is our view that there is another dynamic taking place at the end of the nineteenth century. With the expansion of the state, and the rise of state bureaucracy penetrating into every greater areas of personal and public life, there is a transformation of how the state is viewed and the factors that produce legitimacy. Such a transformation leads to the legitimacy of state power, even as it moves away from the practice of consent as the mechanism of legitimation.

The Transformation of Legitimacy: The Logic of Post-Efficacy Democracy

While suffrage was expanding, and the fear of extending suffrage to the unpropertied class was waning, there was another process taking place. During the nineteenth century the nation-state emerged as the predominant social institution. Church power had been in decline since the Renaissance. Modern science and literacy, coupled with the rise of trade and commerce, had ended the reign of the parallel institutions of monarchy and church hierarchy.

But the emergence of "modern" institutions brought a need for integration and regulation as had never before been the case. Production for self-sufficiency, the production model of the feudal estate, had not produced the need for any regularity or standardization outside of its own environment. Industrialization enhanced a process that had been emerging along with trade, the creation of institutional structures with wider scope and enhanced political power. Efficiency demands some levels of standardization in production, even if only for agreed upon measures of weight and size.

The nation-state emerged as the institution responsible for managing those conditions. It is the locus of institutional power, expanding its reach into every corner of its territory. In the process, it is taking over ever larger domains of life, managing economic activity, promoting the growth of industrial production, standardizing practices, and creating educational infrastructures. As a result, the operational definition of legitimacy is transformed.

Modern political thought, going back to John Locke, has characterized legitimacy as a political phenomenon generated from the consent of the governed. With the expansion of suffrage the question of legitimacy would seem secure within the democratic states. However, the democratic processes that evolved in the Western states afford little opportunity to address the legitimacy of the structures themselves. Rather, legitimacy is associated with the ability to replace personalities within the existing structures. Legitimacy is extended to the actions of individual rulers who, as their popularity wanes, are replaced through the democratic act of voting. If policies are driven by the requirements of the system as a whole, this will only produce marginal impacts on policy. Institutional legitimacy, thus, remains unchallenged, even as the power of institutions expands.

This means the measure of legitimacy is altered and expanded. Institutional legitimacy is transformed from the exclusive domain of the political to a systemic level as the power of economic and social institutions become more concentrated. The performance of individual leaders is increasingly measured by their ability to execute the function of management in the areas of economic performance and security. Political legitimacy takes the character of *systemic performance* as political and economic power is concentrated.

If democracy is defined as a political structure in which all the members of society have the ability to influence the direction of public policy through the acts of political participation, then the concentration of power within the newly centralized institutional setting moves away from this idea. Legitimacy as personal political efficacy is replaced by a model measured by systems maintenance.

The system requires management. Public participation is limited to a referendum on the system managers, not on the systemic logic itself. The centralization of management for the generation of national wealth and power moved political practice into what can be termed *post-efficacy democracy*. Within such a system, the direction of policy is largely dictated by a self-sustaining logic that views the systemic imperatives of the institutional order as the operative substantive values directing the path of binding political decisions. There are still institutions that periodically poll the public's sentiments, but the domain over which the public has real choices is pushed further and further to the margins of social life.

This is not to say that there are not competing models of the growth paradigm. By the late nineteenth century there are differing strategies as to the direction economic management should take. Applied to economic development, the question of performance generated three competing models of progress: socialism, Social Darwinism, and what was called "populism" in the United States. These three models each propose a different strategy of societal integration based on their positions toward the concentration of wealth emerging in the industrial age.

From the socialist perspective there is an internal logic within capitalism that will result in the depression of the wages of the industrial work-force. As the market demands increased profits for expansion, the competition among the workers, increasingly made replaceable by machine production, intensifies and drives down wages.[75] Such a process generates a structural impediment to economic development as an impoverished workforce will not have the means to purchase the goods being produced within the factories. In the end, this results in overproduction of industrial goods and a downward spiral in the economy resulting in a depression.[76] While Lenin asserted that such a collapse can be postponed by imperialist policies, the internal logic of this process remains.[77]

For the socialists, economic progress requires the nationalization production and the replacement of a capitalist economy with a planned economy. This will require an agency to mobilize the resources necessary for the industrial processes, while eliminating the market mechanism for the determination of prices and wages. This prescription is supported by an ethic that stresses the alienating nature of wage-labor and a model of subjectivity that excludes the idea of competitive struggle as endemic to the human condition.[78]

Social Darwinism argues that the maximization of material progress will occur if government allows the natural forces of the exchange economy to manifest a differentiated hierarchy in terms of material rewards and political power. As William Graham Sumner described the process, the concentration of wealth is one step in social evolution which will ultimately include the concentration of power and control, intensified social discipline, and the more perfect integration of society.[79] The benefits of concentrated economic and political power will pass down through all the economic classes.[80]

Sumner criticized democracy because of the power it extends to the poor. Democracy contains the potential to upset this *natural* development because he feared the desire of the masses for the possessions of the wealthy would be manifest in government policies that removed the social steering power of those who have proven their superior skills. Ironically, even while Sumner criticized state intervention,[81] it should be acknowledged that historically the development of concentrated capital has relied on the state to create the structural means for its ascension.

In contrast to the socialist and the Social Darwinist, the progressive era attitude toward the concentration of wealth is decidedly negative. From this perspective, government policy should promote the dispersion of wealth within society, while maintaining the basic structure of private accumulation. It is for this reason the American Populist Party denounced the devaluation of silver in the 1892 platform.[82] From their perspective, economic growth requires a population with the resources to stimulate demand for the economic goods produced.

This position developed into Keynesian economics in the early part of the twentieth century and became part of the economic justification for the creation of the welfare state in both Europe and the United States. By maintaining the purchasing power of the masses, the capitalist system can be sustained, albeit in less than its pure form. The circulation of capital within the national economies will be sufficient to keep the economy growing.

Despite their differences, these three models are based on common themes. Each of these economic strategies is predicated on the concentration of capital that is taking place as a result of industrial production. Each requires the active participation of a central authority to assist in producing the structural conditions for its vision of economic organization. Therefore, in each of these models systemic legitimacy is tied to a measure of economic performance that each seeks to justify within its own model of economic logic. With political legitimacy tied to economic performance, the continued expansion and centralization of institutional power is assured as long as the centralization of production continues. As a result, each of these models requires the enhanced power of the central national institutions.

The state as *manager* of economic and social affairs is the central point of the model of political analysis known as *corporatism*. While the argument of this work is not identical with that of the corporatist literature, we agree with the proponents of the corporatist model that there is a systemic interest in which power is brought to bear in order to manage the functioning of the national institutions.[83] As expressed by Pahl and Winkler, the state expands its regulatory power to promote the goals of order, unity, nationalism, and success.[84] This management can be carried out without the transfer of corporate ownership to the state.

While useful, it is our view that the corporatist model has a tendency to view government as too independent from the historical dimensions of the systemic logic under which it operates. From our perspective, it is sufficient to claim that there is an "affinity" among the interest of the industrial sector and the state in which the argument of who is the most causally significant is functionally irrelevant. Particularly with the age of heavy industrial production, the interest of the state and those of the private financial actors were closely attuned, with the state assisting in the centralization of capital.

Ideology and Material Necessity

The popular view on the relation between democracy and state power is expressed by Roland Stromberg. In the modern period the idea of progress is associated with the growth of democratic institutions.[85] Democratic procedures are defended by liberals, socialists, and nationalists alike, as the mechanism by which their agendas can be

pursued in the most rational process available, given the inherent
equality and rationality of the population. The natural "self-interested"
character of the individual is manifested in the competing organized
interests in the social realm. This is what Robert Dahl refers to as the
structure of "polyarchy."[86]

However, this description of the trends or tendencies of political
behavior should not be confused with the broader developments of
modern institutional life. The creation of democratic institutions has not
caused a decline in the centralization of power nor slowed the expansion
of the *rights of power*. In fact, the contrary is the case. The
democratization of institutions has generated an expansion of state power
and the extension of government activity, as it is now asserted both as
legitimately formulated and reflecting the interest of the whole. This
remains one of the truly remarkable achievements of power in the West:
the ability of institutions to engage the populous in the creation and
extension of instruments for the coordination and mass mobilization of
human activity in service of an institutional ethos. In an age of literacy,
printing, and an exchange economy, it is unlikely that such a project
could be carried out without democracy.

But the process of expanding state power also needs an
accompanying discourse of legitimation. For this process, Immanuel
Kant is more illustrative than Locke. Writing at the end of the eighteenth
century, Kant helps provide the ideological tools for the expansion of
state power. With the assertion of the categorical and practical
imperatives, Kant gives an account of the transcendental nature of
morality. Reason ascends to universal moral law through the use of these
mechanisms. Hence, the outcome of deliberative processes regarding the
law has the character of universal morality.

Kant makes it clear that universal morality informs the content of
justice and the content of law.[87] Therefore, the content of law exists as
the externalization of transcendent reason. This is the basis of the modern
notion of natural law, and has supported the expansion of legal statutes
and state power. If the expansion of law and state power under
constitutional governments reflects the externalization of *reason* itself, it
must be considered the product of the very essence of reason itself. This
is the logical bridge between the political writings of Kant and Hegel.

The externalization of reason, as law, becomes the operative
teleology of the state. The project, which Kant asserted is driven by
nature itself,[88] is the expansion of the state and its powers. The
legitimacy of the law is not grounded in the idea of consent, but in a
principle far more flexible. "...[I]f there is a mere possibility that a

people might consent to a law, then it is a duty to consider that the law is just, even though at the moment the people might be in such a position or have a point of view that would result in their refusing to give their consent to it if asked."[89]

The logic is now complete for the movement away from a notion of democracy as individual or group efficacy. The notion of consent applies to the individual role-players within the system of power relations, not the structure of power relations themselves. Democracy, as the structural objective of political association, gives way to system performance as the measure of legitimacy

What this suggests is that in the eighteenth and nineteenth centuries there was a growing body of ideological work that served as a foundation for the expansion of state power. These works provided the support for the processes already taking place by suggesting its "natural" or "rational" character. Hegel went even further than Kant, extending Kant's mystification of the law to the mystification of the state itself. However, such mystification of the law and the state ignores the material conditions that gave rise to centralized power. These forces are considerable in number, but they can be classified in three general categories; the communicative, the economic, and the territorial.

Administration on any level requires a degree of communicative skill and expertise. The rise in literacy rates during the nineteenth century provides the means by which centralized structures of administration can expand their reach. Literacy helped the process of national integration, as state-sponsored education began to teach the notion of national identity to a population largely consisting of rural peasants. This process was enhanced by the technology of printing and its advances during the eighteenth and nineteenth centuries. Further, the rise in literacy was essential to administration at the center, as the formation of the university and various institutions were created to aid the government in the formation of policy. Finally, some notion of literacy is essential for the creation and gathering of data for the management and control of the various agencies of the state apparatus. The rational-legal form of rule that is associated with bureaucracy would be impossible without the generations of knowledge and the technical means to use it.

The requirements of a competitive economic system built on exchange are manifested in the drive to open up new territories to resource and merchandise extraction, and as the source of new markets for commodities. This process required the broadest possible regularity of law and custom in order to facilitate the processes. Government expanded its power in order to make the environment compatible for the rise of industrial capitalism. This could not be done without the centralization of power, even as governments pursued a strategy of deregulating property under the liberal economic paradigm.

Regularity in the law and the tax code is paralleled by regularity in the production process itself. At first, this process centered on conditions within the nation-states, as mass production required the standardization of technology, railroad gauges, and machine tools. But such a process cannot avoid the imperatives of an exchange economy. The internationalization of agreements, only in its infancy in the nineteenth century, will be driven to new heights in the twentieth century in the service of exchange. The centralization of power will then move to a new stage.

Finally, the material conditions for the centralization of power in the nineteenth century must be addressed within the context of national territory. As a historical product, the nation-state system arose out of the conflict over territory and identity. Once fixed, the boundaries required the turning inward of the processes of identity formation. Nationhood is something that must be conditioned.

However, once successful the power that can be generated by the system of national identification can be enormous. From the Napoleonic invasions to the beginning of World War I, Europe underwent a process of nationalization. To compete against a neighbor required integration and discipline.

Order and efficiency, the substantive values of the economic system, also became the values of the state. This is what Max Weber discussed in his critique of Western rationalism.[90] Both institutions create task-oriented hierarchies, with rational training, formal rules, and a division of labor that separates the workers from the instruments of production. The end of this process of rationalization is the increased concentration of power.

The expansion of activity by the state requires the rationalization and formalization of ever greater aspects of human existence. This is carried out through the generation of laws. The law is used to both discipline and condition. The law legitimates the state's access to the human bodies in order to assure that bodies are put to socially important uses.[91] Following the logic of Weber's position, Michel Foucault asserted that the expansion of state power is exercised through an uninterrupted system of surveillance and hierarchical ordering. The legal system exists to give sanction to the entire system of discipline.[92] The influence of the system of power spreads to the limits of the technical carrying capacity of the system as a whole. In this way, the disciplinary power of the state is expanded along with the *rationality* of its formal structures of organization.

Subjectivity in the Industrial Age

In his book, *Surveillance, Power, and Modernity,* Christopher Dandeker describes the stepwise process of expanding state power.

> In matters of police, health and other aspects of the state supervision of society, the overall patterns of central state intervention were very similar. Each involved a succession of distinct phases. Permissive legislation was followed by compulsory legislation, which was, in turn, followed by partial state funding of official activities. In this third phase, state funding depended on the observation of minimum standards laid down by the central authority, and these standards were monitored by an "inspectorate." Then followed a degree of central coordination in procedure and policy, and finally there was a phase of rationalization in organization, through amalgamations and related measures.[93]

Political institutions are not the inhibitors of this process, but are its enablers. Through the electoral process, the expansion of state power into ever greater areas of human activity is legitimated. The logic of efficiency demands the routinization of behavior and the systemization of all aspects of social life. Instrumental logic has become substantive logic. Efficiency in production and administration is enhanced by an orderly society, disciplined into the necessities of labor and conditioned into the *normal* patterns of social life. The modern state exists, in part, to put the stamp of reason on the processes determined by the historical conditions dictated by industrial production and the nation-state system. As Max Weber saw it, such a process will have a corrosive effect on the range of individual actions, and undermine spontaneity and creative adaptation to new circumstances and conditions dictated by environmental change.

All of these changes have a profound impact on the conditions in which subjectivity is constructed. The subject is transformed into a component of the mass. The expansion of the public sphere shrinks the private. The centralization of the material instruments of dissemination creates mass conformity. Mass production raises the material conditions of existence, but the division of labor in the production process generates a subject whose value is diminished in the work process.

Mass politics reflect the character of these conditions. "Equality" means substitutability within mass politics. One is equal in relation to the collective. However, "position," and "role," are defined by the character of individual responsibility within the institutional order. One carries out the expectations dictated by structure. The space for individual action and private meaning is diminished as the dictates of mass institutional necessities rule the day.

Mass structures sustain themselves by the transformation of the environment in which they exist. Hence, what is defined as "rational" are those practices that enhance the conditions for the maintenance of institutional power. The legal code is modified to resolve the conflicts generated by the centralization of power. Political power is expanded in order to enhance the calculability and stability necessary for the maintenance of mass forms of production and administration.

Conclusion

The period between 1800 and 1914 witnessed the growth and centralization of power to the technical limits of the nation-state system. Literacy and the technology of printing helped spread nationalist identities. The development of industrial systems, both in production and transport, allowed for the economic and political integration of territories.

During this period there was great symbiosis between the interests of expanding corporate entities and the institutions of the nation-state. The increase in corporate profits required the transformation of the legal environment, giving autonomy to corporate entities, and the creation of conditions for the concentration of resources for expanding capital intensive production. The creation of a militarily strong state required a vibrant industrial sector, able to produce both massive quantities of commodities, and the advanced war-fighting hardware necessary for expanding state power. Therefore, both the interests of capital and the national interests of the state profited from the expansion of the state's power.

When this growth in material power was coupled with the spread of nationalism, and its tendency to create the estranged *other* as a foil for state power, the unfolding of the events leading up to 1914 seem less a stumble, and take on an almost inevitable character. The Great War is the culmination of an ongoing process of industrial growth and military expansion coupled with a method of legitimating the existential angst among a people, now carved up into competing camps across Europe. All this takes place at a time in which democratic institutions are expanding. The context for the Second World War was not so different.

However, in the period after World War II, some of the internal contradictions in this symbiosis were beginning to manifest themselves. The nation-state and the corporation do not always have mutually reinforcing agendas, and the marriage of convenience that emerged between the corporation and the state in the nineteenth century began to show signs of strain by the latter half of the twentieth. The nation-state appears increasingly as an obstacle to increasing corporate profits, a nostalgic anachronism in an age of globalized commerce. New technologies are creating the material infrastructure for systemic level transformation.

While the impetus for this transformation is manifesting itself in private capital markets, the state appears increasingly impotent in dealing with the tasks for which it is being held accountable. A performance-based system of legitimacy means that the state is expected to be responsible for a widening array of functions, as the systemic level of complexity expands. At the same time, the globalized nature of these problems leaves the state impotent in dealing with the emerging crises. This is one of the points in Jürgen Habermas's work, *The Legitimation Crisis*.[94] The industrial democracies are in a precarious position. The demands for performance are occurring at a time of decreasing state effectiveness, creating legitimacy problems for the nation-state. These are subjects that will be developed in the next chapter.

Notes

1. Powell, Rebecca, *Literacy as a Moral Imperative: Facing the Challenges of a Pluralistic Society* (Lanham, MD: Rowman and Littlefield, 1999), 59.

2. Dewey, John, *Democracy and Education: An Introduction to the Philosophy of Education* (New York: Macmillan, 1916).

3. Barber, Benjamin, *An Aristocracy of Everyone: The Politics of Education and the Future of America* (New York: Ballantine Books, 1992).

4. Vincent, David, *The Rise of Mass Literacy: Reading and Writing in Modern Europe* (Cambridge, UK: Polity, 2000), 9.

5. Soltow, Lee and Edward Stevens, *The Rise of Literacy and the Common School in the United States: A Socioeconomic Analysis to 1870* (Chicago: University of Chicago Press, 1981), 174.

6. Vincent, 7.

7. Vincent, 9.

8. Soltow, 174.

9. Pacey, Arnold, *The Culture of Technology* (Cambridge, UK: MIT Press, 1983), 20.

10. Weber, Eugen. *Peasants into Frenchman: The Modernization of Rural France 1870-1914* (Stanford, CA: Stanford University Press, 1976).

11. Vincent, 6.

12. Vincent, 6.

13. Eisenstein, Elizabeth L., "Some Conjectures About the Impact of Printing on Western Society and Thought: A Preliminary Report," *Journal of Modern History,* 40:1 (March 1968), 56.

14. Anderson, Benedict, *Imagined Communities* (London: Verso, 1991), 36.

15. Clair, Colin, *The History of European* Printing (London: Academic Press, 1976), 121.

16. Clair, 121.

17. Clair, 121.

18. Clair, 120.

19. Anderson, 39-42 and Fussel, Stephan, *Gutenberg and the Impact of Printing,* trans. Douglas Martin (Aldershot, Hamshire: Ashgate, 2003), 113–145.

20. Clair, 312.

21. Steinburg, S.H., *Five Hundred Years of Printing* (London: Oak Knoll Press and the British Library, 1996), 149.

22. Clair, 313.

23. Buchanan, R. A., *The Power of the Machine* (London: Penguin, 1994), 48.

24. Nussbaum, Frederick L., *A History of the Economic Institutions of Modern Europe* (New York: F. S. Crofts, 1935), 86.

25. Buchanan, 48.

26. Mitchell, B. R., *International Historical Statistics: Europe 1750–1993* (London: Macmillan, 1998), 684-686.

27. Hillstrom, Kevin and Laurie Collier Hillstrom, *The Industrial Revolution in America: Iron and Steel* (Santa Barbara, CA: ABC-Clio, 2005), 12.

28. Henderson, W. O., *The Industrial Revolution in Europe: Germany, France, Russia, 1815–1914* (Chicago: Quadrangle Books, 1961), 158.

29. Buchanan, 106.

30. Henderson, 65.

31. Lebergott, Stanley, "The Patterns of Employment Since 1800" in *American Economic History*, ed. Seymour E. Harris (New York: McGraw-Hill, 1961), 282.

32. DuBoff, Richard B., *Acuumulation and Power: An Economic History of the United States* (Armonk, New York: M. E. Sharp, 1989), 17.

33. Nussbaum, 324.

34. Du Boff, 39.

35. Henderson, 157.

36. Henderson, 62.

37. Nussbaum, 273.

38. Nussbaum, 271.

39. Weber, Max. "Socialism" in *Max Weber: Selections in Translation,* ed. W. G. Runciman, trans. E. Matthews (Cambridge, UK: Cambridge University Press, 1978).

40. Henderson, 64.

41. Henderson, 178.

42. DuBoff, 59.

43. DuBoff, 59.

44. Nussbaum, 346.

45. Nussbaum, 346.

46. Nussbaum, 347.

47. Nussbaum, 278.

48. Nussbaum, 276.

49. Weber, Max, *Economy and Society* (Berkeley: University of California Press, 1978), 1393.

50. Weber, 1978, 1393.

51. Finer, Herman, *Theory and Practice of Modern Government* (Westport, CT: Greenwood Press, 1949), 714.

52. Finer, 710.

53. Finer, 711.

54. Raadschelders, Jos C. N., *Handbook of Administrative History* (New Brunswick, NJ: Transaction Publishers, 1998), 112.

55. Finer, 727.

56. Finer, 794–796.

57. Gladden, E. N., *A History of Public Administration*, Vol. II (London: Frank Cass, 1972), 313.

58. Finer, 764.

59. Finer, 750.

60. Nord, Philip, "Origins of the Third Republic in France," in *The Social Construction of Democracy: 1870–1990*, ed. George Reid Andrews and Herrick Chapman (New York: New York University Press, 1995), 38.

61. Gladden, 311.

62. Weber, 1978, 1401.

63. Weber, 1978, 1402.

64. Weber, 1978, 1402.

65. Mitchell, 569–586.

66. Nussbaum, 280.

67. Nussbaum, 280.

68. Finer, 230.

69. Finer, 228.

70. Stromberg, Roland N., *Democracy: A Short Analytical History* (Armonk, NY: M. E. Sharpe, 1996), 41.

71. Nord, 31.

72. We do not want to suggest here that these parties were not influential in improving the conditions of the working class: expanding working safety, securing better wages, creating social "safety nets," and other benefits. It is simply our contention that they did not produce what the bourgeoisie had feared, the wholesale appropriation of private property in the most advance industrial states.

73. Nord, 32.

74. Eley, Geoff, "The Social Construction of Democracy in Germany: 1871-1933," in *The Social Construction of Democracy: 1870–1990* (New York: New York University Press, 1995), 94.

75. Marx, Karl, "The Communist Manifesto," in *The Marx-Engels Reader*, ed. Robert Tucker (New York: Norton, 1978), 479.

76. Marx, Karl. "The Communist Manifesto," 478.

77. Lenin, Vladimir, "Imperialism, The Highest Stage of Capitalism," in *The Lenin Anthology*, ed. Robert Tucker (New York: Norton, 1975).

78. Marx, Karl, "The Economic and Philosophic Manuscripts of 1844," in *The Marx-Engels Reader*, ed. Robert Tucker (New York: Norton, 1978), 84.

79. Sumner, William Graham, "The Concentration of Wealth: Its Economic Justification," in *Social Darwinism: Selected Essays*, (Englewood Cliffs, NJ: Prentice Hall, 1963), 151.

80. Sumner, "The Concentration of Wealth," 156.

81. Sumner, William Graham, "What the Social Classes Owe to Each Other," in *American Political Thought*, ed. Kenneth Dolbeare and Michael Cummings (Washington, D.C.: Congressional Quarterly Press, 2004), 272.

82. "The Populist Party Platform (1892)" in *American Political Thought*, eds. Kenneth Dolbeare and Michael Cummings (Washington, D.C.: Congressional Quarterly Press, 2004), 298.

83. Schmitter, Phillipe, "Still the Century of Corporatism," in *The Review of Politics* 36, 85-126. Williamson, P. J., *Varieties of Corporatism* (Cambridge, UK: Cambridge University Press, 1985), 167.

84. Pahl, R. E. and Winkler, J. T., "The Coming Corporatism," in *New Society* 10 (October 1974).

85. Stromberg, 39.

86. Dahl, Robert, *Dilemmas of Pluralist Democracy* (New Haven, CT: Yale University Press, 1982).

87. Kant, Immanuel, *The Metaphysical Elements of Justice* (New York: Bobbs-Merrill, 1965), 45.

88. Kant, Immanuel, "Eternal Peace," in *The Philosophy of Kant*, ed. Carl J. Friedrich (New York: Modern Library, 1977), 448.

89. Kant, Immanuel, "Theory and Practice," in *The Philosophy of Kant*, ed. Carl J. Friedrich (New York: Modern Library, 1977), 422.

90. For an extensive discussion of Weber's position see Koch, Andrew M., *Romance and Reason: The Ontological and Social Sources of Alienation in the Writings of Max Weber* (Lanham, MD: Roman and Littlefield, 2006).

91. Foucault, Michel, *Discipline and Punish* (New York: Vintage, 1995), 136.

92. Foucault, 302.

93. Dandeker, Christopher, *Surveillance, Power and Modernity* (New York: St. Martins, 1990), 122.

94. Habermas, Jürgen, *The Legitimation Crisis* (Boston: Beacon Press, 1975).

Chapter 6

Collective Power in the Twenty-first Century

Introduction

In the preceding chapters we have argued that the rise of sovereign political power is tied to material conditions that promote the collectivization and integration of people into administrative units. As we have discussed, such developments can take many forms, from the generation of common languages, the rise of writing and literacy, the advance of effective institutions of administration, and the consolidating tendencies of wealth and production. Each of these will enhance the material conditions that give rise to and expand the institutionalization and centralization of power.

We agree with Michel Foucault that power resides in all organizational structures, and have generally followed the proposition that organizations are the generators and repositories of power. This is the case because organizations incorporate the individual into complexes of expectations, assigned roles, and patterns of behavior. Through this transformative process identity, or subjectivity, is constructed. Individuals carry out tasks in the service of collective organizations in which they have assigned roles and incorporate this recognition as part of their identity. Recent history has demonstrated that national identification is particularly strong, as this association has created populations willing to sacrifice their lives in the service of that construction.

In the last two chapters we have begun stressing the importance of economic factors in the collectivization of sovereign power. In Chapter

Four we examined the intersection of literacy, the nation-state as an institutional order of sovereignty, and the rise of national market economies. It was our contention that these trends all came together to create a unique, interdependent set of forces that enhanced the formation of a common model of domination across the Western states. The territorial state was characterized by a centralized administrative apparatus whose functional stability was tied to a mechanism in which a larger proportion of the population was afforded some influence over the direction of collective action.

In Chapter Five we discuss a changing situation. Democracy, as a process allowing greater input from the population, was expanded as a result of an affinity between two forces. The increased literacy of the population had a transformative effect on the construction of subjectivity. Literacy both increased the likelihood that the population had the technical capacities of rule, while at the same time, restructured the political expectations that tied institutional legitimacy to increased access to power.

However, the nation-state's ability to control the instruments of dissemination directly, as in the case of mass education, or indirectly, as in the case of political information, give it enormous power in affecting the attitudes of the populations that identify with these constructions. When this is coupled with the massive concentration of wealth generated by the advent of heavy industrial production, to which the expanding power of the state is now coupled, the system of domination undergoes a transformation. What emerged was a post-efficacy form of democracy. In practical terms, this means that the greater the distance between the individual actors and the structures that wield sovereign power, the less efficacious practices such as voting tend to be. The result is that economic and political institutions are increasingly managed according to the systemic logic of the institutional structures themselves. The matters over which the public has direct control within the democratic institutions are pushed to the margins in favor of a model of social relations in which the economic and political policies are directed to the goals of growth and stability.

In this chapter we will examine the transformation of conditions that gave rise to the power of sovereign political organizations from the mid-twentieth century into the twenty-first. After World War II, forces that were pushing the structures of power in the direction of globalization prior to the two world wars take on a new impetus. Developments in the area of energy production and new technologies in communications and transportation create the material conditions in which greater institutional consolidation is possible. The systemic imperatives of capitalist production, matters of finance, resource interdependence, trade, and transnational infrastructure development, also push an emerging global system of commerce toward ever greater political integration. By the middle of the twentieth century it is clear that the national structures are simply inadequate to the task of managing a range of issues that are ever more global in nature. As a result, rationality demands the rise of numerous new institutional forms from which an embryonic form of global identity takes shape.

It is impossible to speak of this transformation, still in its infancy, without acknowledging the critical role of technology. The most significant technology leading these changes was electricity. Electricity has transformed the social, economic, and political landscape of the twentieth century. Its enormous impact on society was due to the various uses to which electromagnetism can be put. Electricity has properties that are valuable in manufacturing, as it can be transformed into mechanical power in the production process. It can substitute for the use of coal or petroleum in the generation of heat. However, its most profound impact is in the arena of communications and computerization.   By the middle of the twentieth century electricity had reshaped communications from the transfer of point-to-point wired exchanges via the telegraph to a vast network of one-way information transfer systems via radio and television. The ability of such a medium to socialize a population cannot be overstated. The technologies convey a common history, ideology, and normative pattern by the very act of mass broadcasting. As these technologies largely developed within a national framework, they have tended to reinforce the public's identification with national sovereignty and national interests.

However, by the end of the century the environment made possible by electricity was undergoing another material transformation. The arrival of computers and the digital age creates the possibility for the construction and transfer of data that is not filtered by national institutions. Further, because the new digital network is global in character, it enhances the formation of post-national institutions. This has clearly been occurring in the processes of production, distribution, and consumption. It is our view that economic integration cannot occur without some political integration. We have also seen movement in this direction as well. By the end of the twentieth century the addition of digital media, global data networks, and computerization had altered the scope of organizations and the depth of their power.

This new material reality serves as the background for the construction of new sets of power relations. If the period prior to World War I began the post-efficacy democratic era, because of the emerging imperatives of material growth and political stability, the twenty-first century incorporates a logic that is decidedly post-national. The material conditions generated from the age of globalization create tensions with the national forms of collective power that have been in place since the Peace of Westphalia. In economics, finance capital emerges as a force separate from production. It is a necessary condition of production, but lacking any particular connection to geographic location or national affiliation. Global media, the internet, and the instruments of culture present mounting difficulties for the institutions of national power, as they create alternative images and narratives of identity that compete with national symbols in the contemporary environment. Such developments enhance the tensions among a de-democratized public, the forces of world capital, and national institutions increasingly at the mercy of new structures that wield power on a global level.

An ideology that fully articulates the rationale of the emerging condition has yet to be completely formed. This is the result of instability in the structures out of which identity is manifest. The ideology of national politics was generated in the early modern period and is ill-equipped to address the global nature of these trends. This is largely due to the competing forces that have been unleashed by these developments and the contradictory nature of their prescriptive logics. However, even if a new post-national ideology has yet to be fully formed, the evolution of the institutional structures for its generation and fortification are under way.

Energy and National Power

Energy use has been a component of human settlements since the dawn of civilization. It has taken various forms, from wood to the atom. However, throughout much of history, the appropriation of energy from nature has largely been a local phenomenon. People used what was locally available. As a political force, therefore, there was little influence from the appropriation of energy toward the collectivization of political affiliations. All this changed with the industrial age.

The fuels of the industrial age promoted the centralization of energy production and encouraged the creation of mass industrial processes. These both reflected and enhanced the processes of integration taking place more generally. Such scale required the mass capitalization of investments, which in turn, required the concentration of finance capital. Such concentrated economic power expanded the domain of national governments in the regulation of finance, capital, and the expanding infrastructure.

Coal was the energy source that fueled the industrial revolution. Between 1860 and 1910 the extraction of coal increased dramatically. In Great Britain, coal production increased from 87.9 metric tons annually to 269 metric tons. In France, coal production increased from 8.3 to 38.4 metric tons during the same period. In Germany the rate increased from 18.4 to 222 metric tons.[1]

Coal had an advantage of reinforcing both the national economies and the nationalist aspirations of the European powers. Each of the major powers in Europe, along with the United States, had significant coal reserves which allowed for the growth of domestic industries without the requirements of wholesale international trade and transport. Therefore, the use of coal in the process of industrialization was not a significant economic force in pushing the major powers in the direction of creating international structures, regardless of how significant it was in spurring the growth of national institutions.

However, even by the early twentieth century coal production as a percentage of overall energy consumption began a long and steady decline.[2] After World War II coal production returned to prewar levels but began to decline by the late 1950's and early 1960's. This is largely the result of the use of another fossil fuel, oil. However, the distribution of oil was not as widely dispersed among the Western industrial powers as coal. This began the internationalization of the energy industry.

The period from the end of World War II until the 1970's was what Mason Willrich calls the "cheap energy era."[3] Such a result was largely due to the abundant and inexpensive oil from the Middle East. This facilitated the rapid recovery of the European and Japanese economies, as the price of energy declined in relation to the other factors of production.[4] Oil and natural gas were increasingly used in place of coal for the firing of boilers in factories. Oil was also particularly attractive in the development of transport.

However, because oil was not evenly dispersed across the globe, it needed to be imported, even in the United States. The result was that by the 1970's, oil accounted for 15% of the total value of world trade.[5] In 1960 the major oil-producing countries created The Organization of Petroleum Exporting Countries (OPEC) in order to manage their domestic resource in the wake of expanding demand and the penetration of their economies by foreign corporations and finance capital.

The creation of OPEC is only one example of the growing internationalization of energy and the resulting structures that evolved for the management of energy resources. Energy industries emerged as multinational concerns, initially for the purpose of extraction, but later began the processing of energy resources.[6] Such investments required the opening of financial markets and institutions to promote the development of the industry. These processes have been facilitated by the General Agreement on Tariff and Trade and the World Bank. The creation of the European Common Market was, in part, designed to consolidate the production of energy resources. The International Atomic Energy Agency (IAEA) was created in 1957 to monitor and promote the peaceful uses of atomic energy in the international environment.

The vast range of governmental and business activities that are involved in the energy industry are beyond the scope or focus of this work. However, it is clear that the internationalization of the energy industry is a major force in the direction of creating new institutional structures. Thus, the material conditions of a globalizing economy, more generally, are creating the need for the creation of new international structures and an expansion of the domain of political power. This situation cannot help but generate tension with the nation-state governments that had exclusive claims to sovereignty within their territories.[7]

While the internationalization trade is creating the conditions for a new set of international structures, the developments within the energy sector were also transforming the domestic social and political structures. This is particularly evident in the electric industry. Electricity generation had grown steadily throughout the twentieth century in all the major industrial economies. From 1900 to 1993 France went from 0 output to 454 gigawatt hours. Germany went from 1 to 560 gigawatt hours, and Great Britain from .2 to 301 gigawatt hours during the same period.[8] By the early 1990s the United States was generating close to 3000 gigawatt hours.[9]

Today, much of the discussion surrounding electricity production involves the topics of whether or not the utility should be privately or publicly owned, and the extent to which government should be involved in its regulation.[10] This is the result of the centralization of electricity production during the growth of the industry and its viewed status as a "natural monopoly." Unlike coal and petroleum, electricity requires that the user be connected to a network of wires linking the production facility to the consumer. This is most commonly referred to as the "grid." It is simply impractical, not to mention unprofitable, for more than one organization to string and maintain the wiring for the grid. As a result, the electricity industry developed in a very centralized fashion, with the scale of power generation plants growing throughout the postwar era in order to meet the increasing demand with the efficiency of production.

As Richard F. Hirsh describes it, electricity is the most versatile and diverse of energy sources.[11] It can be converted to mechanical energy through the use of electric motors, converted to heat for homes or industry, or transformed into digital impulses for the expanding telecommunications industry. Therefore, it is essential to industry, the financial sector, and all aspects of telecommunications. It is safe to assume that the role of electric power will expand throughout the twenty-first century.

The growth of the electric industry effects the political culture in several ways. The conditions of industrial generation of electricity have been a component of the consolidation of capital and resources since the beginnings of the industrial revolution. This enhances the centralization of power and domination within an expanding framework, on the national level. The direct influence on the construction of subjectivity needs to be understood on this level of massified culture more generally.

As the society becomes more dependent on the grid, the fragility and vulnerability of this dependence may be part of the impetus toward the development of new technologies. New technologies of power generation are under development. However, most are designed to augment the grid while cutting environmentally destructive production processes. Such a transformation does not alter the centralized form of generation and administration. The development of fusion reactors, wind farms, and large solar installations will only enhance the reliance on centralized production.

Micro generation, small-scale electric generators that produce power *on-site*, has the potential to transform both the means of power generation and the centralization of institutional structures that have dominated the industry since its inception.[12] However, in the United States, both the industry and the government bureaucracy are resisting attempts to decentralize the industry.[13] Despite all of these influences, the major impact of electricity will not be the method by which it is generated, but the uses to which it is put.

Electricity has augmented the processes of mechanical production, as electric motors can be substituted for petroleum or coal-fired steam engines. In that sense electricity does not constitute a revolutionary phenomenon. However, in the second half of the twentieth century the transformative potential of electricity became manifest. This is tied to its uses in varied forms of communication technologies and its role in the development of high-technology industries such as computers and robotics.

Electricity is the central material component in the emergence of these new sectors of the economy and is the foundation for the transformation of the subjectivity at the end of the twentieth century. This issue will be addressed in the next section.

Dissemination in the Electronic Age

Over the course of this work we have discussed a variety of methods by which ideas have been disseminated among the masses in order to provide a shared set of reference points. These reference points create a common arrangement of signs and metaphors for a people as they engage in political discourse. History has witnessed the development of various technologies for the dissemination and articulation of these reference points in the culture, from speech, to writing, to the printing press. Each established a mechanism by which the identity of people is constructed and disseminated across a given territory. In the nineteenth century the rise of mass education furthered the political dimension of this process of integration.

The process of mass education and enculturation continued in the twentieth century, but is augmented by new technologies of dissemination and integration. The twentieth century heralds the electronic age. After a brief discussion of the further centralization of the state's role in education, our attention will turn to the political significance of the electronic age and the new technologies of communication.

Central Administration and State Education

By the end of the nineteenth century, the major countries in Europe, along with the United States, had begun a program of mass literacy.[14] As was discussed in the preceding chapter, this process allowed for the dissemination of a national identity on a scale that had previously not existed. Schools taught national history, national heroes, and organized patriotic exercises, even at the elementary level.[15] This was particularly important in the countryside, as the traditional agents of socialization, churches and families, were replaced by state-sponsored education systems teaching national history as the binding force of the collective.

As Gerd Baumann puts it in the "Introduction" to *Civil Enculturation*:

> Without state schools, there would be no nations as we know
> them in northwestern Europe, no national conscience collec-
> tive, and no effective means of inculcating and rehearsing the
> conventions of the dominant political culture. . .[16]

Bauman continues by quoting A. D. Smith:

> . . . [C]ertainly, most governments since the end of the nine-
> teenth century have seen it as one of their prime duties to es-
> tablish, fund, and increasingly direct a mass system of public
> education -- compulsory, standardized, hierarchical, academy-
> supervised and diplomas-conferring – in order to create [both]
> an efficient labour force and [a] loyal, homogeneous citi-
> zenry.[17]

The political dimension of this argument was explored by Gladys A.
Wiggin in the work, *Education and Nationalism.* Wiggin argued that
education is necessary to the political survival of all states, totalitarian or
democratic. For a democracy, following the Jeffersonian ideal, education
is necessary for an informed electorate to make the best choices in choos-
ing leaders and directing the activities of institutions. In a totalitarian
society, education is necessary as an agent of state propaganda, as the
public must be convinced that the collective is superior to the citizens
that make it up.[18]

While it is our view that these two political functions are not as
neatly separated as Wiggin suggested, the political point, nevertheless,
holds. That mass public education has been indispensable to the rise of
the modern nation-state in the nineteenth and twentieth centuries. Each
state, in order to remain viable within the logic of the nation-state system, must create a legitimating process that includes a narrative that inte-
grates the populous into that administrative unit. Mass schooling becomes the central activity through which the reciprocal links between the
individuals and the nation-state are forged.[19]

Compulsory education, a reality in the major European states in the
nineteenth century, spreads to almost all European states by the 1930s.[20]
Also, by the 1930s most European states had some form of centralized
educational authority to oversee the content and quality of state-
sponsored educational institutions.[21] Even in states with federal constitu-
tions like Germany and the United States there were coordinating functions carried out on both the national and state levels.

The Beginning of Electronic Media

In the previous chapter the mechanical characteristics of electricity were discussed as part of the processes of industrialization. The electromagnetic properties of electricity can be transformed to kinetic energy for the movement of mechanical devices. Electric motors gradually replaced steam power and the internal combustion engine in some of the production processes by the turn of the twentieth century. However, electromagnetism has had a more profound impact on information technologies than in the area of industrial production, as it is the sole basis upon which these technologies developed.

The rise of telecommunications creates the environmental conditions for a transformation of human identity. Along with the growth of railroads, automobiles, steam and petroleum powered ships and aircraft, electronic media shrinks the psychological space in which people form their cultural identities. David Harvey argues time and space are the conditions of social action.[22] As such, a change in the way people perceive the expanse of their material world alters the expanse of their perceived domain of activity. People reorient themselves to the dimensions of their field of action.

These same technologies also alter the construction of time as a social phenomenon. Without the technologies to link distant spaces, all time is local. However, the linking of locales through transport and communications creates the need to standardize time. This takes place at the beginning of the telecommunications revolution in 1844, with the creation of standardized time. By the 1850s, Greenwich Mean Time is the global standard for communications.

The electronic age of communications begins with the telegraph. As with the printing press, a number of people working in different places, notably England, Germany, and the United States, create the final version of the technology. What is significant is the fact that what began as a series of experiments with electromagnetism in the 1820s and 1830s generates a new telegraph industry by the 1840s. In March 1843 the United States Congress passed an appropriations bill to fund the construction of the first segment of the telegraph. The first section, connecting Washington, D.C. and Baltimore, was operational by 1844.

Much the same was taking place on the European continent. Governments were interested in developing the technology for both national security and commercial purposes. By 1860, 730,000 telegrams were sent in Germany and 700,000 in France. By 1870 those numbers had grown significantly. In Germany and the United Kingdom, 8.6 million telegrams were sent, with the number in France at 5.7 million.[23]

There was also a demand for international telegraph service, initially linking the United States and Europe. While the first transatlantic cable was laid as early as 1858, the first reliable service was not completed until 1866. France laid a cable between the continent and a tiny island off of Newfoundland in 1869 to compete with the British-United States venture. In 1871 a Danish company laid line from Denmark through Siberia, into China and Japan.[24] By 1882 cable connected South America to the emerging international network.

The telegraph provided the first technology that created a global network of communications. For the United States and Europe, telegraph traffic continued to grow steadily, peaking in the 1920s. However, by the 1920s it was eclipsed by the growth of another technology receiving wide use, the telephone, and showed steady decline throughout the rest of the twentieth century.

Although there is some dispute over who invented the first telephone, the patent for the device was granted in the United States to Alexander Graham Bell in 1876. Demand for the service grew rapidly, with exchanges in the major cities in the United States developed between 1880 and 1883. However, the first transcontinental call did not take place until 1914.[25]

In Europe demand for the telephone also grew rapidly. By 1890 Germany had 58,000 phones in operation. France had 16,000. Britain had almost no service until the latter half of the 1890s. However, by 1920, the United Kingdom had 980,000 phones in operation. At the same time, France had 439,000 phones connected to the network, and Germany had 1.8 million.[26] By the end of the twentieth century there were tens of millions of phones in operation.

The telegraph and the telephone had the effect of shrinking space and time. News, business, and personal messages could travel from one place to another as fast, theoretically, as the electrons could travel. However, the limited number of wires and the technical boundaries of the equipment meant that the scope of the technology was limited. However, this would change with the invention of wireless technology.

Wireless Technology: Radio and Television

No technology of dissemination can be claimed to characterize the nature of the twentieth century as much as radio and television. These two inventions have the ability to reach mass audiences, listeners who are not required to be literate or educated in any way. These media can inform, entertain, educate, and motivate. Most significantly for the focus of this work, radio and television can transform the identities of the people within reach of their signals. They assign identities, set agendas, and mobilize the public. As such, the potential for centralizing political power implicit in these media is unparalleled in history.

As with the other inventions of the period, there are a number of notable researchers that were significant figures in bringing about the wireless age. However, the person most often credited with developing the commercial application of radio is Guglielmo Marconi. Marconi set up the Wireless Telegraph and Signal Company in London on July 20, 1897. In 1899 Marconi established a presence in the United States with the Marconi Wireless and Telegraph Company of America. By 1903 there were direct wireless telegraph communications between England and the United States.[27] These early units simply used the dots and dashes of Morse Code. However, in 1906 new equipment allowed for the transmission and reception of voice communications, and the radio age was born.

The invention of this new technology required a global standard. As was the case with Morse Code a few decades earlier, new technologies required the development of benchmarks that would apply across national boundaries. In 1906 the Bureau of the International Telegraph Union allocated frequencies for the new radio technology. This body was also charged with creating regulations for the emerging international industry.

As radio developed in the early twentieth century, two alternative models that reflected its potential emerged: the socio-political and the commercial. The socio-political model viewed the development of these new technologies through the lens of their impact on the social and political order of the society. It stressed the significance of the technology for informing the public and its potentials for building a political consensus among the domestic population for the direction of public policy. This model developed in Europe, and fostered direct government involvement in the industry.

The recognition of the political and social significance of the medium caused European governments to ban or restrict the use of paid ad vertising as a means to pay for the development of the industry. Instead, a system of taxes or fees was established for the listeners. Each receiver was registered and a monthly fee paid by the listener. This was the financing scheme behind the development of state-run radio, and later television, in England, France, Germany, and much of Europe. By 1925 the United Kingdom had 1.3 million licensed radios, with 1 million in Germany. By 1935 the number in both countries had increased by 600%.[28]

In the United States the commercial model was employed, but this was carried out with government assistance on a number of levels. In 1919 the government established the Radio Corporation of America with most of its stock going to two firms developing radio technology: General Electric and Westinghouse.[29] However, with the diffusion of radio technology, and little regulation, a large number of small stations proliferated. But most of these were local, nonprofit organizations that were run by religious groups, labor organizations, universities, or civic bodies for the benefit of their members.[30] As such, the early days of radio in the United States were largely commercial free. This would change dramatically in 1928 with General Order 40, announced by the Federal Radio Commission.

In order to address the crowding of the limited number of frequency bands, General Order 40 allocated time on a particular bandwidth to stations based on the popularity of the programming. It argued that rather than having an obligation to provide access to the airways for a variety of viewpoints and agendas, the government's responsibility was to provide the programming that was favored by the largest audience.[31] This opened the frontier to national networks that made profits through the sale of advertising. The potential of the medium for directing mass consumptive patterns was soon realized, and by the 1930s a small number of national broadcasting corporations began generating staggering profits, even during the Depression. These early funding models developed during the days of radio carried over into the television age.

The origins of television go back to the 1880s when a German scientist sent images over a wire.[32] In the 1920s wireless technology and cathode tubes were developed allowing for the emergence of a viable commercial industry. Regular television broadcasts began in France and Germany in 1935.[33] The United Kingdom followed in 1936 with the British Broadcasting Corporation moving into the field of television. By the 1990s Germany had over 30 million registered television sets. The United Kingdom had over 20 million.[34]

In 1941 the first commercial station in the United States went on the air in New York City. Unlike radio, television was a commercial venture from the start in the United States. However, the political implication of television in twentieth century politics soon became apparent. Harry Truman delivered the first televised broadcast from the White House in 1947 and, from that time forward, television has enhanced the power of presidents to put forward their agenda as the national priority.[35]

As with radio, European sensitivity to the vast social and political power of the media led to the development of television with strong governmental oversight. Although the European desire to overtly use the media's political potential had waned since the 1930s, the strong state oversight continued. As late as 1971, the German courts ruled that the state had a strong interest in regulating content because of television's power as a tool of mass communications.[36] However, by the 1980s technological changes were manifesting a transformation of the industry with global implications.

Since the 1960s the United States had been launching communications satellites. These were necessary as microwave transmissions do not curve with the earth's surface. In 1962 the Communications Satellite Act was passed by the United States Congress with the goal of creating a global system of satellite communications. Intelsat was formed as an international organization to manage the developing satellite industry. By 1980 there were 120 nations with 222 earth stations linked to the Intelsat system.[37]

As the reach of satellites increased, and technological developments enlarged the amount of data that the systems could carry, it was a small evolutionary step that brought television into the satellite era. However, as satellite communications became global it created the need for the standardization of both equipment and content, creating an imperative for integration. In some cases this was encouraged, as in Europe with the European Commission's creation of BABEL in 1986 to promote multi-lingual and multicultural program across Europe.[38] In others, satellite television was perceived as a threat to more traditional ways of life.

By 1998 there were 938 million television sets in three-quarters of the world's households.[39] While national governments have sought to control content and stress the transmission of domestic programming, there is an inevitable cosmopolitanism that comes from commercial programming seeking to expand its reach within a global market. This can be witnessed in the success of MTV and CNN as global phenomena.

The standardization of the technology generates both a global medium and an integrated system of production for the emerging technologies. Whether watching the first moon landing, world cup soccer, or military conflicts, this technology begins the process of cultural integration on a global level. While the national focus of identity formation is still predominant, the globalization of this technology can only serve to expand the psychological space which human beings see as the domain of their activity.

The Internet

The internet is the technology that is dominating the global transfer of information as the world moves into the twenty-first century. What started with the telegraph in the early nineteenth century has morphed into a technology that can store and send massive amounts of information and images at the speed of light. The effect of this technology on the distribution of power globally has yet to be fully realized.

The internet had its origins in a program created by the United States Defense Department and the Advanced Research Projects Agency. In the late 1960s they created ARPANET, connecting four research universities in the western United States.[40] By 1972 the number of computers connected to the network was fifty. But there was a problem. These computers did not all use the same operating systems and the transfer codes used required some standardization in order to facilitate data transfers.

In the 1980s the problem of computer-to-computer communication was addressed with the creation of a standardized code to be used by all computers connecting to the network. The 1982 introduction of the Transmission Control Protocol and the Internet Protocol allowed machines using different program language to communicate across the network. The creation of this standardized program language allowed for the rapid growth of the internet. In 1986 the National Science Foundation funded NSFNET with supercomputing centers linking major universities all over the United States.

In the early 1990s a number of searching tools were introduced to allow the user to search and retrieve information that was stored on the network. This led to a further expansion of the number of computers connected to the network, with the doubling of connections almost every year throughout the 1990s. The introduction of the World Wide Web and Mosaic in 1992 and 1993, respectively, allowed for a graphic interface with hypertext links across the network. This led to an explosion in the quantity of web sites, with the number jumping from 130 in 1993 to over

23,000 by 1995.[41] Today the number of web sites numbers in the millions.

The technology continues to evolve. With the introduction of fiber optic cable the amount of code that can be transfer over cable has increased dramatically. Wireless connectivity has expanded the reach of internet access, allowing users to be both connected and mobile. One can expect an increase in the carrying capacity of the network and expanding access for the foreseeable future.

The internet is a global phenomenon. It has the potential to link people across the world in direct communication, unfiltered by government agencies and national institutions. Such a technology allows for the expansion of the space in which people orient their actions. Scientists and academics can communicate their ideas across the globe and consumers can shop for specialized commodities without the limitations of geographic space. The specialized production that Adam Smith saw as a luxury of the urban environment has now broken down. Anyone can get anything from anywhere.

Electronic Dissemination and Political Power

The politics of the internet has been the subject of considerable discussion over the course of the last two decades. These discussions reflect a variety of opinions. The most sweeping view argues that the revolutionary character of this medium of communication will transform the social and political order in such a way as to completely reshape the environment in which people live and conduct their political lives. As asserted by Bob Davis in 1999, the internet will provide so much information to so many people that it will have a greater impact on our lives than the printing press.[42] As this view argues, greater information to the populous will affect the demand for greater democratic influences on the practice of politics around the globe. The decentralized connective features of the technology are such that it will facilitate the organization of alternative movements, mass democratic networks that undermine the effective control of non-democratic regimes.[43] The emerging "network society" will be less hierarchical, more decentralized, with more autonomous components.[44] While not necessarily going as far as McLuhan's concept of a *global village*,[45] carried to its logical conclusion the development of alternative political orders on both the sub-national and transnational basis cannot help but erode the power of the centralized nation-state.

Analysis asserting a less sweeping transformation suggests that the internet will be shaped by the current distribution of power relations in society, mitigating its revolutionary potentials. In their 2006 work, *Who Controls the Internet*, Jack Goldsmith and Tim Wu argue that what has evolved since the origins of the internet is a structure in which the elements deemed subversive to either the political or cultural orders of nation-states are being systematically filtered and neutralized.[46] Under these conditions, the prospects for a cosmopolitan world order seem remote.

Marxist critics of the internet focus on access and the emergence of a new global class structure. They argue that the internet is controlled by wealthy nations and this will determine who benefits from the emerging institutional order.[47] Such a claim has some merit, as a class of people that do not have network access will surely be at a disadvantage in a networked global order.

There is some truth to all of these arguments. However, within the focus of this work, the analytic framework we have established takes us in a different direction. Our question is: what are the material conditions that lead to the growth and concentration of power? Further, if democracy is not viewed as the opposite, or mitigator, of power then what is the relationship between the political potentials opened up by the technology and the levels of domination present in a society and what are its forms?

The idea of the world "shrinking" is something that has been occurring since the days of the Phoenician alphabet, Greek shipping, and Roman roads. Certainly this trend has been enhanced by the advent of electronic communications. As Frances Cairncross argues, the British Empire would have been difficult, if not impossible to rule without the telegraph.[48] In moving from the telegraph to the internet the question, therefore, is at what point does a quantitative change lead to a qualitative one? To address this issue in the context of this work, does the development of electronic communications in its present form constitute such a transformative change that it affects and redirects the social and political forms of power?

There is certainly evidence that such changes are occurring, but not in the way that is usually described. Particularly with satellite television and the internet, it is possible to alter the socialization pattern and the formation of identity that has been dominant since the rise of nationally oriented mass literacy programs. It should be expected that where access to these technologies exist, the population will develop a more cosmopolitan identity, and where they are not readily available, a more national or local orientation will remain. Thus, what the Marxists assert as a class divide in the access to technology will likely produce some fragmentation even within national systems of administration.

However, the most profound effect of these changes in technology will manifest themselves in what they make possible in the interrelated domains of democracy, production, and institutional power. The internet has the ability to store and transmit vast amounts of data, it has the ability to provide access to a limitless variety of one-way communication by users, and it has capacities for two-way interaction among a limited number of users. In this mix, there is the potential to expand democracy through greater access to information and for the organization of political agendas and movements. Therefore, in political terms the technology may be used to either enhance or erode the nation-state.

However, when it comes to the question of power, we have argued throughout this work that power is manifested by connection and coordination of human activity. Even the most favorable views of the impact of the technology, such as McLuhan's *global village*, are predicated on the idea of *connection*. Integration into the network is the precursor to all its political outcomes. One must first enter the domain of subjectivity that is, in part, defined by the medium itself. One must identify oneself by the integrating metaphor of the new technology as a user. This is what Jean Baudrillard identified as a "living satellite," a component of the vast network of simulated interconnectedness itself.[49]

As internet access conditions a more cosmopolitan view of the international political environment, cultural resistance to such a trend can be expected to wane to the extent that populations are exposed to the technology. However, the cosmopolitanism that comes with the integration of the network is not one that resists power, but is one that is more comfortable with the wielding of power on a global level. Conflicts will emerge along the fault line of those that identify with the new system and those who are connected to the old. Therefore, when it comes to the issue of power, democratization and globalization are parallel processes of the same development. The movement toward democratization and the expansion of systemic power are made more manifest by the growth of information technologies.

In the last chapter we argued that democracy was an essential legitimating mechanism for the rise of centralized state power. If power expands to the technical carrying capacity of the system, the internet creates the ability for the systematic arrangement of the formal aspect of power in a way that has never existed. The development of these communications systems creates a technologically functioning global network for the first time in human history. The potential is for an almost instantaneous and transparent transmission of information. While democratization may give the public greater effect on the steering decisions of the society, the integrating effect of the technology demands greater homogenization of power and public policy.

Further, this view raises questions about the outcome of such a process. Democracy means the legitimation of collective action through the influence of the public sentiment. To remain legitimate, even in the Lockean sense, governments will have to perform in a way that meets both the consumptive demands of the public and the imperative of security. Office holders will be measured against a standard of performance in these areas.

In a material sense, information technology puts the nation-state in a paradoxical situation. In order to meet those needs in an interdependent system of production and a global system of security, the nation-state must integrate into the world networks. National power will require reliance on global networks of production, finance, transport, and administration. Material performance will require greater efficiencies, greater flexibility, and greater access to commodities in an increasingly global production environment. As a result, nation-states have to cede elements of sovereign power to international organizations in order to produce the efficiencies that enhance their own legitimacy on the national level. The rise of electronic information technologies makes the transfer of this power to the international level possible as never before.

Electronic communications as the tools of dissemination does not eliminate or reduce the amount of power in the system. It magnifies it. Not only does it make possible the transfer of some power associated with the nation-state to the international level, it also creates new sets of institutions that are the repositories of power. The consolidation of economic power on an international level has been a great catalyst in this transformation.

Global Economic Consolidation

In the preceding section the focus was on the rise of new instruments of dissemination made possible by the harnessing of electric power. This resulted in the creation of a network of telecommunications that linked the globe together, and along with revolutions in transportation, created greater contact and interconnection among the various parts of the world.

These material developments enhanced the capacity of power. This occurred along two dimensions. First, as a "technical-cultural" phenomenon, the interconnectivity has the psychological effect of shrinking the world. Information is no longer exclusively local in its scope. This expands the horizon in which human identity is formed, generating a more global orientation among the population. In doing so, populations are more open to types of formal political arrangements that would have been inconceivable a generation or two earlier. The emergence of the European Union is the most obvious example of the integrating effects of a reformulated process of socialization.

The other dimension that is transformed by these developments in the area of electronic dissemination is what can be termed the "material-political." We have argued throughout this work that the tendency of power is to expand to the technical capacities of the system in which it is manifest. The advent of new information technologies has enhanced the structural capacity of power to expand beyond the nation-state. Such a development takes the potential for an integrated structure of global power well beyond those found in the Athenian's rule of the sea or the Roman system of roads. One can see the beginnings of this potential within the structure of the British Empire and its use of the telegraph to integrate the disparate components of the empire.

However, today the globalization of democratic practices has transformed the landscape in a way that was not present during the days of British dominance. As democratic political institutions have spread, the legitimating mechanism for global structures has also been put in place. This enhances the likelihood of greater political integration on the international level.

In the last chapter we argued that the nineteenth and early twentieth centuries were a time of economic consolidation on the national level. Since the late twentieth century the concentration of capital has been occurring on an international level. Such a development will have considerable influence on the creation of centralized, global institutions that exert power on a world-wide scale.

Capital Aggregation and Imperialism in the Early Twentieth Century

From the late nineteenth century until the onset of World War I, the world was undergoing the beginnings of modern globalization. The national consolidation of wealth had led to the creation of vast pools of capital. New production technologies were able to manufacture products well beyond the needs of the national populations. A series of economic downturns were the result, as the mechanical processes of the industrial age now faced a crisis of overproduction.

However, at the dawn of the twentieth century there were new technologies of communications and transportation that provided the capacity for economic integration on a global scale. This was carried out, largely under British domination, with the creation of a consensus regarding the use of gold as an international benchmark. As Jeffrey Frieden argues in his book, *Global Capitalism*, gold provided stability and predictability within the growing international system and created an objective and material means of adjusting balance of payment deficits that were outside the control of individual governments.[50] As a result, global trade grew from $8 billion in 1896 to $18 billion in 1913.

But this is also the epoch described by Lenin as the "age of imperialism." According to Lenin, this period was characterized by a concentration of capital controlled by a class of oligarchs who sought to expand their holding through the internationalization of capital. Industrial and financial capital were fused through this process and governments were brought into this equation as the agents to *open* foreign markets to the capital from repositories in the core economies. Lenin examined this process by citing the growth in finance capital exported from the major European powers. In 1872 British banks had invested the equivalent of 15 billion francs abroad, while France invested 10 billion. By 1914 Britain had invested up to 100 billion Francs, France had invested 60 billion, and the latecomer, Germany, had invested 44 billion.[51] Lenin then asserted that this financial system spurred the colonization of the world by the European powers such that by 1900, 98% of Polynesia, 90% of Africa, and 56% of Asia were under direct political control of European powers.[52]

The rationale for the process is simple. The logic of capitalism demands industrialists and financiers seek out the cheapest material and human resources in the production process. Further, as capitalism is driven by the exchange process, markets for the exchange of goods must be open for the process of exchange. As Lenin put it, "The interests pursued in exporting capital also give an impetus to the conquest of colonies, for in the colonial market it is easier to employ monopoly methods to eliminate competition, to ensure supplies, to secure the necessary 'connection,' etc. The non-economic superstructure which grows up on the basis of finance capital, its politics and its ideology, stimulates the strivings for colonial conquest."[53]

How long this system of direct political domination could have lasted without the intervention of World War I and World War II is open to debate. However, the inherent political instability of the structure would manifest the limitations of a system largely maintained by military power. As identity is slow to change and requires the resocialization of the public, direct political control of people who have local and national identities required force.

By the late twentieth century, domestic democratic political institutions were found to be much more effective for integrating the population of peripheral countries into the network of global production. Therefore, it is our view that the argument of Christopher Chase-Dunn, that the world economy is today largely integrated by political and military power,[54] is overstated. Though they require more time to develop, in the late twentieth century, democratic practice has generated far more stability in the world system and has allowed the integrating effect of capitalist structures to grow. However, that is not to say that the power of dominant nation-states has not been used as a disciplinary force, even for economic matters. Nevertheless, the new international institutional structures, coupled with the spread of democratic practices within national units, are producing a system in which the rules of the game and systemic stability are being enhanced through alternative means.

The Bretton Woods System

At the end of World War II the process of integrating the world into a global system of production and exchange continued, albeit with some significant differences. World War I had effectively ended the dominance of the British Empire in the international arena, in both economic and military terms. The United States emerged as the strongest global power in the interwar period, but remained relatively isolationist in its orientation. As the end of World War II approached, the United States and Great Britain developed a structure for the post-war environment that would continue the process of global economic exchange that had grown so significantly in the years prior to World War I.

International exchange does not happen in the absence of managing structures and institutions. As was clear in the nineteenth century, there must be international agreements to homogenize the processes of exchange, whether dealing with the standardization of weights and measures, the compatibility of cross-border electronic communications, or the transfer of currencies from one state to another. After World War II, the system of international currency exchange was governed by an agreement negotiated between the United States and Britain and signed in 1944. This was known as the Bretton Woods Agreement.

The final discussions on the Bretton Woods Agreement were carried out by a thousand delegates from forty different countries.[55] It created a mechanism by which countries could carry out exchanges using their domestic currencies (in theory) while adjusting balance of payment deficits by the transfer of gold. This system was to be managed by a new international financial institution called the International Monetary Fund (IMF). The IMF would provide system-wide stability by maintaining fixed exchange rates across the entire international economy.

A second institution, the World Bank, was created to fund development projects in countries where the private capital markets might be reluctant to go. The World Bank would essentially guarantee the loans of private financial institutions for projects in developing countries. This would be especially helpful for longer-term projects where the question of return on investment might cause the private capital to stay away.

Concerns about a return of the protectionist trade policies that had such a ruinous effect during the interwar period prompted the creation of another organization. This institution was the General Agreement on Tariffs and Trade (GATT). The first meeting of GATT took place in 1947 and the negotiators signed over one hundred agreements affecting more than 45,000 products.[56] Tariffs were cut by an average of one third in order to promote a liberal trading regime in the international environment. Further tariff reductions were negotiated in the GATT meetings in 1949, 1951, 1956, and 1967.

The Bretton Woods system, and its accompanying institutions and agreements, produced an explosion of world trade. Through the 1950s global exports were growing at 8.6% per year.[57] Still, the political and economic reality of this system was that it was created and managed by the great powers, and functioned largely to their benefit. Institutionally, the nation-state was the center of economic power as the process of trade and development had no autonomous organizational structures that operated outside the margins of state controls.

Further, power was exercised within these institutions based on national economic might. The United States, as the dominate power within the system maintained an ideological commitment to free trade, but it was also the case that the United States benefited from the open trading posture within the system. It had a near monopoly on industrial goods in the immediate aftermath of World War II, and open trade would keep raw materials and agricultural products inexpensive on free and open markets. This created what Robert Ross and Kent Trachte refer to as an "international division of labor" in which the poorer countries of the world found themselves disadvantaged by the system of trade that puts downward pressure on raw materials and agricultural products, while producing expanded rewards for the industrial economies.[58] Such a view is also expressed by Andrew Gunder Frank[59] and in the work of Fernando Cardoso and Enzo Faletto.[60]

In the early years of this system, the United States was also in a unique position, given the high standing of the dollar internationally. The United States was able to provide currency to the international system without generating either domestic inflation or a demand for gold from its reserves. However, this would begin to change by the late 1950s.

The Bretton Woods system needs to be viewed in its historical context. It was an attempt to restore the open trading system that existed prior to World War I, with gold maintaining the stability of the system. It was a nation-state centered system that required international institutions for its management. As trade and commerce increased, so did the necessity of more highly centralized institutions to manage the growth of trade and finance within the system. As Robert Gilpin describes the dangers, erratic changes in either the monetary system or the financial system can produce instability.[61] However, it can be claimed that this was a system that was ultimately designed around finance capital, as the fixed exchange rates offered the greatest protection to lenders.

The institutional structure created by the Bretton Woods system constituted a major step in the integration of economic power on a global level. It brought the major non-communist state actors together within an institutional framework that integrated and coordinated economic activities using market mechanism as a guide to resource allocation and production. In the end, however, it was only a step in the process of economic integration. It would eventually be overwhelmed by some of the very forces it helped set in motion.

The Collapse of Bretton Woods: From National to International Capitalism

The Bretton Woods system was structured, in part, as a refinement of the pre-World War I model of development. Under this arrangement national economies were integrated into the global economy through financial institutions that participated in global investments. The World Bank was constructed with this in mind, as it became an international bank for finance and development.

However, the Bretton Woods model never completely functioned as it was designed. The use of the dollar on international markets allowed the United States to export deficits without engaging the adjustment mechanisms built into the Bretton Woods system. Nevertheless, the dollar's role in providing international liquidity contributed to the rapid growth of the international economy throughout the 1950s. Eventually the practices of the United States would come back in the form of a crisis, and be one of the contributing factors in the collapse of the Bretton Woods system.

Three factors led to the collapse of Bretton Woods: the chronic United States deficits, the exceptional growth of trade, and the move from finance capital to foreign direct investments by transnational corporations. Each of these developments was more consistent with a model of economic integration that was more open, flexible, and responsive than the Bretton Woods system allowed. In the end, this would require the alteration of the structure to create a system more consistent with the evolution of global capitalism.

The Bretton Woods system established fixed exchange rates among the participating member's currencies, requiring that trade imbalances be adjusted with the transfer of gold fixed at thirty-five dollars an ounce. Through this mechanism, stable exchange rates could be maintained. With the currencies tied to gold, governments would be restrained from printing money and generating inflation as a means of dealing with debt. But the United States was an outlier. With the development of Eurodollar and Petrodollar markets, the United States was able to print dollars that did not immediately return to the United States as demands for gold. However, by the late 1960s the cost of domestic programs and the Vietnam War in the United States were pushing the red ink to an intolerable degree for the rising economies of Europe. As Robert Gilpin notes, the integration of the world's economies means a loss of national macro economic policy autonomy.[62] The system would have to adjust to a new reality.

Also in the 1960s there was an explosion of international trade. From 1962 to 1977 manufacturing exports from sixteen of the leading economies in the developing world went from $2.3 billion to $36 billion. During the same period, manufacturing exports from the leading economic power also increased dramatically, with Japan moving from $4 billion in exports to $77 billion and West Germany increasing from $11 billion to $104 billion in the same period.[63] It is our contention that these increases were simply overwhelming a system that was designed when the volume of trade was significantly smaller.

Finally, there were the beginnings of what would eventually constitute a major influence in the direction of the new international economic order. While GATT was opening much of the world to a liberal trading structure, the United States allowed Europe and Japan some protectionist measures in order to help stimulate industrial growth. Starting in the 1950s American companies sought to bypass some of the tariff and non-tariff barriers to their exports found in these countries. Companies began to make direct investments, establishing production facilities and purchasing local manufacturers, in order to avoid these restrictions. This required an adjustment within the international economic structures to a system that was more compatible with multinational corporations as major actors within the system. (More will be said about this in the next section.)

In 1971 President Richard Nixon ended the convertibility of the dollar to gold, and by 1973 the Bretton Woods era had ended. Despite the concerns over inflation, the capitalist economies moved to a floating exchange rate system. This would begin an evolutionary transformation of the economic system to a structure that was more open and flexible to financial flows. This new system was the handmaiden to global structures for the management of economic matters.

The floating of exchange rates meant that the international financial system was moving away from national dominance of economic matters to a system that was more controlled by markets. The float, coupled with instant and automatic convertibility meant the universalization of capital within a global system. Where currencies are fully convertible, in practice there is only one currency. Thus there is an impetus in the international system to move toward global structures and away from the national structures that governed the system under Bretton Woods.

Evidence of this structural change can be seen in the way in which governments reacted to the internationalization of finance capital. The collapse of Bretton Woods brought structural changes to the global economy and altered the relationships between governments and financial markets. By the 1980s, the internationalization of finance provided a pool of investment capital that allowed governments to sell bonds to finance deficit spending in national budgets. In the United States alone, between 1980 and 1992 government debt rose from under $1 trillion to over $4 trillion. This was assisted by the consolidation of international financial capital, with over $5 trillion in assets going into international markets by the 1990s.[64] Other industrial states followed the lead of the United States and Great Britain, drawing on this international capital to finance their deficit spending. This could not have been carried out without the global financial markets.

Foreign Direct Investment and the Internationalization of Production

By the 1990s a confluence of forces was creating a radically different international economic system. Information technologies had made the transfer of both information and capital nearly instantaneous. Convertibility and the float allowed markets to react in real-time to changes in the financial environment on a global scale. The barriers to the flow of goods were reduced and restrictions on the flow of capital have largely been eliminated. This created a radically different playing field for the activities of capital on a global level. To put it simply, the consolidation of economic power on a national level that took place at the end of the nineteenth century was taking place on a global level at the end of the twentieth.

What was the effect? One representation of the scope of this change is put forward by William Robinson. Robinson argues that the old system was characterized by national economies linked to a world economic system through the structures created by the national governments. The new system is characterized by the fragmentation of production and the integration of these elements into a global system that is external to the national structures.[65] An alternative position on globalization and the nation-state is presented by Robert Gilpin. Gilpin's position, what he terms "state-centric realism," argues that the international system is still dominated by the structure of the nation-state and its concerns for security.[66] Our view is that the national economies are not completely powerless in this evolving system, but that power is waning as they enter the process representing a position that is foreign to the logic of international capital.

One way to understand the scope of the change is to view the international economy from the perspective of foreign direct investment (FDI). FDI is different than the investment by financial institutions, as it is carried out by multinational companies whose sole interest is in maximizing the return on their investment. This can result in both the building of new production facilities in other countries, or in the acquisition of foreign companies and the integration of those assets into the operation of the investor.

In 1982 global foreign direct investment was $57 billion dollars. By 1990 this figure had grown to $202 billion. In 2000 global FDI was

$1.27 trillion. (Frieden puts total foreign investments at over $2 trillion for 2000 when adding investments by financial institutions.)[67] Such an increase required three factors: the breakdown of barriers to trade and financial flows, the infrastructure in global capital markets to handle the volume, and a political climate that was stable and favorable to the integration into the global economy. As a result of GATT, and the World Trade Organization, the political barriers to trade and capital liberalization were falling. The infrastructure was in place as the result of the revolution in information technology. By 1999 the international system was handling $1.5 trillion in foreign exchange transactions every day.[68] The political climate was also increasingly favorable to such transactions.

In 1990 the value of cross border corporate mergers was less than $200 billion. By 2000 the number had reached almost $1.2 trillion.[69] In 1999 the major cross-border mergers included: Air Touch, a United States Company purchased by the Vodafone Group of Great Britain for $60 billion; Astra A B of Sweden, acquired by Zeneca in Great Britain for $35 billion; Chrysler Motors purchased by Daimler-Benz for $41 billion; and Amoco, a United State petroleum company purchased by British Petroleum for $48 billion.[70] Such acquisitions represent the consolidation of wealth on a global scale.

The significance of FDI and mergers can be seen in the value of sales by foreign affiliates in a variety of host countries. In Ireland, from 1985 to 1998 the percentage of total sales carried out by companies with transnational ownership rose from 50% to 74%. In China, from 1990 to 2000 the number rose from 2.3% to 31.3%. In the United States, from 1985 until 1999 the value rose from 10% to 18%.[71] Even these few examples highlight the increasing internationalization of the corporate sector.

The openness of the financial system and the ease and relative cost of cross-border shipping all contributed to the rise of global production. Private industry finds it profitable to fragment the production process, placing different units in countries where it finds the most advantage and then assembling the final products some place else. This denationalization of production cannot help but create demands for institutions that facilitate such processes. These must have the character of global structures.

Democratic Practice and the Rise of Global Economic Institutions

In Chapter Five our central premise regarding democracy was that the development of democratic institutions did not offset the rise of concentrated power at the core of national institutions. In fact, democratic practice was essential to the formation of those institutions as it created a legitimating mechanism for the consolidation of power taking place. It is our contention that the same forces are at work in the international system.

International trade requires a certain homogenization and standardization of institutions and practices across the nation-state system. This cannot be carried out without cooperation on the state level. Such a situation produces an interesting dynamic. The early stages of globalization were met with some resistance, particularly in places like Latin America. The IMF and World Bank were viewed with suspicion, particularly as these institutions demanded elements of economic sovereignty be sacrificed as a condition of integration into the global economy. This was particularly difficult for governments that had non-democratic institutions, as they lacked the legitimacy to carry out reforms even while the public demanded access to higher living standards.

In this regard, the push toward globalization produced a democratic response as both cause and effect. As the regimes created more democratic forms of rule, the demands for greater economic performance were manifest on the national level. In turn, the democratic form of domination enhanced the stability of domestic institutions and provided a safer investment climate, which brought greater growth rates and greater integration into the global economy.

In this respect, the spread of democracy and the spread of globalization cannot be seen as coincidental. Latin America is a good example of this trend. In 1980 Latin America had only two elected governments. By 1990, there were no dictatorships left.[72] Global integration became the agenda of political parties on both the left and the right, in Latin America, East Asia, and even among the left in Europe. It is the perceived engine of economic growth and governments cannot remain in power without delivering the goods. In that regard, democratic institutions have been essential to the consolidation of power on a global level.

The link between democratic institutions and economic globalization can also be seen in the responses of state governments to the internationalization of production. In 1991 thirty-five countries passed a total of 80 pieces of legislation to create a more favorable climate for foreign

direct investments. By 2001, 71 countries had passed 194 pieces of legislation to promote investments.[73] These included liberalizing capital
flows, investment incentive programs, and loan guarantees. As the economies of the world democratize, they are becoming more integrated into
the global system.

The state's response to globalization has also taken another form.
This is the creation of trading blocs. The most advanced of these institutions is the European Union. Having its origins in the 1950s, as the European Coal and Steel Community, the European Union has evolved into a
twenty-seven member trading bloc. Today it has a common currency and
an evolving set of structures for managing trade and finance in a collective fashion. For trade and finance, the creation of the trading bloc generally results in the elimination of tariff and non-tariff restrictions on inter-
bloc transactions.

But the evolution of the European Union demonstrates the impossi-
bility of completely separating economic and political integration. Economic integration required the coordination of tax policy, immigration
policy, production standards, and a host of other agreements. In the case
of Europe, this has resulted in the increasing power of its central political
institutions.

The attractiveness of the trading bloc model for nation-states has
resulted in the creation of the North American Free Trade Agreement
and the Southern Common Market (Mercosur) in Latin America. However, this is a further indication of the financial impetus toward greater
integration of capital and trade on a global scale. In this regard, the trading bloc structure may be seen as a transitional phase to a more global
institutional structure for regulating trade and capital flows.

The world economy took the next step toward globalization in 1994.
The Uruguay Round of GATT concluded with a series of agreements to
liberalize trade and capital flows, but it also created a transnational institution for economic management. The agreement created the World
Trade Organization (WTO) as a permanent institution to replace GATT
and facilitate the liberalization of trade and capital movement. While the
creation of the WTO was with the approval of national governments, it is
a transnational entity, the sole purpose of which is to serve the interests
of trade and transnational capital. Thus, the nation-state governments act
within the paradox of the current system. With democratic domestic political structures, national leaders must respond to the demands for more
consumption coming from their populations. This requires greater integration into the global environment. In the final analysis, this erodes the
sovereignty of the state, chipping off one functional component at a time.

While this may be less obvious within the states that are major powers, it is strongly felt in the smaller states.

As this played out over the last twenty years, resentment against these global institutions, such as the IMF, World Bank, and the WTO, has been manifested. Criticisms of the system have been varied. Where the IMF and World Bank have demanded the reprioritization of national budgets, resentment over the loss of local control has resulted. For countries that export raw materials (excluding oil) and agricultural products, concerns over an unjust system of international trade have resulted. There have also been concerns about core countries exporting pollution and waste products to countries with few options in a global trading environment. Open capital flows also have the potential to leave weaker economies on the periphery vulnerable to speculation.

The East Asian currency crisis of 1997 is an illustrative example of this point. The East Asian economies of Thailand, Malaysia, Indonesia, and South Korea were growing rapidly during the early 1990s, attracting a lot of foreign financial capital and multinational corporation investments. However, by 1996 exports were lagging and inflation was rising. The recognition that the currencies in East Asia were about to be devalued brought in speculators who exploited the situation. This caused economic turmoil throughout the region. The result was some criticism of the open financial system that technology and economic logic had made possible.

However, there were two notable outcomes from this event. The first was that despite the criticism of the global system by the victims of this crisis, they engaged in no wholesale withdrawal from the global economy. Within a few years they were open and participating in the very processes from which they had suffered. The second reaction was that this event, along with the Latin American crisis of 1994-1995 gave impetus to the discussions about creating more elaborate international structures for the management of the global economy. Robert Gilpin has noted that concerns over the lack of structure has brought such diverse voices as those of Susan Strange, Charles Kindleberger, and George Soros to call for a variety of centralized structures to manage the international economy.[74] The 2008 economic crisis in the United States will only increase those calls, as the financial and security markets are increasingly linked within a global network of institutions.

Much of the criticism of the current circumstance centers on the lack of democracy in the new structures. There is no democratically organized political structure that makes the institutional decisions legitimate beyond the interests of the major players. Lacking those legitimat-

ing structures, the rewards of the current arrangement go disproportion-
ately to those with the power to design the system. As is demonstrated by
the complex political discussions surrounding the European Union, the
North American Free Trade Agreement, and the Mercosur, economic
integration reaches a structural limit without the furthering of political
integration.

Today, functional sovereignty is being chipped away in the nation-
state, but there exists no political structure in which the question of *justice* can be addressed in the global economy. Lacking fuller economic
integration and effective structures, responses have been a patchwork. So
far, the existing institutions have been able to restablize the system when
it falls into crisis. However, as was the case with the national consolidation of capital at the turn of the twentieth century, the greater the integration and interdependence without effective institutional management, the
more likely it is that a crisis could emerge that outstrips the effectiveness
of the institutions.

The democratic form of domination in the nation-states produced
the political legitimacy necessary for the creation of effective institutions
for the management of national capital's consolidation phase. Political
sovereignty afforded the nation-states the opportunity to generate systemic legitimacy for this process. The international system lacks sovereign political institutions, despite the push for the increasing integration
of capital. The result of the present circumstance is an empire of capital
in which the major holders of the economic instruments have had a dominant position in determining the distribution of rewards. This can only
lead to tension, as winners and losers contest the level of *justice* afforded
by the current order. It may take a crisis on a global scale to move the
players in the international environment to accept the level of political
integration necessary to manage the system as a whole.

The Rise of the Global System

The material conditions that gave rise to capitalism in the seventeenth
and eighteenth centuries were, in many respects, the same conditions that
gave rise to democracy within the nation-states of Europe. These included: the growth of small scale entrepreneurs and traders, the dispersal
of wealth and power to a broader class of society, the development of
rational science, and the adoption of a rational and empirically based
process of decision making. These conditions led to a diffusion of both

wealth and political power across a wider segment of the population and created the foundation for the rise of democratic institutions.

In the nineteenth century, with the development of mass forms of production, the systemic logic that supported the diffusion of wealth and power began to erode. The efficiency of production demanded the mass ordering of the production environment, the regulation and management of industrial processes, and the consolidation of economic resources. At the same time, the instruments of dissemination are employed to generate consensus around the logic of national politics. The emerging institutions established, reinforced, and enacted the *rational efficiency* of the process of consolidation. Thus, in both the political and economic spheres, the centralization of power had an operative logic.

The cultural dynamic of this process was profound and produced and ideological disconnect between the emerging institutional dynamics and the mythologies of liberalism inherited from the early days of the Enlightenment. The model of subjectivity consistent with the early modern period was infused with notions of free will, creativity, and the autonomy of action. In both the economic and political sense, the individual is asserted to possess an autonomy of will that allows for the calculation of self-interested action. Such autonomy makes democracy essential, as an expression of the ontological conditions of freedom that lies at the core of human identity. This idea of personal independence reinforced the system of capitalism, manifested as another facet of that identity.

In the nineteenth century Karl Marx, with his materialist view of history, began the articulation of two fundamental features of the systemic changes underway. First, Marx understood the constructed nature of subjectivity. Our notions of the self are products of lived experiences. This relativized the notion of the subject and made it contingent upon the contextual conditions informing its construction. Second, the materialist understanding of the relationship between ideology and institutions, discussed by Marx, reprioritizes the relationship between the individuals and organizations. Institutions order and prioritize experience and activity in a fashion that reinforces the goals and aspirations of the institutions themselves. Individual actions take place under the rules that circumscribe and govern the limits of behavior. Further, these organizations do not serve some transcendent truth, but a logic that provides the rationale for their own being.[75]

In the nineteenth century the consolidation of power on the national level, and the expansion of the institutional order, operated under three imperatives: providing security to the citizens of the state, enhancing the material well-being of the national citizenry, and the production of *just* outcomes within the political processes. From the materialist perspective, all of these actions are carried out within the constraints contained in the general environment. Institutions are created to pursue these objectives and collective action is adjusted in the service of these goals in a manner consistent with the institutional dynamics of the time.

Management of actions in service of these goals required the growth of various bureaucracies for the direction of collective action toward these objectives. This rational ordering of social life generated a variety of effects, one of which is the transformation of the foundational support of democratic practice. The *natural* components of democracy give way to *practical* ones. Democracy is reduced to a procedure in the service of institutional performance. This renders the ontological components of democratic practice constructed within the early days of the Enlightenment little more than illusory and nostalgic artifacts of Western culture.

By the early twentieth century, power was adjusting mass behavior to the service of the systemic objectives of the institutional order. Democratic practice was essential to this process as it legitimates the integration and the institutionalization of daily life. The logic of the institutional order, and its rational efficiencies, circumscribe the objectives and direction of social and political choices. As we have argued throughout this work, in historical terms such a process has been limited by the technical mechanisms for the extension of power. By the late twentieth century such technical boundaries have waned.

As a result, the technological limitations on the expansion of power to a global level have largely been overcome. Further, there is a systemic logic at work within the institutional order that makes movement in that direction *rational*. Efficiencies in security, material well-being, and justice have generated an institutional order which is ever more global in nature. These issues are viewed increasingly as matters that require global solutions. In turn, these institutions are redefining the nature of subjectivity and culture in terms that are more universal in character.

This section will address the rise of global institutions over the last one hundred years. It will be argued that contrary to much of the mythology surrounding this process, democracy is not a means of recapturing the ontological autonomy of the will propagated by the Enlightenment view of subjectivity and spreading that to all humanity. Instead, as democracy has been divorced from its ontological underpinnings, it has taken on the character of a practical procedure, a catalyst, for the expansion and consolidation of institutional power. Thus, it has become the mechanism for the reconfiguration of sovereignty, as global institutions take on greater utility. The rational efficiency of a system in pursuit of security, well-being, and justice generates the necessity of collective power on a global level.

The Transformation of Sovereignty

In the West, the modern notion of sovereignty has its origins in the Peace of Westphalia in 1648. This document established the definition of sovereignty as the ultimate power of collective decision making within fixed territorial borders. Within those borders, power is absolute, regardless of the means by which internal decision making is carried out. Such a notion retains its influence even in the twentieth century, as elements of this concept of sovereignty are contained in the United Nations Charter.

Regardless of how absolute this notion of sovereignty appears, the reality of the past one hundred years is less rigid. Both conceptually and empirically the notion of sovereignty has undergone a transformation. The materialist premises that underlie the *constructivist* perspective on international relations suggest that changes in the environment in which concepts are formulated will alter the content of those ideas. Sovereignty is no exception. Institutions interact with evolving cultures. Sovereignty will be altered by the material transformation of the conditions that give rise to culture.[76]

Elements of global culture are not new. They can be traced back in history to the expansion of the earliest civilizations. What is new today is the context in which the universalizing activities take place. Since the nineteenth century, with the rise of new technologies of communication and transportation, the transformation of sovereignty has been underway.

The most profound impact of the forces of integration can be seen on the continent of Europe. Through wars, treaties, and trade, modern Europe has been on the path of integration since the end of the Middle Ages. As was discussed in Chapter Five, the process of integration received great impetus with the growth of industrialization in the nineteenth century. Trade necessitated the rise of organizational structures to manage, standardized, and regulate the transfer of commodities across national borders.

However, there were political forces that were unleashed by this increasing contact. In his book *Swords into Plowshares*, Inis L. Claude identified three political changes in the nineteenth century moving Europe toward greater integration. He describes them as: The Concert of Europe (1815), the rise of international unions of various sorts, and the development of the Hague system for settling disputes.[77] The Hague Convention of 1899 also created a permanent international court. This institution would evolve into the International Court of Justice. These structures provided the context for the creation of the League of Nations after World War I.

The failure of the League of Nations should not overshadow its historical significance. The League is the first universal political body created for the settling of international disputes. Its rationale, purpose, and significance are evidenced by the creation of the United Nations at the end of World War II. The United Nations is open to all nations and is the primary international institution for dealing with matters of security, well-being, and justice on a global scale. Its role and size have increased significantly since its inception. It is the centerpiece of global authority and is a significant force in the transformation of sovereignty.

However, the United Nations is only one dimension of the process that is undermining the Westphalian notion of sovereignty. With the rise of functionally differentiated international organizations the traditional notion of sovereignty is transformed. The absolute power afforded to states within a specific territory is giving way to a notion of global authority. This occurs as sovereignty is fragmented into functional differentiated areas and reconstituted within specialized institutions whose authority is global in scope.

Normative and Rational Underpinnings of Global Authority

In the work, *Constructing World Culture: International Non-Governmental Organizations Since 1875*, John Boli describes the model of authority associated with the nation-state as "rational legal," borrowing the term from Max Weber. But Boli seeks to go beyond Weber by developing a concept that describes the move toward globalization. To this end, Boli introduces the concept of "rational-voluntarist" authority.[78] Rational-voluntarist authority describes the development of legitimacy on the global level of activity. The actions of international institutions have legitimacy because they are viewed as being both morally and practically superior to the institutions constructed to serve the interests of individual states.

In normative terms, the international institutions have moral weight for a variety of interconnected reasons. Their orientation is universal in scope. Membership is open to all. They tend to be oriented toward the promotion of a universal good in the area of security, well-being, or justice, without regard to the interests of individual actors. They also tend to be democratically organized, at least when it comes to the non-governmental institutions, which gives the outcomes of their deliberations a *just* quality in the international community. As a result, the perceived legitimacy of these institutions in the eyes of the world promotes their further expansion and influence in shaping a global culture, even while acknowledging the dominance of the Westphalian system.

In practical terms, the international non-governmental organizations are viewed as superior due to their functionally differentiated and specialized orientations, as well as their universal scope. In confronting problems such as disease, pollution, human rights, and a host of others, on a global scale these organizations are pursuing a strategy that is more *rational* in the sense that the chances to have a significant impact are enhanced. Even in the area of standardization in manufacturing, the global nature of organizations extends the rationality of efficient production by making goods that have trans-border utility.[79] Global well-being is enhanced by the transfer of standardized products.

However, this form of authority that Boli assigns to non-governmental agencies can also be applied to the international organizations created by governments. In their book, *Rules for the World: International Organizations and Global Politics*, Michel Barnett and Martha Finnemore argue that international government-sponsored bureaucracies exhibit the same tendencies. Government-sponsored international organizations operate according to missions that are assigned by the institutions themselves. These bureaucracies construct the world in a way that makes their activities rational.[80] These agencies affect governments directly through their policies, but they also represent a cultural transformation in that they create a lens through which the world is viewed. In the case of international bureaucracies, that view is global. In generating knowledge about the social world, the bureaucracies construct a social reality that is used to orient the action of actors within the system.[81] The world polity is increasingly operating under an image of a world as a single integrated society.

All of these activities feed back into the system as inputs, generating the growth of new institutions that possess this orientation. Therefore, in terms of morals, practical efficiencies, and cultural perspectives, there is a reorientation taking place. The result is more consolidated institutions on the international level. Given the rational efficiencies for security, well-being, and justice, that can be generated in a world state, such an outcome of human social evolution may be the final product of these developments. However, in the short term a global state is not necessary for global authority to be concentrated, rational, and effective.[82]

The Growth of Global Political Institutions

International political institutions are generally divided into the two groups: governmental and non-governmental. Governmental organizations receive their authority directly from the nation-states in the international environment. In theory, they are directly responsible to those governments. However, as Barnett and Finnemore argue, once these agencies are created they tend to follow a mandate that is more directly in line with their mission.[83] The category of non-governmental organizations covers a wide range of potential structures and activities. These may be organizations for the promotion of human rights, health care, industrial standards, or a host of other topics. Participation is voluntary, but may be limited by a member's expertise.

The United Nations

Though technically an intergovernmental organization, the unique place of the United Nations within the global political environment warrants special attention. It is the focal point and organizational hub for much international activity that takes place among governments. Formalized in 1945, the UN is the international organization with the broadest scope and mandate from the participant nations. It is the umbrella organization under which much of the internationalization of politics and economics is taking place. It is open to all nations and most of the countries of the world are members.

Structurally, the UN is made up of numerous bodies organized under six major organs: the International Court of Justice, the General Assembly, the Economic and Social Council, the Security Council, the Trusteeship Council, and the Secretariat. The agencies of the UN deal with matters that are of interest to the member states, focusing on health, economic development, peace and security, and global norms and standards of behavior. The UN General Assembly is also particularly important in the creation of international law. While not a world legislature, the General Assembly has been important in articulating the principles that become encoded in international law.[84]

The UN is organized to promote a rational approach to the matters of security, well-being, and justice on a global scale. Does the organization represent a Western bias? It can be argued that it extends the Western *rationality project* in the Weberian sense, with the focus on rational procedures and organization. Barnett and Finnemore argue that the content of its activity tends to center around Western liberal values such as individual rights, private property, and the operation of market forces.[85] While these may be debatable points, the role of the United Nations regarding the exercise of collective power is less ambiguous.

The United Nations exists in a paradoxical universe. Article Two of the United Nations charter codifies the nation-state as the basis of the international system. However, the creation of the Security Council and numerous UN agencies not only undermine the notion of national sovereignty, in a practical sense, the existence of the UN and its constituent agencies are creating a set of global norms and processes to which the member states are increasingly expected to comply. The point is not to say whether this is overtly positive or negative to the human condition, but to identify the UN system as part of a broader project of rational organization that is taking place globally.

Between 1951 and 1995, 3666 new multilateral treaties were concluded.[86] These covered a range of topics including the environment, whaling, ocean use and ownership, arms control, human rights, and trade. The United Nations was at the center of most of these activities. These treaties outline the expectations of behavior on an international level. They represent the extension of both rationality and power to international units of administration.

The open, and largely democratic, processes at the UN enhance the legitimacy of this movement to collective power on an international level. While participation in the United Nations is technically voluntary, as a practical matter compliance with UN mandates are difficult to resist. The Security Council has coercive power that can be exercised over noncompliant states. Even on economic matters, the rejection of proposals from the International Monetary Fund is often not practical, especially for smaller states.[87]

Intergovernmental Units and Regional Organizations

According to *The Yearbook of International Organizations*, in 2005 there were 246 intergovernmental international bodies. Of those, 178 were regional organizations, 33 were intercontinental, and 34 were intergovernmental organizations open to universal membership.[88] These intergovernmental organizations were created to deal with a wide spectrum of issues that can generally be categorized as pursuing security, well-being, and justice. They include regional security arrangements, trading blocs, technical agreements, border management, and capital flows. In general, these organizations are government-to-government agreements that create a formal structure for the management of specific areas of concern.

In the post World War II environment, a number of regional security units were created. These included the North Atlantic Treaty Organization, the Warsaw Pact, the Southeast Asia Treaty Organization, and others. More general regional organizations include the African Union, the Arab League, the Gulf Cooperation Council, and the Organization of American States. A number of regional economic organizations have been created including the North American Free Trade Agreement, Mercosur, the Asia-Pacific Economic Cooperation organization, and the Central American Common Market. This list only highlights a few of these organizations. Nevertheless, the trend towards an integrated approach to security, well-being, and justice appears preeminent.

In this regard, the most advanced of these regional intergovernmental organizations is the European Union. The EU has its origins with the six members of the European Coal and Steel Community in 1952. That organization sought to manage the reconstruction of Europe with the most rationally efficient use of resources in the post-World War II environment. By 2008 the European Union contained twenty-seven members, representing 500 million people.

The EU is by far the most developed of the regional organizations. It has a hybrid structure designed to account for the unique questions of sovereignty raised by the evolving nature of state/EU relations. The EU structure consists of a number of agencies that are designed to balance the interests of the nation-states with the integrating forces of the EU. The European Commission presides over the EU bureaucracy. The European Commission members are nominated by the national governments, but are to promote the transnational objectives of the European Union. The Council of the European Union is an organization that consists of state representatives that are brought together to deal with specific issue areas and approve the proposals presented by the European Commission. The European Parliament is directly elected by the voters in the member states, and is the most democratic of the EU's institutions, but it cedes real legislative power to the Council of the European Union.[89]

Is this movement one that will take Europe to full political integration? In functional terms, Europe is on the verge of becoming a fully articulated confederation. The current negotiations toward common tax, immigration, military, and foreign policies push it further in that direction. If one views these developments historically, it is hard to deny the movement in that direction over the last 50 years.

Is this the way in which all regional blocs will develop? Given the vast span of history, such a development is possible. However, the question will be whether or not the movement toward regionalism will be overtaken by the creation of global institutions.

Non-Governmental Institutions and the Rise of Global Democratic Culture

The growth of intergovernmental organizations and regional blocs has been dwarfed by the rise of international non-governmental organizations. In 1900 there were approximately 200 active NGOs.[90] By 2005 there were 7306.[91]

There are many types of international NGOs. The sectoral analysis presented by Boli and Thomas concludes that one-fourth of the international NGOs are for business and economic activity, one-third promote coordination of science and technology, and only 7% are organized around individual rights and public welfare.[92] Examples of international NGOs include labor unions, the Red Cross, the International Chamber of Commerce, the International Organization for Standardization, the International Electrotechnical Commission, Greenpeace, Amnesty International, and a host of others.

Though these institutions have no direct political power, they have a great deal of influence over the actions of states. This indirect power stems from two major sources: the creation of universal cultural norms for the international system, and the consensus building processes among area experts. The international NGOs accumulate data that is relevant to state actors in the formulation of policy.

Further, by constructing an image of the world organized around the objectives of the organization, they alter the perception of political actors and the public. This expands the creation of a global culture as international NGOs pursue goals and create norms that are premised on the existence of a global civil society.[93] For example, Oxfam and Amnesty International operate under standards that are universal in scope.

In areas in which international NGOs are essentially unions of technical experts, especially science and manufacturing, governments rely on the NGO's expertise and incorporate their standards into national practices. International trade in electronic products would be impossible without an organization such as the International Electrotechnical Commission establishing standard measures for such electromagnetic phenomena as volts, resistance, current, and frequency. The goal of these organizations is to remove the technical barriers to trade. While this may enhance the revenue of multinational capitalist enterprises, the global standardization of production cannot be reduced to the economic logic of capitalism.[94] Standardization expands the systemic capacity of global production and it would be the *rational* course to pursue regardless of the economic model employed. Given the rationality of standardization for the increase in global production, it is impossible for governments to resist. This generates the coordination of production decisions at a global level.

Agreements to facilitate trade and commerce can be traced back to the Hanseatic League in Europe. However, there are qualitative differences with the processes taking place in the twenty-first century. The NGOs today operate outside of the specific directives of national governments and are in the processes of reshaping the world culture according to standards that are rationally constructed, universal in scope, and premised on global citizenship. It is impossible to imagine such a development without the emergence of the communications technologies advanced during the twentieth century. It is equally impossible to imagine this trend not continuing given the material conditions present in the twenty-first.

Conclusion

This chapter began by addressing the emergence of new technologies and assessing their impact on the centralization and collectivization of power. Global telecommunications has transformed the material conditions that give rise to culture, creating a basis for the emergence of a world culture. This is true even in territorial units that are still struggling with the replacement of local identities with those premised on the Westphalian model. Identity is formed through institutional contact in the process of socialization. The greater the impact of global institutions, the greater will be the reorientation of the public away from the nation-state system.

The structural conditions present today provide advantages to the appearance of this global culture. Not only does the emergence of communications technology make the transfer of global cultural images and values more pronounced, but it also makes the daily practice of globalizing activities within reach of greater segments of the population. People consume goods from all over the world, but also find themselves linked to international systems through employment, international television feeds, financial investments, and leisure travel.

In terms of political institutions, the functions once assigned as the exclusive domain of nation-states increasingly are carried out on the international level by specialized and functionally differentiated organizations. OPEC provides oil, Amnesty International watches for violations of universal rights, and Oxfam feeds. Such a process cannot avoid eroding the power of the state, as increasingly national power is fragmented and reconstituted on the international level.

While still in the early stages of this process, it is a trend that is likely to continue. The reason for this is simple. The global approach is more efficient. Rational efficiency will ultimately drive the globalization project. If this is the case, even capitalism will find itself subsumed under the directives of the rationality project.

Integration in the modern period has required democratic procedures. Only democracy can create the legitimacy for the process, whether at the national or international level. The culture of the emerging international institutions has been decidedly democratic, both reinforcing the significance of democratic culture and replicating those processes in emerging institutions. As a result, the legitimacy in the process of integration is tied to the democratic nature of its institutions.

Capitalism as an economic practice cannot legitimate itself through the same mechanisms. Its practice is not inherently democratic. Therefore, its legitimacy is tied to its performance in promoting well-being through the production of commodities. It can only be legitimized indirectly through the broader political process, which can toss it aside if a more rational form of economic system emerges.

Therefore, it is a mistake to read global integration simply through the lens of capitalist expansion. The processes taking place are far more profound, and the globalization of capital is only one facet of that trend. The invention of new technologies has created the material conditions for the expansion of power to new levels of human associations. These new institutions emerge as a reaction to the psychology of a shrinking world, and the material reality of problems that can only be addressed within a global framework.

It should be clear to all but the most myopic of onlookers that the very survival of the species will drive this process of integration forward. Pollution, disease, and environmental degradation are matters that cannot be addressed by the nation-state system. The spread of weapons technology threatens the entire planet, not just individual states. The consumptive patterns of an ever-increasing population appear ever more unsustainable without some rational plan of action that can only be addressed on a global level. Capitalism's logic presents a problem in the development of rational action in this area more that it offers a solution.

Rational efficiencies in the areas of security, well-being, and justice will drive the development of global institutions in the twenty-first century. This will mean greater integration and the transfer of a larger number of functions to the international level. Democracy is the key component for the generation of global institutions through peaceful means. It makes the process legitimate, even as it slows down the integrative process itself.

Notes

1. Mitchell, B. R., *International Historical Statistics, Europe 1750-1993* (New York: Macmillian, 1998), 426–429.

2. Peirce, William Spangar, *Economics of the Energy Industry* (Westport, CT: Praeger, 1996), 102.

3. Willrich, Mason, *Energy and World Politics* (New York: Free Press, 1975), 29.

4. Willrich, 30.

5. Willrich, 13.

6. Willrich, 12.

7. Willrich, 14.

8. Mitchell, 562–565.

9. Pierce, 182.

10. Dubash, Navroz, *Power Politics: Equity and Environment in Electricity Reform* (Washington, D.C.: World Resource Institute, 2002), x.

11. Hirsh, Richard F., *Technology and Transformation in the American Electric Utility Industry* (Cambridge, UK: Cambridge University Press, 1989), x.

12. Munson, Richard, *From Edison to Enron: The Business of Power and What It Means for the Future of Electricity* (Westport, CT: Praeger, 2005), 146.

13. Munson, 154–157.

14. Vincent, David, *The Rise of Mass Literacy* (Cambridge, Uk: Polity Press, 2000).

15. Wiggin, Gladys A., *Education and Nationalism* (New York: McGraw-Hill, 1962), 14.

16. Baumann, Gerd, "Introduction," in *Civil Enculturation: Nation-State, School and Ethnic Difference in The Netherlands, Britain, German, and France,* eds. Werner Schiffauer, Gerd Baumann, Riva Kastoryano, and Steven Vertovec (New York: Berghahn Books, 2004), 2.

17. Smith, A. D., *Nations and Nationalism in a Global Era* (Cambridge, UK: Polity Press, 1995), 91.

18. Wiggin, 13.

19. Ramirez, Francisco O. and Marc J. Ventresca, "Building the Institution of Mass Schooling: Isomorphism in the Modern World," in *The Political Construction of Education: The State, School Expansion, and Economic Change* (New York: Praeger, 1992), 49.

20. Ramirez and Ventresca, 56.

21. Ramirez and Ventresca, 58.

22. Harvey, David, "From Space to Place and Back Again: Reflections on the Conditions of Postmodernity," in *Mapping the Futures: Local Culture, Global Change*, eds. J. Bird, et. al (London: Routledge, 1993), 3.

23. Mitchell, 750–753.

24. Oslin, George P., *The Story of Telecommunications* (Macon, GA: Mercer University Press, 1992), 178.

25. Oslin, 268.

26. Mitchell, 765–772.

27. Oslin, 275.

28. Mitchell, 776–778.

29. McChesney, Robert W., *Telecommunications, Mass Media, and Democracy: The Battle for the Control of U. S. Broadcasting, 1928–1935* (New York: Oxford University Press, 1993), 12.

30. McChesney, 14.

31. McChesney, 27.

32. Oslin, 321.

33. Noam, Eli, *Television in Europe* (New York: Oxford University Press, 1991), 74, 96.

34. Mitchell, 777–779.

35. Foote, Joe S., *Television Access and Political Power: The Networks, the Presidency, and the Loyal Opposition* (New York: Praeger, 1990), 25–45.

36. Noam, 80.

37. Oslin, 397.

38. Noam, 294.

39. Cairncross, Frances, *The Death of Distance* (Boston: Harvard Business School Press, 2001), 31.

40. Wolinsky, Art, *The History of the Internet and the World Wide Web* (Berkeley Heights, NJ: Enslow Publishers, 1999), 9.

41. Wolinsky, 41.

42. Davis, Bob, "Think Big: What is the Greatest Technological Innovation of the Past 1,000 Years," in *Wall Street Journal*, January 11, 1999.

43. Rosenau, James N. and David Johnson, "Information Technologies and Turbulence in World Politics," in *Technology, Development, and Democracy*, ed. Juliann Emmons Allison (Albany: State University of New York Press, 2002).

44. Castells, Manuel, "The Network Society: From Knowledge to Policy," in *The Network Society: From Knowledge to Policy,* ed. Manuel Castells and

Gustavo Cardoso (Washington, D. C.: Johns Hopkins Center for Transatlantic Relations, 2006), 4.

45. McLuhan, Marshall, *Understanding Media: The Extensions of Man* (New York: New American Library, 1964).

46. Goldsmith, Jack and Tim Wu, *Who Controls the Internet: Illusions of a Borderless World* (New York: Oxford University Press, 2006).

47. Poster, Mark, "Cyberdemocracy: The Internet and the Public Sphere," in *Masters of the Wired World: Cyberspeak Speaks Out*, ed. Anne Leer (London: Pitman Publishing, 1999), 212-228.

48. Cairncross, 25.

49. Baudrillard, Jean, "The Ecstasy of Communication," in *The Anti-Aesthetic: Essays on Postmodern Culture*, ed. Hal Foster (New York: New Press, 1998), 128.

50. Frieden, Jeffrey A., *Global Capitalism* (New York: Norton, 2006), 17–18.

51. Lenin, Vladimir, "Imperialism: The Highest Stage of Capitalism," in *The Lenin Anthology*, ed. Robert Tucker (New York: Norton, 1975), 226.

52. Lenin, 234.

53. Lenin, 240.

54. Chase-Dunn, Christopher, *Global Formation: Structures of the World-Economy* (Oxford, UK: Basil Blackwell, 1989), 88.

55. Frieden, 259.

56. Frieden, 288.

57. Frieden, 288.

58. Ross, Robert J. S. and Kent C. Trachte, *Global Capitalism: The New Leviathan* (Albany, New York: State University of New York Press, 1990), 74.

59. Frank, Andre Gunder, *Capitalism and Underdevelopment in Latin America* (New York: Monthly Review, 1967).

60. Cardoso, Fernando and Enzo Faletto, *Dependency and Development in Latin America* (Berkeley: University of California Press, 1979).

61. Gilpin, Robert, *Global Political Economy* (Princeton, NJ: Princeton University Press, 2001), 235.

62. Gilpin, 240.

63. Ross and Trachte, 105.

64. Frieden, 381.

65. Robinson, 10.

66. Gilpin, 15.

67. Frieden, 417.

68. Frieden, 396.

69. United Nations, *World Investment Report: Transnational Corporations and Export Competitiveness* (Geneva, Switzerland: United Nations Publication, 2002), 12.

70. Robinson, 61.

71. United Nations, *World Investment Report*, 2002, 17.

72. Frieden, 375.

73. United Nations, *World Investment Report*, 2002, 7.

74. Gilpin, 268.

75. Here it should be noted that Marx failed to appreciate that this would be true for communism as well as capitalism.

76. Reus-Smit, Christian, *The Moral Purpose of the State: Culture, Social Identity, and Institutional Rationality in International Relations* (Princeton, NJ: Princeton University Press, 1999).

77. Claude, Inis L., *Swords into Plowshares: The Problems and Progress of International Organizations* (New York: Random House, 1964).

78. Boli, John, "Conclusion: World Authority Structures and Legitimations," in *Constructing World Culture: International Non-Governmental Organizations Since 1875* (Stanford, CA: Stanford University Press, 1999). 273.

79. Loya, Thomas A. and John Boli, "Standardization in the World Polity: Technical Rationality over Power," in *Constructing World Culture: International Non-Governmental Organizations Since 1875* (Stanford, CA: Stanford University Press, 1999), 183.

80. Barnett, Michael and Martha Finnemore, *Rules for the World: International Organizations in Global Politics* (Ithaca, NY: Cornell University Press, 2004), 18.

81. Holzner, Burkhart and John Marx, *Knowledge Applications: The Knowledge System in Society* (Boston: Allyn and Bacon, 1979).

82. Loya and Boli, 194.

83. Barnett and Finnemore, 2.

84. Karns, Margaret P. and Karen A. Mingst, *International Organizations: The Politics and Processes of Global Governance* (Boulder, CO: Lynne Rienner, 2004), 103.

85. Barnett and Finnemore, 168.

86. Karns and Mingst, 5.

87. Barnett and Finnemore, 167.

88. Union of International Associations, *The Yearbook of International Organizations* (Munich: K. G. Saur, 2005), 2966.

89. Karns and Mingst, 168.

90. Boli, John and George M. Thomas, "INGOs and the Organization of World Culture," in *Constructing World Culture*, eds. John Boli and George M. Thomas (Stanford, UK: Stanford University Press, 1999), 14.

91. Union of International Associations, *The Yearbook of International Organizations*, 2966.

92. Boli and Thomas, 41.

93. Karns and Mingst, 223.

94. Loya and Boli, 196.

Concluding Remarks

Introduction

We began the Introduction to this work with a simple observation: that power stems from the organization of human activity. Through the various chapters we have reinforced the idea with numerous historical examples from the development of institutions in the Western world that serves as the evidence for such a claim. Mass forms of social organizations do not occur in a vacuum. They require certain material conditions to be present. Political power is the residue of those conditions, even if it is not the impetus behind the creation of various organizational practices.

Our methodological perspective was informed by the idea of genealogical analysis, developed by Nietzsche, Foucault, and others. The point was to explore the material conditions that enhanced or detracted from the centralization of power across the span of time. It was our intention that the analysis be conducted without either a fixed view of human nature or the assumption that there has been some underlying teleology within the historical process. Ideology and identity were treated as the residual by-products of the materiality of collective power.

From a materialist perspective, the centralization of institutions can be addressed as a series of problems to be solved. There must be a common means of communications. People must have some medium by which they can communicate the experiences of collective life and initiate a common sense of collective responsibility. This shared set of symbols, metaphorical and historical reference points, is essential to the coordination of efforts for a common purpose.

For the collective organization to grow into a political union there are infrastructure conditions that must be satisfied. Historically, there have been technical limitations to the reach of an integrating narrative. This has circumscribed the scope of political consolidation. Further, the collectivization of people within political unions requires their concentration, at least to some degree. This required the construction of urban centers, the building of roads, bridges, water and sewage systems, and some organization of production for the satisfaction of human needs.

Finally, the collectivization of people within political units requires some procedure which bestows legitimacy on the integrating process itself. Force, or conquest, is not sufficient to bring about the legitimacy necessary for stable integration. It is for that reason that tracing military expansion has not been a major component of this work. Only when there is acceptance that the organizational activities of the collective political entity are *just*, can the substantive values of the rational order be extended.

Historically, the generation of institutional legitimacy has taken many forms. It has been manifested in political institutions due to ethnic identification, and the common language and culture that are represented by the governing structures in a society. Legitimacy can be created in the structures that emerge from the common myths and religions developed by people in the course of their constructing an identity. Legitimacy can also be generated by procedures in which people give either direct or indirect consent to the structures and statutes to which they are subject.

Integration and Disintegration in Western History

The history of the West has been marked with periods of integration and disintegration. What we have sought to show is that the waxing and waning of centralizing tendencies has been tied to a broad array of material conditions that have affected this process. Considered as the result of empirical influences, rather than an ideological or teleological revelation, the collectivization of power can be analyzed as part of the material development of the human species. To that end, we have tried to identify those material elements that were significant in promoting the integration and disintegration of this larger process.

In the societies of Greece and Rome, literacy among the governing class was essential in producing centralized institutions. Literacy of ancient Greek societies made democratic practice possible organizationally and philosophically. A common language and customs within ancient Greek city-states helped to give the populous a common identity. The shared sense of identity was a necessary condition for the centralization of power. With writing and more widespread literacy came an increase in the transmission of knowledge more precisely and to a greater level of abstraction.

The use of the phonetic alphabet made it possible for further social integration as the community could advance more complex issues of social and material life to the scrutiny of a wider collective. Therefore, with literacy came the belief that the society could be organized around the practice of *reason*. The debate in Greek society was never over the value of organizing society along the lines of reason, it largely focused on who were the possessors of that reason. With reason, social goals could transcend individual interests. A rational citizenry was assumed to possess the requisite skills to participate in the decisions directing the course of collective activity. This became the foundational premise for democratic practice.

Under Pericles, governance was a collective undertaking. Decisions were arrived at by the consensus of the *politai*. There was not a legal code of precedents to follow in coming to a decision. *Justice* was the product of consensus. The citizens were not constrained by tradition or legal precedent. Rational beings should not be constrained by the law or precedent. Such a practice led Plato and Aristotle to associate democracy with "mob rule."

The Romans inherited much from the Greeks, but departed from them in terms of goals, organization, and political structures. Rome, in its conquests, sought to extend Rome and its influence to the entire known world. Technological activities such as urban planning, public administration, civil engineering, establishing a written code of laws, and military skill were highly valued accomplishments for the extension of central power. Writing and literacy were used as a systemized and uniform means of organization and were employed in practical matters of record keeping for the Roman state.

Roman literacy, like Greek literacy, allowed for the concentration and centralization of power. Education of the Roman elite included rhetoric, as it was a tool that was useful in making the case for one's argument. Politically, rhetorical skill in constructing a persuasive argument was crucial to acquiring and maintaining influence in Roman society and politics. Only the powerful and wealthy in Roman society could afford the comprehensive education that was the prerequisite to being influential in Roman politics and administration.

Writing and literacy were the technological means of disseminating culture. In the case of Rome, writing aided in the centralization of administration by spreading the content of Roman culture into the territories. By generating a perception of *Roman-ness*, the central power of the Roman state could be extended.

The power and influence of the Roman Empire went into decline in the third and fourth centuries. Plunder acquired from the various provinces was not sufficient in supporting the central infrastructures. As Rome's centralized administration was deteriorating, the structure that supported the integration of the Empire began to erode. This resulted in declining literacy rates, faltering repair of the road network, and the collapse of the domestic economy. A new organization of society emerged that was not dependent upon literacy and the rational organization of social life.

Administration during the Roman Empire was quite centralized. With the disintegration of the conditions that maintained the Empire, regional monarchies arose in the fragments of the old order. These were loosely held together by the Catholic Church that had developed in the final centuries of the Roman Empire. This fragmentation resulted from the collapse of the technical means of administration. Without professional administrators, a literate class of engineers and builders, and a system for the rational organization for collective action, a splintering of the central state took place.

The Middle Ages reversed the process of integration that had been occurring since the time of the Egyptian, Persian, and Greek Empires. With the decline in transportation and education, communities reverted to oral traditions in local languages. Absolute rule by local monarchs was the norm in the absence of written statute. What little check there was on the power of the monarchs came from the church in Rome. However, with the church seeking to protect its own power, it often produced its own forms of subjugation for the local populations.

The reconstitution of the forces of integration did not occur for almost a thousand years. By the fourteenth century material conditions were beginning to manifest a new dynamic. The power structure that was previously based on the feudal system and the church gave way to the new set of political arrangements. By the fifteenth century the European estates were beginning to be eclipsed by a new form of social life. This resulted from the rise of a class of traders and merchants, the invention of the printing press, and the birth of the nation-state system. These developments rekindled the process of rational integration.

The logic of a trading economy expanded the circle of contacts and promoted integration on a national level. The distribution of printed material allowed for the dissemination of the technical aspects of a common grammar, and extended the integrating aspects of a common identity and culture. Trade required infrastructure, and infrastructure necessitated technical education and administration. The process of integration had returned to the West, although this time it had its logic tied to the rationality project; with the substantive goals of efficiency and order rather than simple conquest.

The construction of subjectivity was transformed in this switch from medieval to modern society. The medieval subject is acted upon by events and forces, by the structures of power and the dynamics of history. The view of the modern subject developed during this period is one that is both the *creator* of the social and political structures embedded within history and the *actor* who controls the direction of historical progress. History is viewed as the product of human will and the actions in support of it.

This process created the basis for the modern form of democratic practice. Democracy is based in the transcendent equality of community members, who are assumed to possess relatively equal amounts of a universal faculty of reason. The consent of the free, equal, and rational citizens becomes established as the legitimating mechanism for collective decision making in the modern period.

As rational science replaced mysticism, there was a universalization of the rules that governed the production of knowledge. Reason was viewed as a unified phenomenon, leading people to conclude that individuals with similar orientations and similar problems would come to the same conclusions. This was the modern basis of natural law. This meant that the application of reason in the modern period began to create the possibility of generating laws, institutions, and practices that transcend the nation-state barriers.

This cultural development had an affinity with the material processes of integration taking place in the West. The logic of capitalist production had assisted the process of institutional centralization on the national level. Markets had to be opened and a more advanced infrastructure was needed for that process to continue. This reinforced the trend toward social, cultural, and political integration on the national level.

The efficiency of the machine would expand factory production and further the process of integration in the West. By the late nineteenth century, industrial activity was already beginning to exceed the demand for industrial products in the advanced economies. Trade was the answer, but trade required both greater infrastructure and a new set of institutions for the coordination of international commerce. The integrating logic of the new material reality manifested itself at the systemic level. However, when this systemic force was coupled with the nationalistic identities manifested within the states, a series of conflicts emerged over control of the integrating processes themselves.

Democracy emerges in the post-war environment of the twentieth century as a mitigating force that slowed the process of integration, while providing it with the legitimacy lacking in the attempts at integration by force. This process was dependent on the new technologies that had emerged in communications, transportation, and production. By the late twentieth century democratic states had begun ceding power to a new set of international institutions that were increasingly providing the administrative apparatus for a global structure.

Efficiency of production demands compatibility and interchangeability among the various technologies of the new industrial economy. Capital flows demand the regulation of markets and the establishment of institutions to monitor these transactions. The system requires stability in order to carry out its functions. Democracy is the political practice that promotes the systemic stability and reinforces the construction of subjectivity emerging from these practices.

The new material conditions that emerged have an affinity with a post-national orientation, where individual states are increasingly unable to challenge the forces of global integration. The ease of global travel, the increasing use of the internet, and a globalized media are in the process of re-socializing the populations of the major industrial states away from the confines of national culture. Global trade and commerce require the internationalization of institutional structures oriented to the world stage. Environmental crises, nuclear proliferation, and terrorism all necessitate international structures in order to create an efficient and rational response. The model of a single hegemonic state responding to these crises violates the conditions of subjectivity constructed in the contemporary historical epoch. For this reason, all attempts by hegemonic states to impose a solution to a crisis will appear illegitimate and unjust within the evolving institutional order. Only democratically formed institutions will have the legitimacy to provide a *just* response.

While still in its early stages, the globalization of human institutions will complete the process of integration that had begun centuries ago with the incorporation of people into villages, towns, and territories. However, this will require the extension of a common model of subjectivity to every part of the globe. Today, the struggle over competing models of the subject continues, even as the integrating effects of global institutions emerge.

The Normative Question

It has been our intention to avoid overtly normative judgments in the discussion of the evolution of collective power. This is the case for several reasons. From the perspective of poststructuralist epistemology it is difficult, if not impossible, to find that foundational platform on which to stand to offer such critiques. It would be necessary to construct an essentialist model of the subject in order to suggest that human nature was somehow violated in the march of history. Such a claim would contradict the basic assumptions of the methodology employed in this project.

Further, it would be difficult to assert that the development of collective power is either all good or all bad based on the historical evidence. For example, the expansion of networks of colonial power in the nineteenth century brought subjugation and exploitation to much of the non-Western world. However, they also brought with them more efficient farming techniques, medicines, and rational science. In the twenty-first century the globalization of power has the potential to enhance the agenda of peace and prosperity, even as its dark potentials lurk close under the surface.

However, there is a difference between the assertion of normative prescriptions and the articulation of normative implications. Several normative implications are worth noting. Over the course of history, the development of higher structures of power has created competition among differing levels of association for the allegiance of the population. Today, the global consolidation of power is in its infancy, yet it is possible to discern the growing tension between nationalism, ethnic fidelity, and religious devotion, and the emerging logic of globalization represented in a new institutional order. The normative components of this process are expressed in the loyalties that populations display for one of the competing narratives that legitimate the exercise of power.

Further, it is possible to identify the substantive values that are prevalent within the system. Since the Enlightenment, the West has been in the process of establishing *order* and *efficiency* as its prime organizational values. The formal ordering of social and political structures has been underway since the time of ancient Greece, but the enterprise took on a messianic character with the support of authors such as Kant and Hegel. Extending the rational order was then presented as the teleology of history, with human beings as the agents of the natural order. Challenging these substantive values can only occur from the perspective of alternative and competing values systems. Such a challenge is difficult to mount when the entire institutional order has embodied the alternative.

If the emerging global institutions embody the substantive values of order and efficiency it is likely that their affinity with the capitalist form of economic organization is likely to wane. As has been discussed by Max Weber, capitalist economics and the growth of rational institutions have mutually reinforced one another in the modern period. However, this is not outside the scope of the historical process. As institutions address the questions surrounding the pursuit of security, well-being, and justice, the pure form of capitalism that was embedded in the logic of modernity has been transformed.

If the development of global institutions continues to pursue the Western rationality project, the pursuit of objectives by rationally efficient means, capitalism will increasingly find itself representing a substantive irrationality within the system. The capitalist economic system that is predicated on increasing consumption as its fundamental logic will be in a state of tension with the well-being of the biological entities that inhabit the planet. Capitalism will appear increasingly irrational within this framework and will require alteration.

Finally, something must be said about the normative content of democracy. Democratic practice arose in the West with the support of the narratives of rationality and equality. From the time of Greek society, the idea of human rationality has been embedded (albeit, sometimes well below the surface) within Western culture. In the modern period this view of subjectivity has been reinforced by rational science, the efficient ordering of production, and the spread of literacy. Without these material reinforcements, the premises that support democratic practice would lack the empirical foundation for its generation.

Equality has had different meanings. In ancient Greece equality was measured in the practical activities of citizens in the community. In the Middle Ages, the practical gave way to the transcendental, as equality was addressed as part of humanness itself. The definition and prioritization of these components of equality alter the perception of democracy's limitations.

At its core, democracy is a mechanism for generating legitimacy for collective decision based on some form of mass participation. However, as it arose out of historical conditions that reinforced its practice, it must be viewed relativistically and historically, rather than ontologically and transcendentally. It is a technique of collective politics rather than its *truth*. It should also be noted, that it is a technique that is particularly suited to the emerging processes of collectivization and integration in the present age.

Three Narratives Surrounding Integration

Tying the process of collectivization to the material elements that supports it provides a means to understand the sources and impacts of global integration today. Clearly the material factors for a global political system are emerging. A globalized economic system is well into the process of development.

Is there a normative framework that can be applied to this development? As has been previously stated, a final pronouncement is impossible given the mix of positive and negative factors inherent in the consolidation process. However, it is possible to outline broad frameworks that are derived from competing assumptions regarding human nature, social life, and the function of political institutions. For the sake of simplicity, only three such narratives on integration will be presented here.

The Cosmopolitan Narrative

Key to the understanding of the cosmopolitan narrative is the assertion of a fundamental difference between power and authority. The extension of institutional existence to a global level expands the role played by a central authority in establishing political procedures, in creating social institutions, and in the administration of resources. In general, this view asserts that the extension of institutional existence to the global environment expands the role of reason in human affairs.

As a result, the arbitrary and capricious acts of power can be banished from the political scene. Brute force will be eliminated as an expression of political will. Institutions rely on fixed processes for the resolution of disputes. The creation of a network of global political organizations will allow human beings to banish forever the wars that have plagued our collective existence from the time of the earliest communities. As long as these institutions are organized democratically, human freedom will be protected, as the decisions will be the result of the collective will of the global community.

The material foundations of global democracy are present in the technological infrastructure that has been created by the revolution in high-tech communications. With the complete wiring of the world into a single global network, it will be possible for anyone to become an informed citizen of the world and participate in the collective decision making processes that determine the direction of combined action. While this may require the emergence of a common language, the technology raises the possibility for such an outcome. Global institutions would be able to pursue that agenda as a rational course of action with the goal of enhancing the integration of the world community.

Access to information among the global citizenry will enhance the cultural support for democratic practice across a wide spectrum of institutional life. This will promote a model of *rational subjectivity* that will be reinforced at every level of the global culture. We would see a spontaneous movement toward more uniformity in global institutions. Open discourse, rational inquiry, and the use of science and technology to solve contemporary problems will enhance open-mindedness and reasonableness. As a result of this model of the subject, ethnic and religious intolerance will fade as a political force that generates conflicts around the world.

Armies have historically been the means by which communities have expanded their power. People have fought over territory, resources, and ideological purity. The creation of a global political entity ends that chapter in human history. The resources wasted on such activity can be recaptured and put to use in the service of humanity.

The geographic accident of birth will no longer determine one's life prospects. As world citizens, there will be rights common to all and opportunities guaranteed as a part of global citizenship. These rights will be embedded in the institutional structure, as the written embodiment of rational association itself. Even while recognizing the state as an artificial construction, its cosmopolitan nature will be sufficient to realize a common standard of justice across the globe.

The Narrative of Wealth and Power

In a narrative centered on the interests of wealth and power, the difference between power and authority is viewed as largely illusory. This is the case because from the perspective of this model the advances in technology are not manifested in the empowerment of a citizenry within the institutional structures. Rather, technology is used to manage the public in a way in which order and efficiency can be maintained with a veneer of democratic legitimacy that masks a deeper structure of power and manipulation.

World government will only compound the human subjugation already present in society. Democratic ideals cannot be realized in a political context that is as broad as world government. By locating the legitimate exercise of force in institutions that are so far removed from the influence of the citizens, and the context in which they actually live, force cannot be replaced with democratic consensus. As a result, a global structure will emerge that mirrors the hierarchy and domination already present within the nation-state. In a world government, institutional managers will direct policy for the benefit of political and economic elites already present in the system.

The safeguards against the subjugation of the population that are supposed to be the hallmark of democratic practice are surmounted by a combination of means. The population will be controlled by socialization, elaborated in schools and social institutions, continual propaganda, found in the daily pronouncements from media outlets, and the use of outright force, enhanced by high-tech forms of surveillance. This form of oppression will be carried out in defense of the *legitimacy* of the institutional order, as the facade of democracy will justify the oppression of all that challenge the status quo.

The global government will actually be a Western government that seeks to create a condition that both maintains its power in relation to the rest of the world, and opens up the markets and resources of the globe into trading arrangements that enhance the power of the ruling elites. With the institutional arrangements stacked against them, underdevelopment will remain a problem for those nations that are excluded from the benefits of the global system.

As a result, the principles of democracy will not be achieved, even though they remain the stated agenda of the global institutional structure. The liberal internationalism that is represented in Enlightenment cosmopolitanism exists as little more than an illusory façade over a system of hierarchy and domination generated around the interests of a ruling elite. While a laudable goal, democratic practice lies outside the reach of the vast majority of human beings.

The Social Conditioning Narrative

If subjectivity is viewed as a construction that stems from a combination of material conditions and cultural attitudes, the emergence of the democratic ideal must be placed in the context of history. The growth of integrating technologies has created the material possibilities for the collectivization of power. It has been our contention that the cultural support for the modern form of democracy resulted from an amalgamation of elements, especially the idea of transcendental human equality found in the Middle Ages, and the unified view of reason developed in the early

Enlightenment. As products of the evolution of material and cultural changes, both of these foundational supports for the status afforded to democracy in the modern period are subject to challenge. This raises a question about democracy at its most fundamental levels and suggests that the dynamic currently used as a vehicle to the creation of global institutions needs to be understood as part of a different narrative than those suggested above.

Each of these narratives is rational, in the sense that they rely on empirical markers that are selected and compiled into a story of development. However, only the social conditioning narrative suggests that the content of rationality by which democracy itself is judged, is a historical construction. To put this claim another way, democratic practice generates the structural conditions for its own reinforcement by promoting the institutions in which the logic of its practice is reinforced by the institutional rules. Democracy is rational only in relation to those institutions and the historical conditions which they manifest.

From this perspective, democratic practice does not have its origins in an essentialist construction of human ontology. It origins are in an organizational progression that requires a legitimating mechanism for the process of consolidating institutional power. The rational efficiencies that are generated by the creation of institutional consolidation do not speak to the necessity of either freedom or self-determination. This would explain why so many of the global institutions already created operate at great political distances from the populations of the globe.

If identity is shaped by social conditioning, both materially and culturally, then it is possible to move the population in the direction of a global society. However, if this is the case then the question of what character that society will take remains open. Given the influence of institutional maintenance in the overall systemic logic of the political structures, it can be expected that the instruments of socialization, the law, schools, and media, will be organized to reflect overall systemic needs. In this context, democracy may challenge only the speed of integration, not its overall systemic logic. The public is conditioned to the new institutional order through the process of socialization. In such a circumstance the real political struggles in society are not over the institutions, which operate according to their own internal logic, but over the societal instruments of dissemination.

Such a position is overtly foreign to a model of subjectivity that asserts the transcendent freedom of thought as a component of human ontology. Such an essentialist view cannot be sustained within the model of social conditioning. The social conditioning narrative asserts that the societal danger comes in the form of a collective in which the vast majority of the population is conditioned to be unaware of its own subjugation. In such a state, domination can be packaged as liberty, and exploitation as justice. All will give their obedience to the institutional order without question, as these ideas are continually reinforced by all the technical means possible. To paraphrase Nietzsche, if one were to think differently, they would go voluntarily to the madhouse.

As we have argued throughout this work, democracy should be viewed as one of the techniques of domination. From this perspective, the potential dangers of institutional existence at the local, national, or global level are not mitigated by democratic practice. By examining the historical roots of democracy we are in a better position to understand these processes and how they operate.

Bibliography

Anderson, Benedict. *Imagined Communities*. London: Verso, 1991.

Aquinas, Thomas. *Summa Theologiae*. New York: Benziger Bros., 1947-1948.

Augustine. *City of God*. trans. Marcus Dods. New York: Random House, 1950.

Augustine. "City of God," *Classics in Political Philososphy*. Ed. by Jene Porter. Scarborough, Ontario: Prentice-Hall, 1989.

Ayers, M.R. "The Foundations of Knowledge and the Logic of Substance: The Structure of Locke's General Philosophy." In *Locke's Philosophy: Content and Context*. Ed. by G.A.J. Rogers. Oxford, UK: Clarendon Press, 1994.

Barber, Benjamin. *An Aristocracy of Everyone: The Politics of Education and the Future of America*. New York: Ballantine Books, 1992.

Barnett, Michael, and Finnemore, Martha. *Rules for the World: International Organizations in Global Politics*. Ithaca, NY: Cornell University Press, 2004.

Barker, Ernest, ed. *The Politics of Aristotle*. New York: Oxford University Press, 1977.

Baudrillard, Jean. "The Ecstasy of Communication." In *The Anti-Aesthetic: Essays on Postmodern Culture*. Ed. by Hal Foster. New York: New Press, 1998.

Baumann, Gerd. "Introduction." In *Civil Enculturation: Nation-State, School and Ethnic Difference in The Netherlands, Britain, German, and France*." Ed. by Werner Schiffauer, Gerd Baumann, Riva Kastoryano, and Steven Vertovec. New York: Berghahn Books, 2004.

Biller, Peter, and Hudson, Anne. *Heresy and Literacy, 1000–1530*. Cambridge, UK: Cambridge University Press, 1994.

Black, Jeremy. "Warfare, Crisis, and Absolution." From *Early Modern Europe: An Oxford History*. Ed. by Euan Cameron. Oxford, UK: Oxford University Press, 1999.

Bobbio, Norberto. *Thomas Hobbes and the Natural Law Tradition*. Trans. Daniela Gobetti. Chicago: The University of Chicago Press, 1993.

Boli, John. "Conclusion: World Authority Structures and Legitimations." In *Constructing World Culture: International Non-Governmental Organizations Since 1875*. Stanford, CA: Stanford University Press, 1999.

Boli, John, and Thomas, George M. "INGOs and the Organization of World Culture." In *Constructing World Culture*. Ed. by John Boli and George M. Thomas. Stanford, CA: Stanford University Press, 1999.

Bowra, C.M. *Periclean Athens*. New York: The Dial Press, 1971.

Buchanan, R. A. *The Power of the Machine*. London: Penguin, 1994.

Buchanan, Scott, ed. *The Portable Plato*. New York: Penguin Books, 1976.

Cairncross, Frances. *The Death of Distance*. Boston: Harvard Business School Press, 2001.

Canning, Joseph. *A History of Medieval Political Thought: 300-1450*. London: Routledge, 1996.

Cardoso, Fernando, and Faletto, Enzo. *Dependency and Development in Latin America*. Berkeley: University of California Press, 1979.

Carlyle, Alexander J. "The Sources of Medieval Political Theory and Its Connection with Medieval Politics." *The American Historical Review*, 19: 1, 1913.

Castells, Manuel. "The Network Society: From Knowledge to Policy." In *The Network Society: From Knowledge to Policy*. Ed. by Manuel Castells and Gustavo Cardoso. Washington, D. C.: Johns Hopkins Center for Transatlantic Relations, 2006.

Chambliss, J.J. *Imagination and Reason in Plato, Aristotle, Vico, Rousseau, and Keats: An Essay on the Philosophy of Experience*. The Hague: Matinus Nijhoff, 1974.

Chase-Dunn, Christopher. *Global Formation: Structures of the World-Economy*. Oxford, UK: Basil Blackwell, 1989.

Chevallier, Raymond. *Roman Roads*. Trans. N.H. Field. Berkeley: University of California Press, 1976.

Clair, Colin. *The History of European Printing*. London: Academic Press.

Claude, Inis L. *Swords into Plowshares: The Problems and Progress of International Organizations*. New York: Random House, 1964.

Coates, Wilson H., Hayden V. White, and J. Salwyn Schapiro. *The Emergence of Liberal Humanism: An Intellectual History of Western Europe*, Vol. I. New York: McGraw-Hill Book Co., 1966.

Cohen, Joshua. "Reflections on Rousseau: Autonomy and Democracy." In *The Social Contract Theorists: Critical Essays on Hobbes, Locke, and Rousseau*. Ed. by Christopher W. Morris. Lanham, MD: Rowman and Littlefield Publishers, 1999.

Dahl, Robert. *Dilemmas of Pluralist Democracy*. New Haven, CT: Yale University Press, 1982.

Dandeker, Christopher. *Surveillance, Power and Modernity*. New York: St. Martins, 1990.

Davis, Bob. "Think Big: What Is the Greatest Technological Innovation of the Past 1,000 Years." *Wall Street Journal*. January 11, 1999.

Derrida, Jacques. *Dissemination*. Chicago: University of Chicago Press, 1981.

————. *Writing and Difference*. Chicago: University of Chicago Press, 1978.

Dewey, John. *Democracy and Education: An Introduction to the Philosophy of Education.* New York: Macmillan, 1916.

Diamond, Jared. *Guns, Germs, and Steel: The Fates of Human Societies.* New York: W.W. Norton and Company, 1999.

Dreyfus, Hubert L., and Paul Rabinow. *Michel Foucault: Beyond Structuralism and Hermeneutics.* Chicago: The University of Chicago Press, 1982.

Dubash, Navroz. *Power Politics: Equity and Environment in Electricity Reform.* Washington, D.C.: World Resource Institute, 2002.

DuBoff, Richard B. *Acuumulation and Power: An Economic History of the United States.* Armonk, NY: M. E. Sharpe, 1989.

Eisenstein, Elizabeth L. "The Emergence of Print Culture in the West: 'Defining the Initial Shift.'" In *The Renaissance in Europe: A Reader.* Ed. by Keith Whitlock. New Haven, CT: Yale University Press, 2000.

———. "Some Conjectures About the Impact of Printing on Western Society and Thought: A Preliminary Report." *Journal of Modern History,* 40:1. March 1968.

Eley, Geoff. "The Social Construction of Democracy in Germany: 1871–1933." In *The Social Construction of Democracy: 1870–1990.* New York: New York University Press, 1995.

Finer, Herman. *Theory and Practice of Modern Government.* Westport, CT: Greenwood Press, 1949.

Foote, Joe S. *Television Access and Political Power: The Networks, the Presidency, and the Loyal Opposition.* New York: Praeger, 1990.

Foucault, Michel. *The Archaeology of Knowledge.* Trans. A.M. Sheridan Smith. New York: Pantheon Books, 1972.

———. *Discipline and Punish.* New York: Vintage, 1995.

———. *The History of Sexuality, Volume 1: An Introduction.* Trans. Robert Hurley. New York: Vintage Books, 1990.

———. *Power.* Ed. by James D. Faubion. New York: The New Press, 2000.

———. *Power/Knowledge.* Ed. by Colin Gordon., trans. Colin Gordon, et al. New York: Pantheon Books, 1980.

Frank, Andre Gunder. *Capitalism and Underdevelopment in Latin America.* New York: Monthly Review, 1967.

Frieden, Jeffrey A. *Global Capitalism.* New York: Norton, 2006.

Fukuyama, Francis. *The End of History and the Last Man.* New York: The Free Press, 1992.

Fussel, Stephan. *Gutenberg and the Impact of Printing.* Trans. Douglas Martin. Burlington, UK: Ashgate, 2003.

Gilpin, Robert. *Global Political Economy.* Princeton, NJ: Princeton University Press, 2001.

Gladden, E. N. *A History of Public Administration,* Vol. I & II. London: Frank Cass, 1972.

Goldsmith, Jack, and Wu, Tim. *Who Controls the Internet: Illusions of a Borderless World.* New York: Oxford University Press, 2006.

Grant, Arthur J. *Greece in the Age of Pericles*. New York: Charles Scribner's Sons, 1893.

Green, Arnold W. *Hobbes and Human Nature*. New Brunswick, CT: Transaction Publishers, 1993.

Gurevich, Aaron. "Heresy and Literacy: Evidence of the Thirteenth-Century 'Exempla.'" In *Heresy and Literacy, 1000–1530*. Ed. by Peter Biller and Anne Hudson. Cambridge, UK: Cambridge University Press.

Habermas, Jürgen. *The Legitimation Crisis*. Boston: Beacon Press, 1975.

———. "Modernity: An Incomplete Project." In *The Anti-Aesthetic*. Ed. by Hal Foster. Port Townsend, WA: Bay Press, 1983.

Harvey, David. "From Space to Place and Back Again: Reflections on the Conditions of Postmodernity." In J. Bird, et. al., eds. *Mapping the Futures: Local Culture, Global Change*. London: Routledge, 1993.

Hearnshaw, F.J.C. "Introductory: The Social and Political Problems of the Sixteenth and Seventeenth Centuries." In *The Social and Political Ideas of Some Great Thinkers of the Sixteenth and Seventeenth Centuries: A Series of Lectures Delivered at King's College University of London During the Session 1925–26*. Ed. by F.J.C. Hearnshaw. Port Washington, WA: Kennikat Press, Inc., 1967.

Henderson, W. O. *The Industrial Revolution in Europe: Germany, France, Russia, 1815–1914*. Chicago: Quadrangle Books, 1961.

Herbert, Gary B. *Thomas Hobbes: The Unity of Scientific and Moral Wisdom*. Vancouver: University of Columbia Press, 1989.

Hildinger, Erik. *Swords Against the Senate: The Rise of the Roman Army and the Fall of the Republic*. Cambridge, MA: Da Capo Press, 2002.

Hillstrom, Kevin, and Hillstrom, Laurie Collier. *The Industrial Revolution in America: Iron and Steel*. Santa Barbara, CA: ABC-Clio, 2005.

Hirsh, Richard F. *Technology and Transformation in the American Electric Utility Industry*. Cambridge, UK: Cambridge University Press, 1989.

Hobbes, Thomas. *De Cive, The English Version, Entitled in the First Edition Philosophicall Rudiments Concerning Government and Society*. Ch. I. Oxford, UK: Clarendon Press, 1983.

———. *Leviathan, or The Matter, Forme, and Power of a Common-wealth Ecclesiasticall and Civill*. Ch. XIII. New York: W.W. Norton and Company, Inc., 1997.

Hollinger, Robert. *Postmodernism and the Social Sciences: A Thematic Approach*. Thousand Oaks, CA: Sage Publications, 1994.

Holzner, Burkhart, and Marx, John. *Knowledge Applications: The Knowledge System in Society*. Boston: Allyn and Bacon, 1979.

Jennings, Jeremy. "Rousseau, Social Contract and the Modern Leviathan." In *The Social Contract from Hobbes to Rawls*. Ed. by David Boucher and Paul Kelly. London: Routledge, 1994.

Jensen, De Lamar. *Renaissance Europe: Age of Recovery and Reconciliation*. Lexington, KY: D.C. Heath and Company, 1981.

Kagan, Donald, ed. *Sources in Greek Political Thought: From Homer to Polybius.* "Pericles on Athenian Democracy—The Funeral Oration (Thucydides 2, 35–46)." New York: The Free Press, 1965.

Kant, Immanuel. "Eternal Peace." In *The Philosophy of Kant.* Ed. by Carl J. Friedrich. New York: Modern Library, 1977.

———. *The Metaphysical Elements of Justice.* New York: Bobbs-Merrill, 1965.

———. "Theory and Practice." In *The Philosophy of Kant.* Ed. by Carl J. Friedrich. New York: Modern Library, 1977.

Karns, Margaret P., and Mingst, Karen A. *International Organizations: The Politics and Processes of Global Governance.* Boulder, CO: Lynne Rienner, 2004.

Keens-Soper, Maurice. "Rousseau: The Social Contract." In *The Political Classics.* Ed. by Murray Forsyth and Maurice Keens-Soper. Oxford, UK: Oxford University Press, 1992.

Koch, Andrew M. *Poststructuralism and the Politics of Method.* Lanham, MD: Roman and Littlefield (Lexington Books), 2007.

———. *Romance and Reason: The Ontological and Social Sources of Alienation in the Writings of Max Weber.* Lanham, MD: Roman and Littlefield (Lexington Books), 2006.

———. *Knowledge and Social Construction.* Lanham, MD: Roman and Littlefield (Lexington Books), 2005.

———. "Power, 'Text,' and Public Policy: The Political Implications of Jacques Derrida's Critique of 'Subjectivity.'" *Southeastern Political Review,* 26:1, 1998.

Kohn, Hans. *The Idea of Nationalism: A Study in Its Origins and Background.* New York: The Macmillan Company, 1944.

Lebergott, Stanley. "The Patterns of Employment Since 1800." in *American Economic History.* Ed. by Seymour E. Harris. New York: McGraw-Hill, 1961.

Lenin, Vladimir. "Imperialism, The Highest Stage of Capitalism." In *The Lenin Anthology.* Ed. by Robert Tucker. New York: Norton, 1975.

Locke, John. *Concerning Civil Government, Second Essay.* In *Great Books of the Western World.* Vol. 35. Ed. by Robert Maynard Hutchins. Chicago: Encyclopaedia Britannica, Inc., 1952.

———. "Natural Rights and Government by Consent." In *Political Philosophy.* Ed. by Alan Gewirth. New York: The Macmillan Company, 1965.

Logan, Robert K. *The Alphabet Effect: The Impact of the Phonetic Alphabet on the Development of Western Civilization.* New York: St. Martin's Press, 1986.

Lopata, Benjamin. "Property Theory in Hobbes." *Political Theory.* 1: 2. May 1973.

Loya, Thomas A., and Boli, John. "Standardization in the World Polity: Technical Rationality over Power." In *Constructing World Culture: International Non-Governmental Organizations Since 1875.* Stanford, CA: Stanford University Press, 1999.

Lucki, Emil. *History of the Renaissance: Book I, Economy and Society.* Salt Lake City: University of Utah Press, 1963.

Machiavelli. *The Prince.* Ed. and trans. by Thomas G. Bergin. New York: Appleton-Century-Crofts, 1947.

Marcus, Joyce. *Mesoamerican Writing Systems.* Princeton, NJ: Princeton University Press, 1992.

Marsiglio de Padua. *The Defensor Pacis.* Trans. by A. Gewirth. Toronto: University of Toronto Press, 1956.

Martin, John. "Inventing Sincerity, Refashioning Prudence: The Discovery of the Individual in Renaissance Europe." From *American Historical Review,* 102 (5). December 1997.

Martinich, A.P. *Thomas Hobbes.* New York: St. Martin's Press, 1997.

Marx, Karl. "The Communist Manifesto." In *The Marx-Engels Reader.* Ed. by Robert Tucker New York: Norton, 1978.

———. "The Economic and Philosophic Manuscripts of 1844." In *The Marx-Engels Reader.* Ed. by Robert Tucker. New York: Norton, 1978.

McChesney, Robert W. *Telecommunications, Mass Media, and Democracy: The Battle for the Control of U. S. Broadcasting, 1928–1935.* New York: Oxford University Press, 1993.

McLuhan, Marshall. *Understanding Media: The Extensions of Man.* New York: New American Library, 1964.

Miskimin, Harry A. *The Economy of Early Renaissance Europe, 1300–1460.* Cambridge, UK: Cambridge University Press, 1975.

Mitchell, B. R. *International Historical Statistics: Europe 1750–1993.* London: Macmillan, 1998.

Morris, Ian. "Equality and Origins of Greek Democracy." In *Ancient Greek Democracy: Readings and Sources.* Ed. by Eric W. Robinson. Malden: Blackwell Publishing, 2004.

Munson, Richard. *From Edison to Enron: The Business of Power and What It Means for the Future of Electricity.* Westport, CT: Praeger, 2005.

Murphy, James J. "Roman Writing Instruction as Described by Quintilian." In *A Short History of Writing Instruction: From Ancient Greece to Twentieth-Century America.* Ed. by James J. Murphy. Davis, CA: Hermagoras Press, 1990.

Myres, John L. *The Political Ideas of the Greeks.* New York: The Abingdon Press, 1971.

Nietzsche, Fiedrich. *The Birth of Tragedy and The Genealogy of Morals.* Trans. by Francis Golffing. Garden City, NJ: Doubleday and Company, 1956.

———. "On Truth and Lies in a Non-Moral Sense." In *Nietzsche Selections.* Ed. by Richard Schacht. New York: Macmillan, 1993.

———. *Will to Power.* Ed. by Walter Kaufmann. New York: Vintage, 1968.

Noam, Eli. *Television in Europe.* New York: Oxford University Press, 1991.

Nord, Philip. "Origins of the Third Republic in France." In *The Social Construction of Democracy: 1870–1990*. Ed. by George Reid Andrews and Herrick Chapman. New York: New York University Press, 1995.

Nussbaum, Frederick L. *A History of the Economic Institutions of Modern Europe*. New York: F. S. Crofts, 1935.

Oslin, George P. *The Story of Telecommunications*. Macon, GA: Mercer University Press, 1992.

Pacey, Arnold. *The Culture of Technology*. Cambridge, MA: MIT Press, 1983.

Pagden, Anthony. "Prologue: Europe and the World Around." In *Early Modern Europe: An Oxford History*. Ed. Euan Cameron. Oxford, UK: Oxford University Press, 1999.

Pahl, R. E., and Winkler, J. T. "The Coming Corporatism." *New Society* 10, (October 1974).

Paterson, Jeremy. "Politics in the Late Republic." In *Roman Political Life 90 B.C.-A.D. 69. Exeter Studies in History No. 7*. Ed. by T.P. Wiseman. Exeter, UK: University of Exeter Press, 1985.

Pearson, Lionel. "Party Politics and Free Speech in Democratic Athens." *Greece and Rome*, 7: 19. (Oct., 1937).

Peirce, William Spangar. *Economics of the Energy Industry*. Westport, CT: Praeger, 1996.

Pelikan, Jaroslav. *The Excellent Empire: The Fall of Rome and the Triumph of the Church*. San Francisco: Harper and Row, 1987.

Philosophy and Power in the Graeco-Roman World. Ed. by Gillian Clark and Tessa Rajak. Oxford, UK: Oxford University Press, 2002.

Philp, Mark. "Michel Foucault." In *The Return of Grand Theory in the Human Sciences*. Ed. bu Quentin Skinner. Cambridge, UK: Cambridge University Press, 1985.

The Political Writings of St. Augustine. Ed. by Henry Paolucci. Washington, D.C.: Regnery Publishing, Inc., 1962.

The Populist Party Platform. (1892). In *American Political Thought*. Ed. by Kenneth Dolbeare and Michael Cummings. Washington, D.C.: Congressional Quarterly Press, 2004.

Poster, Mark. "Cyberdemocracy: The Internet and the Public Sphere." In *Masters of the Wired World: Cyberspeak Speaks Out*. Ed. byAnne Leer. London: Pitman Publishing, 1999.

Powell, Rebecca. *Literacy as a Moral Imperative: Facing the Challenges of a Pluralistic Society*. Lanham, MD: Rowman and Littlefield, 1999.

Raadschelders, Jos C. N. *Handbook of Administrative History*. New Brunswick, NJ: Transaction Publishers, 1998.

Raaflaub, Kurt A. "Democracy, Oligarchy, and the Concept of the 'Free Citizen' in Late Fifth-Century Athens." *Political Theory*, 11: 4, (Nov., 1983).

Ramirez, Francisco O., and Ventresca, Marc J. "Building the Institution of Mass Schooling: Isomorphism in the Modern World." In *The Political Con-*

struction of Education: The State, School Expansion, and Economic Change. New York: Praeger, 1992.

Reeves, Marjorie. "Marsiglio of Padua and Dante Alighieri." In *Trends in Medieval Political Thought.* Ed. by Beryl Smalley. New York: Barnes and Noble, Inc., 1965.

Reus-Smit, Christian. *The Moral Purpose of the State: Culture, Social Identity, and Institutional Rationality in International Relations.* Princeton, NJ: Princeton University Press, 1999.

Robinson, Charles Alexander, Jr. *Athens in the Age of Pericles.* Norman: University of Oklahoma Press, 1959.

Rosenau, James N., and Johnson, David. "Information Technologies and Turbulence in World Politics." In *Technology, Development, and Democracy.* Ed. Juliann Emmons Allison. Albany: State University of New York Press, 2002.

Ross, Robert J. S., and Trachte, Kent C. *Global Capitalism: The New Leviathan.* Albany: State University of New York Press, 1990.

Rousseau, Jean-Jacques. *Emile.* Trans. by Barbara Foxley. London: J.M. Dent and Sons, 1911.

———. *The Social Discourse on the Origin and Foundation of Inequality Among Mankind.* Ed. by Lester G. Crocker. New York: Washington Square Press, 1967.

Rowe, Christopher, et. al., eds. *The Cambridge History of Greek and Roman Political Thought.* Cambridge, UK: Cambridge University Press, 2000.

Sagan, Eli. *The Honey and the Hemlock: Democracy and Paranoia in Ancient Athens and Modern America.* New York: Basic Books, 1991.

Savigear, Peter. "Niccolo Machiavelli: The Prince and the Discourses." In *The Political Classics: A Guide to the Essential Texts from Plato to Rousseau."* Ed. by Murray Forsyth and Maurice Keens-Soper. Oxford, UK: Oxford University Press, 1992.

Saxonhouse, Arlene W. "Hobbes and the Beginnings of Modern Political Thought." In *Three Discourses: A Critical Modern Edition of Newly Identified Work of the Young Hobbes.* Ed. by Noel B. Reynolds and Arlene W. Saxonhouse. Chicago: The University of Chicago Press, 1995.

Schmitter, Phillipe. "Still the Century of Corporatism." *The Review of Politics* 36, 85–126. Ed. by Williamson, P. J. *Varieties of Corporatism.* Cambridge, UK: Cambridge University Press, 1985.

Shiner, Larry. "Reading Foucault: Anti-Method and the Genealogy of Power-Knowledge." *History and Theory.* 21: 3 (Oct. 1982).

Shotter, David. *The Fall of the Roman Empire.* London: Routledge, 1994.

Sibley, Mulford Q. *Political Ideas and Ideologies: A History of Political Thought.* New York: Harper and Row Publishers, 1970.

Skinner, Quentin. *Reason and Rhetoric in the Philosophy of Hobbes.* Cambridge: Cambridge University Press, 1996.

Smith, A. D. *Nations and Nationalism in a Global Era.* Cambridge, UK: Polity Press, 1995.

Soltow, Lee, and Stevens, Edward. *The Rise of Literacy and the Common School in the United States: A Socioeconomic Analysis to 1870.* Chicago: University of Chicago Press, 1981.

Staccioli, Romolo Augusto. *The Roads of the Romans.* Los Angeles: Getty Publications, 2003.

Steinburg, S.H. *Five Hundred Years of Printing.* London: Oak Knoll Press and the British Library, 1996.

Stevenson, William R. Jr. *Christian Love and Just War: Moral Paradox and Political Life in St. Augustine and His Modern Interpreters.* Macon, GA: Mercer University Press, 1987.

Stromberg, Roland N. *Democracy: A Short Analytical History.* Armonk, NY: M. E. Sharpe, 1996.

Sumner, William Graham. "The Concentration of Wealth: Its Economic Justification." In *Social Darwinism: Selected Essays.* Englewood Cliffs, NJ: Prentice Hall, 1963.

——— "What the Social Classes Owe to Each Other." In *American Political Thought.* Ed. by Kenneth Dolbeare and Michael Cummings. Washington, D.C.: Congressional Quarterly Press, 2004.

Swanson, R. N. "Literacy, Heresy, History and Orthodoxy: Perspectives and Permutations for the Later Middle Ages." In *Heresy and Literacy, 1000–1530.* Ed. by Peter Biller and Anne Hudson. Cambridge, UK: Cambridge University Press, 1994.

Tacitus, Cornelius P. *A Dialogue on Oratory.* Trans. by Sir William Peterson. Princeton, NJ: Loeb Classical Library, Harvard University Press, 1946.

Thompson, James Westfall. *The Literacy of the Laity in the Middle Ages.* New York: Burt Franklin, 1963.

Troll, Denise. "The Illiterate Mode of Written Communication: The Work of the Medieval Scribe." In *Oral and Written Communications: Historical Approaches.* Ed. by Richard Leo Enos. Newbury Park, CA: Sage Publications, 1990.

Union of International Associations. *The Yearbook of International Organizations.* Munich: K. G. Saur, 2005.

United Nations. *World Investment Report: Transnational Corporations and Export Competitiveness.* Geneva, Switzerland: United Nations Publication, 2002.

Velkley, Richard L. *Being After Rousseau: Philosophy and Culture in Question.* Chicago: The University of Chicago Press, 2002.

Vincent, David. *The Rise of Mass Literacy: Reading and Writing in Modern Europe.* Cambridge, UK: Polity, 2000.

Virgil. *Aeneid.* Trans. by Robert Fagles. New York: Viking, 2006.

von Hagen, Victor W. *The Roads that Led to Rome.* Cleveland, OH: The World Publishing Company, 1967.

Ward, John O. "Rhetoric, Truth, and Literacy in the Renaissance of the Twelfth Century." In *Oral and Written Communication.* Ed. by Richard Leo Enos. Newbury Park, CA: Sage Publications, 1990.

Ward-Perkins, Bryan. *The Fall of Rome and the End of Civilization.* Oxford, UK: Oxford University Press, 2005.

Weber, Eugen. *Peasants into Frenchman: The Modernization of Rural France 1870–1914.* Stanford, CA: Stanford University Press, 1976.

Weber, Max. *The Methodology of the Social Sciences.* New York: Free Press, 1949.

———. *Economy and Society.* Berkeley: University of California Press, 1978.

———. "Socialism." In *Max Weber: Selections in Translation.* Cambridge, UK: Cambridge University Press, 1978.

White, Richard. "The Return of the Master: An Interpretation of Nietzsche's 'Genealogy of Morals.'" *Philosophy and Phenomenological Research,* 48: 4 (Jun., 1988).

Wiggin, Gladys A. *Education and Nationalism.* New York: McGraw-Hill, 1962.

Willrich, Mason. *Energy and World Politics.* New York: Free Press, 1975.

Wiseman, T.P. "Competition and Co-operation." In *Roman Political Life 90 B.C.–A.D. 69,* Exeter Studies in History No. 7. Ed. by T.P. Wiseman. Exeter, UK: University of Exeter Press, 1985.

——— "Introduction." In *Roman Political Life 90 B.C.-A.D. 69,* Exeter Studies in History No. 7. Ed. by T.P. Wiseman. Exeter, UK: University of Exeter Press, 1985.

Wolinsky, Art. *The History of the Internet and the World Wide Web.* Berkeley Heights, NJ: Enslow Publishers, 1999.

Wood, Ellen Meiksins, and Wood, Neal. *Class Ideology and Ancient Political Theory: Socrates, Plato, and Aristotle in Social Context.* New York: Oxford University Press, 1978.

Index

About the Authors

Andrew M. Koch is professor of political philosophy at the Department of Government and Justice Studies at Appalachian State University in Boone, North Carolina. He received his Ph.D. from the University of California at Santa Barbara and is a former Fulbright Scholar and Friedrich Ebert Foundation Fellow. His main areas of research are in continental philosophy and technology.

Among his published works are: *Poststructuralism and the Politics of Method*; *Romance and Reason: The Ontological and Social Sources of Alienation in the Writings of Max Weber*; *Knowledge and Social Construction*; *Poststructuralism and the Epistemological Basis of Anarchism*; *Cyber Citizen or Cyborg Citizen: The Problem of Political Agency in Virtual Politics*.

Amanda Gail Zeddy is currently working on her Ph.D. in political science at the University of California, Santa Barbara. She received a B.A. in History and M.A. in Political Science from Appalachian State University in Boone, North Carolina, and is a former Capstone Research Fellowship recipient. Her primary area of research is Western political philosophy, focusing on continental political thought, poststructuralism, and democratic theory. She also has a secondary interest in comparative politics.